D0759020

AN ILLUSTRATED DICTIONARY
OF ORNAMENT

AN ILLUSTRATED DICTIONARY OF ORNAMENT

by

Maureen Stafford, ARCA and Dora Ware

D#146083

With an Introduction by John Gloag
FSA, Hon. FRIBA, Hon. FSIA

ST. MARTIN'S PRESS

New York

Library of Congress Catalog Card Number: 74-21095

ISBN: 0-312-40776-9

First Paperback Edition

10 9 8 7 6 5 4 3 2 1

to Helen C. Johnson

CONTENTS

ACKNOWLEDGEMENTS

We should like to thank John Gloag, L. E. Kenyon, CBE, Roy Lewis and Ronald Eames for their help and advice; and to record, with gratitude, our debt to the many libraries and admirable works of reference we have consulted. These are included in the bibliography on pages 243 and 244.

M.S.
D.W.

INTRODUCTION

by John Gloag

FSA, Hon. FRIBA, Hon. FSIA

THE CHARACTER OF ORNAMENT

One of the best definitions of ornament was written in the mid-nineteenth century by Ralph Nicholson Wornum, who said: 'Ornament is essentially the accessory to, and not the substitute of, the useful; it is a decoration or adornment; it can have no independent existence practically.'[1] When that was written Victorian taste was already confusing ornament with design, for the Great Exhibition of 1851 had encouraged a fashion for profuse decoration, and the aesthetic merit of an article was often assessed by its ornamental extravagance and complexity. Only in periods of artistic decadence has ornament become an end in itself, as exemplified by the final phase of the rococo style in France under Louis XV and the reincarnation in mid-Victorian England of Gothic, Elizabethan, Jacobean and Carolean forms, grotesquely distorted to create an effect of exuberant opulence. Only in periods of repressive moral earnestness has ornament been condemned and rejected, as it was under the puritan regime in the seventeenth century and during the growing pains of the Modern Movement in design in the 1920s and 1930s, when many exponents of that movement exhibited an almost pathological aversion to anything save the bleak purity of functional shapes and the monotony of plain surfaces.

A few years before the Modern Movement mellowed, the late Percy Smith, an eminent designer, had voiced a profound truth. 'Ornament,' he said, 'is an ancient human need, which should not be denied.'[2] That need has been amply satisfied in the past, and the history and development of the various components of decoration and the nature and selection of ornamental motifs reveal the artistic sensibility of such ancient civilisations as the Egyptian, Minoan and Assyrian, and reveal even more vividly the national characteristics that emerged in European countries when they were released from the standardised taste and conventional ornament imposed by the Roman Empire. Today the capabilities and limitations of a scientific industrial age are disclosed by the subtle use of surface variations, texture and colour in the external and internal treatment of buildings and the design of other artifacts, such as furniture, vehicles and domestic appliances. An anthropologist when comparing the taste of the Celtic inhabitants of Britain with that of their post-Roman conquerors, once said that 'the Celtic Cymry were artists and craftsmen who did not suffer from that dread of blank space, which so often led to an overloading with unnecessary ornamentation of the work of their Teutonic successors'.[3] The pioneers of modern design tended to reinforce that barbaric 'dread of blank space', until with the passage of time the movement matured; concessions to human foibles were approved, and in the 1950s some timid attempts made to originate new forms of ornament that would be attuned to the fashionable mechanistic approach to design and innocent of any traditional bias. Various experiments were tried, some of them inspired by the facetted geometrical shapes found in quartz crystals. They were neither attractive nor original, though respectable in the eyes of dedicated modernists because they had a quasi-scientific basis. Tidily free from the liveliness of organic prototypes, they were an acceptable substitute for such natural subjects as plants, flowers, birds and animals. All those things had been used in the past, and tradition was an obscene word to many designers in the middle years of this century

The use of geometrical patterns is almost as old as mankind. They were used in an elementary form by our Neolithic ancestors, who decorated their clumsy utensils, and engraved surfaces of polished bone, with lines and scrolls and chevrons, which were formalised arrow-heads, conjoining the latter to form zigzags, and by using interlacing lines they occasionally produced primitive versions of such sophisticated devices as the Greek fret. The history and evolution of ornament confirms the view of Sir William Flinders Petrie that it is difficult for man to be really original. In his study of Egyptian decoration that great archaeologist classified the ornamental elements of decoration under four main divisions. 1) the 'simplest geometrical ornament of lines and spirals and curves, and of surfaces divided by these into squares and circles'; 2) the 'natural ornament of copying feathers, flowers, plants and animals'; 3) structural ornament arising from 'the structural necessities of building and manufacture'; and 4) symbolic ornament.[4]

Nearly all types of ornament fit into one or other of those four categories. Open any page in this dictionary, and you will find some entry that proves this. Strapwork, for example, is basically geometric, perhaps because it was devised on the drawing board, engraved for printing pattern books, and ultimately given three-dimensional form by a wood carver on a piece of furniture or a chimney-piece or by a plasterer on a ceiling. Crosses of all kinds are basically geometrical, even such departures from the simple use of a vertical and a horizontal member as the Maltese cross, and all the varieties that occur in the science of heraldry.

Some ornamental devices may claim inclusion in more than one category, as for example the linenfold pattern. This has no architectural affiliations or natural prototype, for it was invented on the bench by woodcarvers and not, like strapwork and rococo ornament, on a drawing board by draughtsmen and engravers. It first appeared in the late fifteenth century as a stylised representation of linen arranged in vertical folds, though some variations suggest scrolls of parchment. Because it has geometrical regularity and is a symmetrical arrangement of vertical lines, it could qualify for the first division, but as it was probably used originally on the doors or lids of receptacles where either linen or parchment scrolls were stored, it might also be regarded as symbolic. The pattern was so intrinsically decorative, that it was not confined to panels on chests and presses, but was used on bed heads, chair backs, wall panelling and chimney-pieces. Some forms of ornament invented by wood carvers were suggested by the aptitude of some particular type of cutting tool, such as gouge work, scooped out on a flat surface with a gouge, and the geometrical patterns of chip carving, set out with compasses and then chipped out with a chisel.

The second category is thronged with examples. Natural objects have always stimulated the human inclination to imitate, and when flowers and foliage have been carved or incised or painted, they have frequently been formalised, like the lotus, 'the largest and most complex' motif in Egyptian ornament, 'so widely spread', according to Flinders Petrie, 'that some have seen in it the source of all ornament.'[5] Its medieval descendant, used in heraldry, is the *fleur-de-lys*. Of all plants, the acanthus, with its leaves arranged in scrolls and sinuous foliations, has an ornamental ubiquity far transcending its original use on the Corinthian order of architecture and in architectural decoration. The whorls of the nautilus shell are stylised to form the Persian and Ionic volutes; the honeysuckle is conventionally repre-sented in the Greek anthemion ornament; the vine with its leaves, tendrils and bunches of grapes has been delineated by carvers, painters and metal workers for at least four thousand years. It was one of the oldest cultivated plants in ancient Egypt, and all the designs copied from it were 'based on the idea of its climbing and trailing over houses'.[6]

Birds, animals and reptiles have for centuries been included in ornamental compositions or displayed as individual ornaments; how often and how variously may be gathered from many entries in the pages that follow; familiar creatures like eagles, hawks, cranes, storks, lions, leopards, deer, horses and goats have enlivened or dignified the design of furniture and interior decoration in civilisations as different as those of ancient Egypt, France under Louis XIV, and early Victorian England. Some were used symbolically, like the eagle in the French Empire period and the federal style that arose in the young American republic of the late eighteenth and early nineteenth centuries; some merely with an engaging frivolity, like the simian figures, popular in mid-eighteenth century furnishing and decoration, which reflected a modish craze for keeping small monkeys as pets. Serpents, fishes, and such sea creatures as dolphins have figured prominently in the long history of ornament, especially dolphins. In different ages and places, men have improved or debased the form of living creatures, hence the diverse family of fabulous monsters, sometimes graceful, like the unicorn, occasionally intimidating, like the Chinese dragon, and the winged lions and bulls of Assyria with their bearded human heads, or broodingly mysterious like the impassive Egyptian sphinx. All the eccentric hybrids of classical antiquity were resurrected during the Renaissance and welcomed by the ornamentalists who created and developed the baroque and rococo styles. The chimera and the griffin, the winged sphinx with the head and breasts of a woman, the harpy, the satyr, the centaur and hosts of chubby, hilarious cherubs invaded the ornate salons of great houses in France and other European countries from the late seventeenth century to the close of the eighteenth. Earlier still, in the sixteenth and early seventeenth centuries, the mixed and improbable fauna of heraldry had been appropriated by carvers and used for decorative purposes on furniture and such internal features as chimney-pieces. The arrangement and postures of birds, animals and double-headed or truncated versions of them, and such inventions as the cockatrice and wivern, had special significance in heraldry, which was a graphic language in the fourteenth and fifteenth centuries, with a code of tinctures, lines and innumerable symbols, conveying a visual message to illiterate people about families entitled to bear arms and merchants, guilds and companies that had been granted the right. Coats of arms painted or carved or engraved on vehicles, furniture or silver, have continued in use to denote ownership from the Middle Ages to the present day.

Heraldic emblems used ornamentally come into the fourth category. In the third, Flinders Petrie mentions as an example of structural influence the bosses that extrude from walls in Moslem architecture, 'which imitate the projecting ends of pillars torn from ruins and built into the wall, though rather too long for the position'.[7] The triglyphs on the frieze of the entablature in the Doric order of architecture are survivals in stone of a long-discarded wooden prototype. We should, perhaps, include in the third category structural elements in architecture that are detached and used as surface ornament, such as arcading—arches with pointed or semi-circular heads applied on furniture or wall panelling either singly or in series—also columns, pilasters, and entablatures belonging to one or other of the classic orders, employed solely for their decorative properties and bereft of functional significance.

Throughout the Graeco-Roman civilisation, the orders of architecture had established a standardised code of ornament; each order was distinguished by characteristic forms of enrichment for mouldings and the treatment of the capitals that crowned the columns;

and this code was revived during the Renaissance, but greatly amplified and liberated from the rigidity that had restricted Roman (but not Greek) decorative art. Periodically, oriental ideas refreshed and invigorated European ornament; Chinese art was linked with the rococo style, and Indian forms of decoration also exerted a perceptible influence in the eighteenth century.

Many byways in the history of ornament are opened up by the information so ably condensed in Dora Ware's entries and by Maureen Stafford's lucid illustrations, for their dictionary is considerably more than a work of reference and to dip into their pages is a rewarding experience.

1 *Analysis of Ornament* (Chapman and Hall, 1855).

2 In the course of a discussion following an address given before the Royal Society of Arts.

3 *The Earlier Inhabitants of London* by F. G. Parsons, FRCS, FSA (Cecil Palmer, 1927), Chapter III, p. 96.

4 *Egyptian Decorative Art* (Methuen & Co. Ltd, 1895). (Quoted from the second edition, 1920.) Chapter I, pp. 10–11.

5 Op cit., Chapter III, p. 61.

6 Op. cit., Chapter III, p. 79.

7 Op. cit., Chapter I, p. 10.

DEFINITIONS

A

Abbotsford period: Late 19th century term, invented by furniture historians, to describe the imitation Gothic furniture made during the 1820s and 1830s. Such furniture was often composed of fragments of 15th and early 16th century Gothic carving, clumsily assembled on chairs and other articles. The name is derived from the house in the Gothic taste designed in 1816 by Edward Blore for Sir Walter Scott, and completed by William Atkinson in 1822–3. See also *Gothic Revival*.

Acanthus: The deeply serrated and scalloped leaves and strong, graceful, curving stems of this European plant inspired the formalised decorative motif used with such ubiquity throughout the world since Graeco-Roman times. In classical Greek and Roman ornamentation, its appearance on the capitals of columns of the Corinthian and Composite orders was so usual as to make the motif synonymous with formal classic architecture: it has also been used to enrich mouldings, surfaces, cresting, borders, scrolls and convolutions, often interwoven in continuous coiling spirals of leaves, and as a termination for chair and table legs, sometimes called acanthus feet. *Acanthus spinosus* (prickly-leaved), and *Acanthus mollis* (soft-leaved), are the two varieties on which the motif is based; in England the plant is a hardy herbaceous perennial, called brank-ursine, bear's breech, or bear's foot.

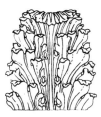

ACANTHUS SPINOSUS

GREEK
based on acanthus spinosus

ROMAN
based on acanthus mollis

BOOK-PLATE. EYNES late 16th Cent.

FRENCH
LATE RENAISSANCE

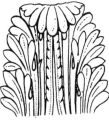

ROMAN

THOMAS SHERATON. ENGLISH 1791

ROMAN

Achievement: in heraldry, the achievement, or achievement of arms, means the complete armorial bearings, *q.v.*, of a person entitled to them. See also *Hatchment*.

ALEX: IRVINE OF DRUM 1457

SHIELD; HELM CROWNED AND CRESTED
WITH MANTLE AND SUPPORTERS

RALPH de MON THERMER. 1301
SHIELD OF ARMS, HELM WITH CREST AND MANTLE,
HORSE-CREST AND ARMORIAL TRAPPERS.

Acorn ornament: from the 16th to 18th centuries, acorn-shaped ornaments were used as decorative terminals and pendants on furniture, notably back stools and chairs, and in the 18th century on the hoods of long case clocks: hence the terms acorn chair and acorn top: in the late 18th, 19th and early 20th centuries blind and curtain cords often ended in a small ornamental acorn. The club device on playing cards is a development of the acorns that represented the suit on German packs. See *Clubs* and *Split Baluster*.

from TABLE, WELSH

JACOBEAN

Acrostolium: an ornament on the prow of a galley, often a spiral or volute shape, but occasionally the snout of an animal, a helmet or a buckler.

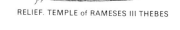

RELIEF. TEMPLE of RAMESES III THEBES

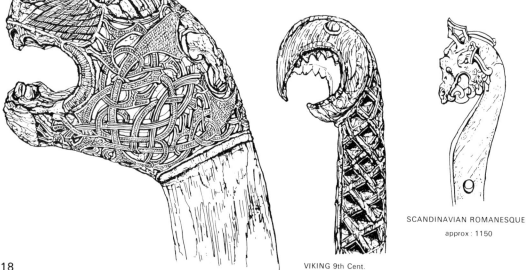

SCANDINAVIAN ROMANESQUE
approx : 1150

VIKING 9th Cent.

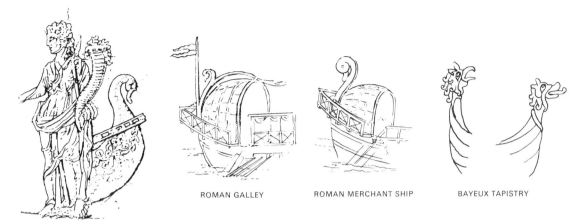

ROMAN GALLEY   ROMAN MERCHANT SHIP   BAYEUX TAPISTRY

from ROMAN COIN. reign of TITUS. 79–81 AD

Acroterion or **Acroterium**: the usual architectural meaning of this word is the block or pedestal, with or without an ornament, that rests on the top or ends of a pediment: it can also mean the ornament with which it may be decorated or which it may bear.

Adam style: the name given to the style that changed English taste in architecture, interior decoration, furniture and allied arts, during the last third of the 18th century: its characteristics are great delicacy and lightness, derived from a new and elegant interpretation of classic ornament. Created and developed by the architect Robert Adam (1728–92), following his detailed studies of classical remains in Italy and Dalmatia, it became for some thirty years a national style.

ROBERT ADAM DESIGN. late 18th Cent.

Aegicrane: see *Ram's head*.

ALTAR VATICAN MUSEUM

Aesculapius, rod of: the rod round which a serpent is coiled, used as an emblem of healing. The motif derives from Aesculapius, the Greek god of healing and medicine, represented in classical art as an elderly bearded man leaning on a serpent-entwined staff: the serpent, *q.v.*, then a symbol of rejuvenation, and allegedly able to discern healing herbs, was sacred to him.

Agnus dei: a religious symbol ; also known as the Holy Lamb, Lamb of God, or Pascal Lamb : a symbolic representation of Christ : the lamb is crowned by a nimbus containing a cross or the monogram of Christ (see *Monogram*), and bears a staff terminating in a cross, on its shoulder : the lamb is sometimes shown standing on a rounded hill with four streams flowing from the base, symbolising the gospels of the four Evangelists. As the badge of the Order of the Knights Templars, that originated with the Crusades and flourished from 1118 to 1309, the Agnus Dei has become the device of the Middle Temple. See *Lamb*.

Aldine leaf: an early binders' ornament, *q.v.* consisting of one or two leaves, with a stalk varying in length and curve. The name is derived from Aldus Manutius, a famous 15th century printer and binder in Venice. The motif was also used as a printers' flower, *q.v.* when it acted as a punctuation sign or to indicate the beginning or ending of a line.

SUB-TITLE FROM THE FIRST PRAYER BOOK
OF THE REFORMED CHURCH OF ENGLAND

TITLE PAGE. FIRST SEPARATE EDITION OF THE PSALTER ENGLISH

Alerion or Allerion: an archaic name for an eagle : in heraldry, it is applied to an eagle displayed, without beak or feet. See also *Aquila* and *Eagle*.

Allegorical ornament: emblems, figures or motifs that convey, by their visual message, not only a recognisable characteristic, but also an abstract or hidden meaning or principle implied by this characteristic.

ITALIAN RENAISSANCE

Alternation: descriptive term for two separate motifs, repeated successively in the same order.

American Colonial: the term for the style of architecture, furniture and related arts before and at the time of the American Revolution in the thirteen originally British colonies. Though closely identified with the periods from Jacobean to Chippendale in England, it was more than an understanding of the orders of architecture, and the design system so represented or a reflection of current English taste. Architects and craftsmen of different regions developed distinctive and personal interpretations of the classic idiom; as their furniture designs gave leading reputations to the cabinet-makers of Albany, Boston, Philadelphia and Salem. The description "colonial" ended with the establishment in 1789 of the Federal Government.

NEWPORT. WRITING-TABLE. MAHOGANY. 1765–75

PHILADELPHIA STYLE. HIGHBOY. MAHOGANY. 1765–1780

American Empire style: a modern term for furniture made in the United States in the early 19th century, that was influenced by the contemporary French Empire style: such furniture was ornamented with boldly carved classical motifs.

American Federal style: a modern term sometimes used for furniture made in the United States *c.* 1790–1820, in which national symbols such as the eagle were associated with military trophies.

Ammonite: this coiled shellfish fossil originally inspired the motif used in 18th century architectural ornament: the name is derived from the ancient Egyptian ram god, Amon, whose horned head resembled the fossil. See also *Nautilus shell* and *Volute.*

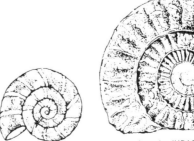

from the JURASSIC PERIOD

Amorini: winged cupids, also called putti, used in carved ornament and decorative sculpture during and after the Renaissance. Some authorities suggest that amorini evolved from the winged angels of early Christian and medieval art.

IVORY DIPTYCH. Cover for the ETCHMIADZIN GOSPELS. BYZANTINE. 6th Cent.

CHANDLER

Amphisbaena: a fabulous monster in the form of a dragon with a head and wings at either end of its body, symbolising the devil's ability to move back and forth at will: used in medieval symbolic ornament.

Anchor: combined with an egg, the fluke of an anchor forms the architectural ornament known as egg-and-anchor, that decorates much classical moulding. See *Egg-and-tongue.* The anchor is also used as an heraldic device, and as a ceramic mark, notably on 18th century Chelsea china: it symbolises hope, patience and faith, also commerce and navigation, and is an attribute of SS. Clement of Rome and Nicholas of Bari, the patron saint of Russia.

EARLY CHRISTIAN, OF SALVATION

BEWDLEY

DERBY. CHELSEA

Andro-sphinx: the Greek name for the Egyptian sphinx, that had a lion's body and the head of a man. See *Sphinx.*

Angulated lines: sharp-angled, zigzag lines which may be arranged to form a pattern of steps: this ornamentation appears on Druidical monuments, Celtic crosses, and in early Celtic MSS, and was used in Britain and Ireland from the 5th to 11th centuries. See *Line.*

'Ankh: originally an ancient Egyptian religious symbol signifying life, it survived after Egypt became a Roman province, and was adopted by the Coptic sect, who often used it in conjunction with the cross, with which it was at times confused. Sometimes called the Crux Ansata, or the Key of Life.

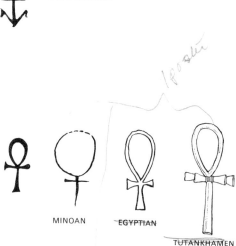

MINOAN   EGYPTIAN

TUTANKHAMEN

Annulet: in architecture, a narrow, flat band or fillet encircling a column: it may be used alone, combined with other mouldings, or repeated in series: it is also used thus, as ornament, by cabinet-makers: sometimes called a cincture, or shaft ring. In heraldry, where it signifies a fifth son, it appears as a plain ring that may be used singly, in groups, or conjoined: when two or three are interlaced they are sometimes called gemel or gimmel rings.

CLUSTERED COLUMN WITH
*ANNULETS AND *FILLETS

FIFTH SON

ANNULETS CONJOINED

Antefix: of classical origin, an ornamental block fixed to the lower edge of a roof where it conceals the tile ending: normally used in series, generally in the form of an anthemion, *q.v.,* antefixae may also appear as lions' heads carved on the upper mouldings of a cornice, where they act as water-spouts as well as decorative units.

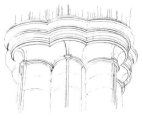

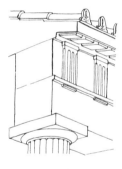

ON GREEK DORIC TEMPLE

GRECIAN, time of PERICLES

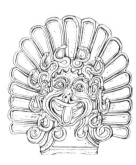

SATYR'S HEAD ANTEFIX
SICILY early 5th Cent. BC

GORGON ANTEFIX
MUSEO DI VILLA GUILIA

Anthemion: a conventional floral motif of great antiquity, probably based on the honeysuckle flower and leaves, though some authorities believe it to have originated in the Egyptian lotus and buds, or the palm tree branch of leaves stretched out like an open hand: the formalised flowers and leaves may appear as a single ornament or in a continuous band, joined by a running scroll. A form of anthemion ornament, combined with pine cones, embellished the Sacred Tree, *q.v.,* but the formalised palmette, or honeysuckle ornament, as it is sometimes called, is universally known as a typical classical motif, used decoratively in sculpture and architecture, on furniture, ceramics or painted surfaces, by Etruscans, Greeks, Romans, and later in Romanesque, Renaissance and late 18th and early 19th century ornamentation. The ornament gave its name to an 18th century chair with an oval back containing a formal honeysuckle device of curved bars. The alternate names of honeysuckle and palmette derive from the alleged plant origins of the two versions of the motif.

GREEK STELE HEAD with ANTHEMION

ERECHTHEION

GREEK

GRAVESTONE. TROAD LATE 6th Cent. BC

RENAISSANCE   RENAISSANCE   CHAIR BACK ENGLISH 1780–85

Aplustre: an ornament forming the upper part of the poop in an early ship: thin planks of wood, joined to the stern by a circular boss, curved upwards into a kind of fan: apart from its decorative appearance, it gave the helmsman some protection in bad weather, and was also used as a maritime device or naval trophy.

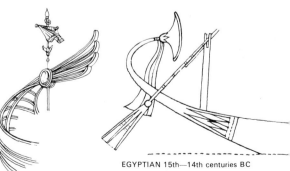

EGYPTIAN 15th—14th centuries BC

Apophyge: see *Congé*.

Applied ornament: a term that became popular in the mid 19th century, which describes ornament in the form of plain or enriched mouldings, or pieces of wood in diamond, lozenge or triangle shapes, applied to a flat surface for decorative effect: cresting, *q.v.*, may also be carved separately and applied to frames, yoke rails, and the tops of cabinets.

Aquarius: the water-carrier: the eleventh sign of the Zodiac. See *Zodiacal devices*.

Aquila: the Latin word for eagle: an alternative term for the ornamental reading desk, carved in the form of an eagle with outspread wings, and generally known as a lectern.

GERMAN RENAISSANCE

Arabesque: the word means Arabian, and in that sense is used to describe the intricately interlaced, geometric patterns evolved in the Arabian civilisations of the Middle East and North Africa, and in the Moorish states of Spain established after the Arab invasion of the 8th century. This Oriental style had classical affinities: flowing lines, fanciful combinations of figures, animals, foliage, landscapes, scrolls, flowers and fruit, were used for surface decoration by the Greeks, Romans, and in the Byzantine Eastern Empire. After the Roman Empire collapsed, and the province of Egypt was conquered by the Arabs, the characteristics of the style were appropriated by the invaders, who, in compliance with the Moslem faith, omitted all human and animal forms, leaving only complex geometrical patterns. The word arabesque, or moresque, became the accepted description of this intricate interwoven ornament. About AD 1500 the Baths of Titus in Rome (built AD 80), were excavated, revealing the original arabesque ornament, both there, and in ancient caves and grottoes. Raphael's adoption of this form of decoration for the Vatican loggias revived this ornamental style, which was widely used in Renaissance art, while its character became more fantastic and complicated: its alternative description as grotesque, *q.v.*, or grottesche, arose from the discoveries made in ancient Roman houses, tombs and theatres. This form of decoration influenced typographical design in 16th century Italy. See *Printers' flowers*.

ARABESQUE WINGS. ITALIAN

Arabian Fret: closely related to the raking fret, *q.v.*: a motif characterised by the use of an oblique line and right-angled key: it may also appear as a pattern of interlaced diagonal lines.

Arabian ornament: see *Arabesque*.

Arcading: this term describes the ornamentation of walls or furniture by a series of arches springing from columns, piers or pilasters: the arches may intersect each other, and be enriched with decorated mouldings. When free-standing, this arrangement is called an arcade, and when closed, or joined to the basic surface, it is known as a blind arcade. This form of decoration is characteristic of Romanesque and medieval ornament, and in the late 16th and 17th centuries was widely used on furniture and chimney-pieces. See *Split Baluster*.

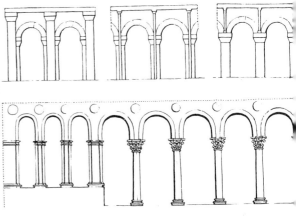

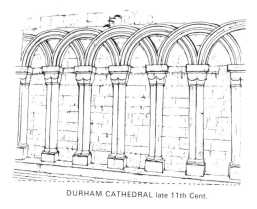

DURHAM CATHEDRAL late 11th Cent.

Archbishop's cross: another name for a patriarchal cross, *q.v.*

Aries: the ram: the first sign of the Zodiac. See *Zodiacal devices.*

Armorial bearings: the heraldic term for the arms, helmet, crest, mantling, supporters, coronet and insignia of Orders: this complete display is called an achievement of arms.

Armorial style: during the late 18th and early 19th centuries this term was sometimes used to describe half-timbered buildings of the Tudor period, with beams decorated by carved heraldic motifs. Later in the 19th century, when the works of Sir Walter Scott had awakened fresh enthusiasm for heraldry, the term was occasionally applied to furniture, which was often adorned with misplaced and inaccurate heraldic devices.

Arms: in heraldry, the most important and essential part of armorial bearings, *q.v.* The arms are the heraldic devices emblazoned on a shield, and also formerly on a surcoat, hence the terms shield of arms and coat of arms.

Arrow: as a form of triangular motif, the arrow-head was used in primitive decoration, to signify war, and as a directional sign. In heraldry, arrows may appear singly, in groups, or bound in bundles: the barbed head or pheon, may be shown with engrailed, *q.v.*, inner edges, but with plain edges it is sometimes called a broad arrow: the heraldic term for a ball-headed arrow is bird-bolt. The arrowtail also has an affinity with the triangle, and a highly formalised feathered tail is a Japanese heraldic device used on crests. As a Christian emblem, the arrow sometimes symbolises martyrdom, and is an attribute of SS. Sebastian, Christina and Ursula: it also signifies death, destruction and disease. It has been used as a rebus, *q.v.*, on the name Fletcher, which was the medieval term for an arrow-maker. The arrow back type of American

Windsor chair, made in the late 19th century, is so-called because of arrow-shaped spindles in the back. Crossed arrows, sometimes headless, an arrow-head with a half-shaft, or an arrow combined with initials, are some of the many variations in which this motif appears as a ceramic mark. See also *Blunt arrow*.

Art Nouveau: sometimes called New Art. A late 19th century attempt to create an original style, that became an aesthetic and cultural movement, anti-traditional, anti-historical, and presenting a revolutionary challenge to all accepted artistic conceptions. Though hints of its character were anticipated in England in the work of William Blake, the Pre-Raphaelites, and the designs of Walter Crane and, to a lesser extent, those of Arthur H. Mackmurdo, the first exponents of the style, which flourished during the last two decades of the 19th century, were the Belgian architects, Victor Horta (1861–1947) and Henry van de Velde (1863–1957): their work quickly influenced design in architecture, furniture, interior decoration, printing and allied arts. The style of ornamentation that characterised the movement had a varied terminology, but the accepted term in France, England and America, became Art Nouveau, derived from the name of a shop opened in Paris in 1895, part of which had been designed by van de Velde. The characteristic decorative features of Art Nouveau are the flowing, snaky, asymetrical lines, with naturalistic motifs, heart-shaped inlay and pierced apertures, and inserted patches of enamel and copper. See also *Quaint style, Roseball,* and *Yachting style.*

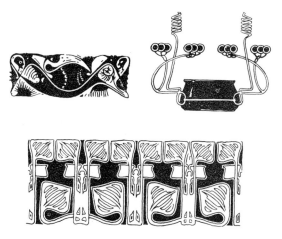

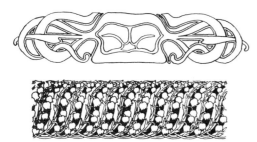

Asp: often winged, the asp was an ancient Egyptian motif, symbolising dominion: asps were incorporated in the winged globe, *q.v.*; they appeared one on each side of the cartouche bearing a king's name in hieroglyphics: and entire friezes consisted of series of the cobra de capello, or swelling asp. Later, the asp became a favourite subject in medieval Christian sculpture where, placed beneath the feet of Christ, it represented victory over malice. The tail covering one ear symbolised disbelief, and it was also shown as a squat lizard, or a winged reptile, or with short legs and a serpent's tail.

VIPERA ASPIS   ROMAN. from ISIAC PROCESSION

Asterisk: a star used as a printers' flower or ornament in 15th century Italy, and this remains its true function: during the 16th century it was inserted to denote a corrupt text, and as a discreet substitute for the letters of a proper name: later still, the sign became a footnote reference mark: it was also substituted for a line, and used thus, in series, once more fulfilled its original function of a printers' flower. In modern usage the asterisk may refer to a footnote: to the names of deceased persons in college lists: to mark a paid-up newspaper advertisement: to divide verses into parts: to indicate the responses in religious service books: to identify a new form of word in philology: and to indicate various typographical requirements on proofs. In the 18th century the asterisk was called an asterism, *q.v.*

Asterism: a group of asterisks, *q.v.*, used thus to draw attention: the 18th century term for an asterisk.

****

****

****

****

Astragal: a small, semi-circular convex moulding, used around the top or base of a column, to embellish an architrave, or to cover a joint: often enriched with bead and reel, *q.v.*, and sometimes called a bead: other names are bagnette, baguette, roundel, or tondino (archaic). The word is derived from the Greek word for an animal's knuckle bone.

WITH BEAD AND REEL

Astroid: see *Star*.

Atlantes: carved male figures or half-figures, used as supports in place of columns: in medieval times the word was sometimes used to mean a column: derived from the name of the god Atlas, who in Greek mythology, held up the heavens. Also called gigantes, perces, or telamones.

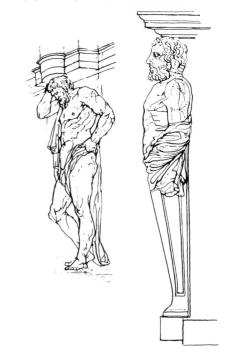

Auger flame: a twisted spiral ornament like an auger, and used as a finial, *q.v.*, on furniture: an American term. See *American Colonial*.

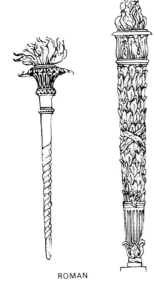

ROMAN

AMERICAN COLONIAL STYLE

from 'DE PROPRIETATE VERUM' 1495

Aureole: a form of halo that surrounds the complete body in personifications of only God, Christ, and the Virgin Mary: it may also envelop delineations of the souls of saints or of Lazarus, but not of their bodies. If the subject represented is seated, the aureole is circular, if standing it becomes oval or almond-shaped, and sometimes appears as lobes, separately enclosing the head, arms and feet of the figure: it may also be oblong, or crossed by a rainbow. Rarely used in classical ornament, this device has become a common Christian symbol; sometimes known as a glory, mandorla, nimbus, or vesica piscis, but is not, correctly, a nimbus, *q.v.*

from THE COVERDALE BIBLE 1535

from THE BOOK OF CANTICLES

Auricular ornament: a macabre form of ornamentation in which devices that simulated portions
of the human body combined with many ear-
shaped curves, were used for the decoration,
first of silver, and later of furniture. Originating in
early 17th century Holland, with the designs of the
van Vianens, silversmiths, and encouraged by an
increased knowledge of anatomy, the style also
became popular in Germany, where it was called
knorpelwork.

B

Bacchante: the Roman term for the Greek maenad. A decorative female figure associated with Bacchus and his rites.

GREEK

ROMAN TOMB H. ST PETER'S NECROPOLIS

Badge: in heraldry the word means a device that could be included in an achievement, *q.v.*, or worn as a distinguishing mark by servants, retainers and followers not entitled to armorial bearings but who were attached to a royal or noble family possessing such bearings: also called a cognizance. Badges were in use before shields of arms, and the devices of the latter were sometimes derived from a badge: they often commemorated a family alliance or exploit, or were a rebus, *q.v.*, on the name. Badges are now an ornamental identification of societies, schools, universities, corporations and of the armed forces, where, as successors to the regimental badges that have existed since Roman times, they also have a recognition value in modern warfare. See *Wheat*.

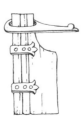

DACRE OF GILSLAND and
DACRE OF THE NORTH

WILLOUGHBY

Bagnette or Baguette: an alternative name for astragal, *q.v.* Also used for a little ring-like moulding, like the astragal, but smaller, and usually carved with foliage or pearl enrichment: thus embellished it is sometimes called a chaplet.

Ball finial: the high backs and back uprights of Norman and medieval settles often terminated in a ball, or ball and cross, and a ball finial appeared as a similar device on the back uprights of turned chairs in 17th century England and the American colonies.

Ball flower: a carved ornament in the form of a globular, three-petalled flower, enclosing a ball: used singly, or in series, sometimes joined by stalks, and usually to encircle a hollow moulding, this is a characteristic motif of the Decorated period of Gothic architecture in the 14th century. Its origin is obscure, but it may be derived from the horse-chestnut fruit, or the pomegranate.

Ball turning: a series of balls or spheres, of equal size, formed the ornamental turning on chair stretchers in the ancient world, and a comparable motif was used on Norman and medieval chair legs and stretchers often combined with rings, and later, from the 17th to the 19th centuries, ball turning was a common decorative device for furniture legs. The spherical foot used on heavy furniture in the 17th and 18th centuries was called a ball foot. See also *Ball finial* and *Turned ornament*.

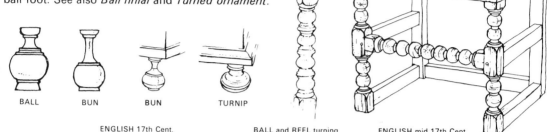

BALL   BUN   BUN   TURNIP

ENGLISH 17th Cent.   BALL and REEL turning   ENGLISH mid 17th Cent.

Ballaster: see *Baluster.*

Baluster: the architectural term for a small column or pillar, usually circular in plan, and swelling in the middle or at the base: used in series to form a balustrade. Its shape has inspired a number of ornamental forms used in furniture design: baluster turning, and the baluster leg on tables, were characteristic of 16th and 17th century work, while the self-explanatory terms, baluster back, and baluster-and-spindle, are de-rived from the baluster-shaped splats in the backs of 18th and 19th century Windsor chairs: baluster-and-bobbin and baluster-and-ring turning, in which bobbins and rings were combined with balusters, adorned long-case clock hoods.

Baluster stem is the term applied to a glass with a baluster-shaped stem, sometimes called a Portuguese swell. Ballaster and banister are corruptions of the term. See *Turned ornament* and *Queen's House.*

ENGLISH 18th Cent.

RINGED.
circa 1670

ELONGATED
ENGLISH
STOOL
mid 17th Cent.

PANETIÈRE. PROVENCAL. early 19th century

TURNED BALUSTERS.
STICK-BACK CHAIR 19th Cent.

early   and late 18th Cent.
(BALUSTER)-SHAPED CHAIR-SPLATS

PIERCED BALUSTER,
BOW-BACK ARMCHAIR
1850—onwards

TRUE

INVERTED

TRUE and
RINGED

GLASS

LIGHT, NEWCASTLE
BALUSTER GOBLET

BALUSTRADE. NAPLES

BALUSTER and SEAL TOP
1563, silver

VILLA D'ESTE

WROUGHT IRON.

Baluster-and-bobbin: see *Baluster*.

Baluster-and-ring: see *Baluster*.

Baluster-and-spindle: see *Baluster*.

Bamboo: decorative motifs, based on the bamboo, have been used since early times in China and Japan, where the reed had symbolic associations with myth and folklore. Later, furniture made from the variety *bambusa arundinacea*, was imported into England from the East, and from the mid-18th century onwards much simulated bamboo furniture was made, in an attempt to reproduce the decorative qualities provided by the colour and variations in stem thickness, of the natural wood. The bamboo cane was imitated in the 'Bamboo Ware' busts and statuettes produced by Josiah Wedgwood in 1770, and during the 18th and early 19th centuries, other potters produced simulated bamboo decoration on dishes, jugs, bulb pots, bowls and imitation piecrusts.

CHIPPENDALE STYLE BED 1765

from 'BRITISH FURNITURE THROUGH THE AGES' by MAUREEN STAFFORD and KEITH MIDDLEMAS by kind permission of ARTHUR BARKER LTD

Band: a narrow moulding, of square or rectangular section, encircling the shaft of a column: also called a fillet. A band also describes a continuous flat ornamental form, usually consisting of a geometrical or plant pattern, applied to flat surfaces or as a border to textiles, ceramics, or typographical designs: in medieval times it was sometimes called a tablet. See *Bandelet,* and *Chain, Evolute spiral, Foliated, Fret, Interlacement, Palmette, Rosette, Undulate* and *Vertebrate bands.*

Bandelet or Bandlet: in architecture, a very narrow flat moulding: also used as a diminutive of band, *q.v.* See also *Tresse.*

Banderolle or Bannerolle: in architecture, an ornamental flat band bearing an inscription or motto: the word may also mean an heraldic banner used at the funeral of an important personage.

HELM MANTLE and CREST with BANDEROLLES

Bandy legs: see *Cabriole profile.*

Banister: see *Baluster.*

Banner: a square or oblong flag, attached to the upper part of a pole, and bearing symbolic ornament or heraldic arms. Banners were used in ancient Rome, and, after Christianity became the official religion of the Empire, to display the Labarum or monogram of Christ (see *Monogram*), and in the Middle Ages by religious foundations, in processions, at tournaments, battles, and other military occasions: in heraldry, a banner is borne by the Sovereign, princes and barons, ornamented with their arms: the Sovereign's banner is the Royal Standard. The Union Jack combines the national banners of England, Scotland and Ireland, the crosses of St George, St Andrew, and St Patrick

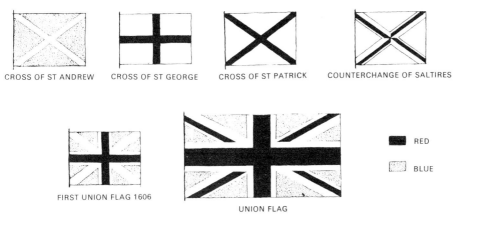

CROSS OF ST ANDREW   CROSS OF ST GEORGE   CROSS OF ST PATRICK   COUNTERCHANGE OF SALTIRES

FIRST UNION FLAG 1606

UNION FLAG

■ RED

☐ BLUE

Bar: in heraldry, an ordinary, *q.v.*, consisting of two or three or more horizontal bars in the centre of a shield, dividing it: the barrulet and closet are narrower versions of the bar.

TWO BARS   BARRY

Bar tracery: in this development of plate tracery, *q.v.*, which it eventually replaced, slender members rise from window mullions, and interlace in a geometrical pattern to fill the window head. See also *Tracery.*

Barley sugar twist: decorative turning, in the form of a spiral twist like a stick of barley sugar, developed in the mid 17th century, and used on the legs and underframes of furniture, and occasionally on clock hoods: also called double rope or double twist. See *Turned ornament.*

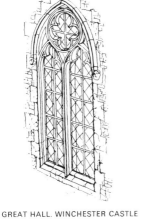

GREAT HALL. WINCHESTER CASTLE

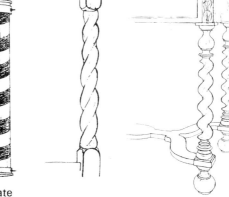

SPIRAL-TURNING or BARLEY-SUGAR TWIST
ENGLISH TABLE late 17th Cent.

Barber's pole: the pole, decorated by alternate spirals of red and white, is an old sign, indicating a barber's shop: some authorities suggest that the red pole, with its white, bandage-like stripes, has a connection with the barber-surgeons of the past.

Baroque style: a vigorous architectural style that developed in 17th century Italy, and, with national variations, spread throughout Europe, where it influenced decoration until the end of the 18th century. The word 'baroque' means irregular or imperfect. It was a florid style, characterised by an exuberant profusion of motifs—festoons of flowers and fruits, masks, scrolls, wreaths, and trophies of weapons and musical instruments: although the style was a reaction against Palladian formality, baroque ornament retained its classical affinities. See also *Rococo*.

Barrulet: see Bar.

Basilisk: a fabulous monster of mythological origin, whose gaze caused instant death: it appears as a gigantic cock with brass beak and claws and a three-pointed serpentine tail, and in heraldry, is portrayed as a wyvern, *q.v.*: an emblem of evil. See *Olive*.

Battlement: see *Castellated* and *Embattled*.

Bay leaf: the leaf of the bay tree, *laurus nobilis*, is used as a decorative enrichment, in a festoon, or, in garland form, on a torus moulding, *q.v.*

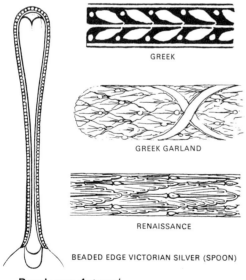

GREEK

GREEK GARLAND

RENAISSANCE

BEADED EDGE VICTORIAN SILVER (SPOON)

Bead: see *Astragal.*

Bead and quirk: see *Quirked bead.*

Bead and reel: a decorative motif consisting of a string of alternate beads and reels, used as an enrichment on a moulding, especially on the astragal, *q.v.*

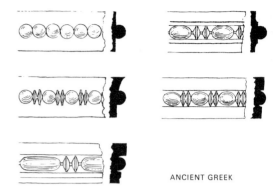

ANCIENT GREEK

Beading: see *Pearling.*

Beakhead: a characteristic Norman ornament, used as a moulding enrichment, and usually consisting of a continuous series of long-beaked birds' heads: a variation, in which the bird's head and beak are replaced by an animal's head and lolling tongue, is known as a cat's head.

Bell-and-baluster: the term describes a form of decorative turning, probably of Dutch origin, used in England in the late 17th and early 18th centuries, on the legs of small stands and side tables: a bell formed the upper part of the leg, and the lower part was shaped like a slender baluster, *q.v.*

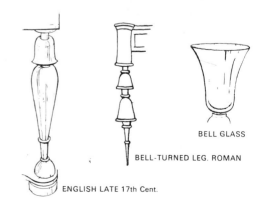

BELL GLASS

BELL-TURNED LEG. ROMAN

ENGLISH LATE 17th Cent.

Bellflower: an ornamental motif, used by American cabinet-makers, in the 18th century, in carved and inlaid work: basically it was a formal, three-petalled flower, with variations in the shape of the petals. See also *Husks*.

AMERICAN CABINET-MAKERS VARIATIONS

Bend: an heraldic term, meaning an ordinary, *q.v.*, consisting of one or two diagonal lines crossing a shield, *q.v.*, from the top right hand corner to the lower left hand edge: the bend sinister crosses a shield in the opposite direction, i.e. from the top left to the lower right. The term bendy describes a shield crossed diagonally by several bends. A bend of half the normal width is called a bendlet. The left (or sinister) and the right (or dexter) sides of a shield are described thus from the standpoint of the man behind it.

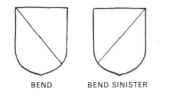

BEND   BEND SINISTER

Bendlet: see *Bend*.

Biedermeier: a style of furnishing and interior decoration, opulent and coarse, that originated in Germany after the Napoleonic Wars: the name is derived from a philistine character who appeared in the pages of the journal, *Fliegende Blätter*. Biedermeier was a debased form and parody of the style known as French Empire (see *Empire Style*), and was characterised by an excessive use of metal ornament, heavily embossed, and used in conjunction with black horsehair upholstery: it owed its popularity largely to the uneducated and meretricious taste of the newly rich classes then emerging in England and Europe.

Bifrons: this word means, literally, double-faced: a device widely used in classical Roman ornament, whereby a bust presented two heads, placed back to back, each face looking in an opposite direction: these busts were erected at crossroads, and used as terminal ornaments in gardens and libraries. The device is derived from the Roman god, Janus, the guardian deity of gates, and to whom the first month of the year, January, with its implication of looking backwards and forwards at one time, was sacred. See *Janus*.

Biga: the term that describes two draught animals yoked together and harnessed to a vehicle: originally applied to a Roman processional chariot, it has since become an ornamental sculptural form.

GOAT DRAWN BIGA from SEAL: MINOAN

Billet: in architecture, a characteristic Romanesque and Norman ornament, used as an enrichment to hollow mouldings; and in the late 15th and early 16th centuries it sometimes appeared on the moulding at the top of a wall panel. Billet ornament consists of a series of short cylinders or square-sectioned blocks, arranged at regular intervals in a row, or rows, in the latter case alternately in each row. In heraldry, the term describes an upright oblong figure.

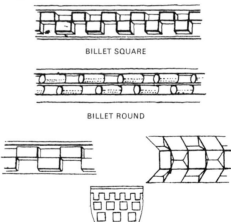

BILLET SQUARE

BILLET ROUND

10 BILLETS (HERALDIC) CHIPPENHAM (ct.-of-arms)

Binders' ornaments: Decoration of covers and backs of books began shortly after the introduction of leather-covered boards and leather backs to protect vellum pages, circa 500 AD. Early ornamentation, consisting of metal-impressed points and lines, was followed by the use of small decorative patterns stamped by intaglio-cut tools, known as "blind-stamping". The development and improvement of binders tools and the growth of the binders technical skill resulted in an increased variety of adornments. From the Aldine leaf, *q.v.* there followed geometrical, heraldic, mythological and naturalistic motifs, and, in the late 15th century, gold leaf tooling.

ST CUTHBERT'S GOSPELS. 7th-8th Cent.

ENGLISH. 19th Cent.

ENGLISH 1660

ENGLISH

GERMAN. late 19th Cent.

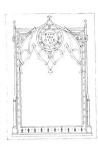

FRENCH. 19th Cent.

Librairie Larousse Paris

Bird-bolt: see *Arrow*.

Birdsbeak: a supporting moulding that has the appearance of a downward curving bird's beak in section: used on the Greek Doric and Ionic orders. See *Moulding*.

Blind arcade: see *Arcading*.

Blind fret: a light decorative fret carved on or applied to a solid surface. See also *Card-cut*.

Blind tracery: Gothic tracery, *q.v.*, carved on a solid surface.

Blunt arrow: an American term applied to the turned legs of mid 18th century Philadelphia Windsor chairs. The pattern resembled an arrow without a pointed head.

Bobbin turning: ornamental turning in the form of a series of bobbins, used to decorate legs and underframing of furniture in the latter half of the 17th century and, in a more delicate form, 19th century American 'Cottage style' furniture. In America, such turned ornament on chairs and table frames has produced the name bobbin furniture. See also *Turned ornament*.

RING AND BOBBIN TURNING, mid 17th Cent. ENGLISH TABLE

LATE 17th Cent

lection moulding: a projecting moulding, ually of bold, heavy section, that covers a joint tween two surfaces at different levels. See oulding.

oltel: see *Bowtell*.

ook plate: a decorative label gummed inside a ook, with the name and arms or initials of the vner, the latter often in the form of a monogram, ith the words 'Ex Libris' and sometimes a design of aves, flowers, or a scene with figures and uildings. See *Acanthus*.

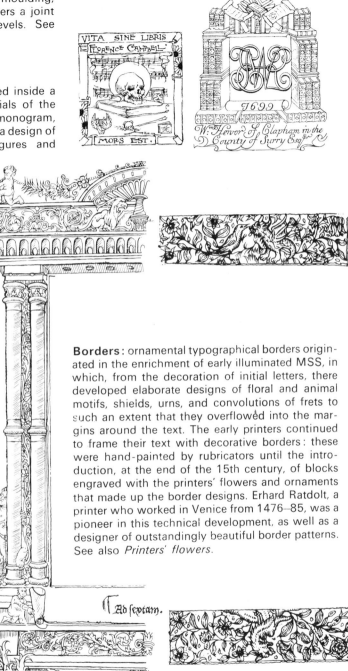

SALTER
57

Borders: ornamental typographical borders origin-ated in the enrichment of early illuminated MSS, in which, from the decoration of initial letters, there developed elaborate designs of floral and animal motifs, shields, urns, and convolutions of frets to such an extent that they overflowed into the mar-gins around the text. The early printers continued to frame their text with decorative borders: these were hand-painted by rubricators until the intro-duction, at the end of the 15th century, of blocks engraved with the printers' flowers and ornaments that made up the border designs. Erhard Ratdolt, a printer who worked in Venice from 1476–85, was a pioneer in this technical development, as well as a designer of outstandingly beautiful border patterns. See also *Printers' flowers*.

This and above as used by W. CAXTON 1490

VOSTRÉ. PARIS *circa* 1515

from BOOK OF 'HOURS' with ORNAMENTS in the ITALIAN RENAISSANCE STYLE

IRST PRINTED
EBREW BIBLE   PIGOUCHET
488   PARIS 1488

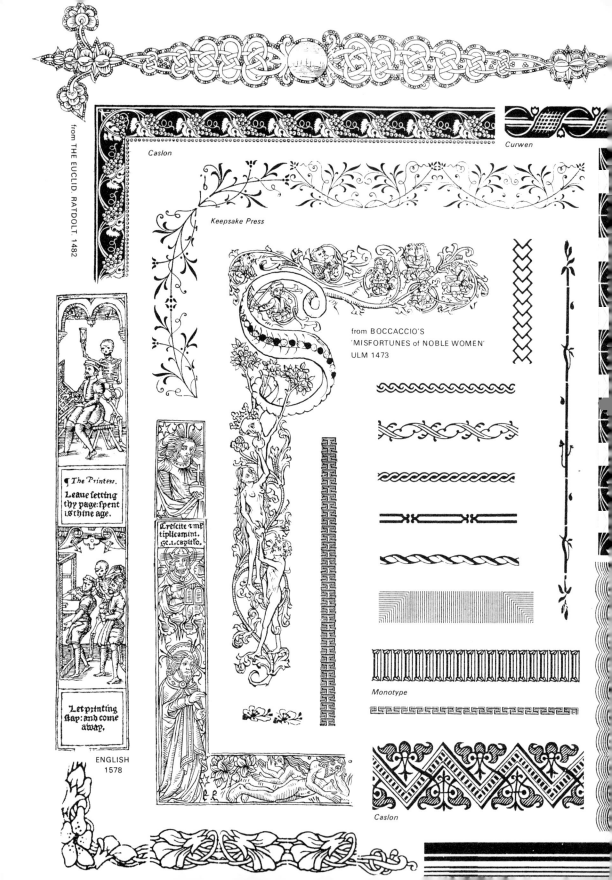

from THE EUCLID. RATDOLT. 1482

Caslon

Curwen

Keepsake Press

from BOCCACCIO'S
'MISFORTUNES of NOBLE WOMEN'
ULM 1473

¶ The Printers.

Leaue fetting
thy page: fpent
is thine age.

Crefcite & mul
tiplicamini.
ge.1. capitfo.

Let printing
ftay: and come
away.

ENGLISH
1578

Monotype

Caslon

Boss: in architecture, a carved projecting ornament that covers the intersection of ribs or beams in roofs and ceilings: it may also form a decorative termination to a dripstone or to mouldings, or, particularly in cabinet-making, may cover the intersections of mouldings. In Early English Gothic architecture, the roof boss consisted of a floreated embellishment, in which the stems were continuations of the rib mouldings: from this an intricate design developed, with foliage, heads, animals, heraldic devices and armorial bearings, associated in many complex and beautiful variations. The word also means an ornamental stud projecting from the centre of a warrior's shield, and sometimes ending in a spike, used as a weapon at close quarters.

Bottel: see *Bowtell*.

Boultin or Boultine: an archaic name for an ovolo moulding, *q.v.*: it has been used to describe a small convex moulding a quarter of a circle in section, also known as quarter round and quadrant bead. See *Moulding*.

Boutel: see *Bowtell*.

Bowtell: the medieval term for a roll moulding about three-quarters of a circle in section, that frequently occurs in Norman architecture: it may also describe a shaft in a clustered column, a jamb or a mullion, and occasionally any cylindrical moulding: a pointed bowtell shows a blunt edge in the centre where the two faces join. The name is derived from its resemblance to an arrow shaft, and variations of the word are boltel, bottel, and boutel. See *Moulding*.

Brace: a typographical term for the symbol formed of conjoined parantheses, that connects two or more lines. Sometimes used to describe a bracket moulding, *q.v.* See also *Toad back moulding*.

Braced, Brased or Brazed: an heraldic term describing the interlacing of identical devices: brased and brazed are archaic forms of the word.

Bracelet: modern American term for a narrow encircling band on the leg of a table or stand, separating it from the foot.

Bracket moulding: a Gothic moulding with the convex faces of two ogee mouldings, *q.v.*, adjoining, giving the appearance of a typographical brace or bracket, *q.v.* Double ogee or brace are alternate names.

Brackets: in typography, the upright curves called correctly parentheses, signify the insertion of a word or sentence into a passage: brackets, strictly speaking, are square, and are used within a quotation, to indicate a comment not contained in the original passage. Page numbers are sometimes set within brackets and parentheses to enhance the appearance of a printed page. Crotch or crotchet are alternate printers' terms for a bracket. See also *Brace* and *Corbel*. In architecture an alternative term for a console. In cabinet-making an eighteenth-century name for a type of case-furniture foot: and for a projecting shelf-support.

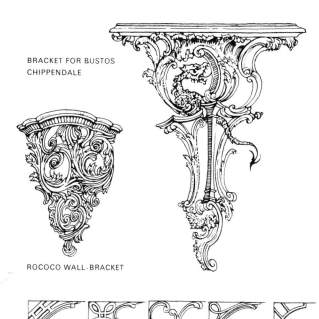

BRACKET FOR BUSTOS
CHIPPENDALE

ROCOCO WALL-BRACKET

CHIPPENDALE, fret-work BRACKETS

WROUGHT IRON.
ENGLISH 18th Cent.

MODILLION, plain
ROMAN

BRACKET FOOT
ENGLISH WALNUT CHEST of DRAWERS 1705

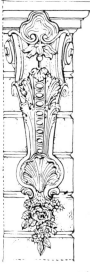

CONSOLE BRACKET.
LOUIS XV style. PARIS

Bracketed style: a mid 19th century American term for a popular style of architecture, based on the structural features of a Swiss châlet, with the projecting eaves of roofs resting on brackets: towards the end of the century it had a slight influence on furniture design.

Braganza toe: a scrolled foot sometimes found on late 17th century chairs. See *Scroll*.

Branched work: a term formerly used to describe carved leaves and branches.

Brased or Brazed: See *Braced*.

Brattishing: an architectural term describing the ornamental cresting on wall parapets, also used on 16th century panelling and screens. The design might consist of miniature battlements, leaves or the motif known as Tudor flower, *q.v.*: brattishing is indeed sometimes called Tudor flower.

Broad arrow: see *Arrow*.

Broken cabriole: cabinet-makers' term for a leg of cabriole profile, *q.v.*, when the curve inside the knee is broken by a straight section.

Buccina: an ancient horn trumpet, straight or curved, originally made of the spiral twisted shell of the crustacean *buccinum*: tritons are sometimes represented holding or blowing this instrument.

HERALDIC

Bucentaur: a variation of the centaur, *q.v.*, and sometimes called a tauro-centaur: a mythological creature, half man, half bull.

Buckle: see *Mask*.

Buckle back: a modern descriptive term for a variation of the Victorian balloon back chair, in which the curve of the back and the ornamentation of the cross-bar suggest the shape of a belt buckle.

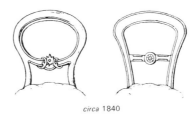

circa 1840

Bucranium: the skull of a bull or ox, garlanded, and used as an ornamental motif on a frieze, and particularly the zoophorus frieze, *q.v.*, of Greek Doric architecture. The device also appeared in conjunction with festoons in Roman ornament, on friezes, sarcophagi or sepulchral urns. The association with wreaths and garlands is derived from their use to bedeck animals that were to be sacrificed.

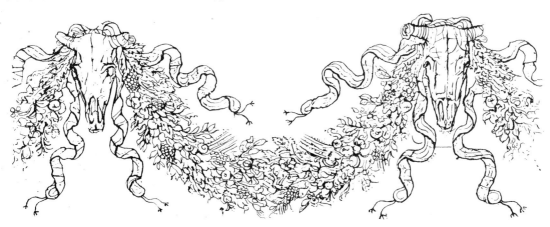

ARA PACIS: AUGUSTAE. ROME

Buddhist emblems: certain ancient Buddhist religious symbols are also used as decorative motifs. Those known as the Eight Ordinary Symbols may adorn porcelain and textiles: the Eight Auspicious Signs, or Emblems of Happy Augury, that, in the form of wood or clay models, stand on Buddhist altars, are also used as architectural ornaments.

Buddhist emblems

THE EIGHT ORDINARY BUDDHIST SYMBOLS

DRAGON PEARL

GOLDEN COIN

LOZENGE

MIRROR

STONE-CHIME

BOOKS

RHINOCEROS' HORNS

ARTEMISIA LEAF

OR

JEWEL

CASH

SYMBOL OF VICTORY

A PAINTING

MUSICAL STONE OF JADE

PAIR OF BOOKS

RHINOCEROS HORN CUPS

ARTEMISIA LEAF

THE (EIGHT) BUDDHIST EMBLEMS OF HAPPY AUGURY

WHEEL AND FLAMES

CONCH—SHELL

UMBRELLA

CANOPY

LOTUS BLOOM

VASE

PAIR OF FISH

ENDLESS KNOT OR ENTRAILS

OR

JAR

CONCH-SHELL

UMBRELLA

CANOPY

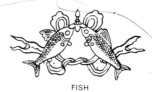

LOTUS

WHEEL

FISH

MYSTIC KNOT

Bulb: an ornamental oval swelling, used as a central ornament on the legs of tables, the supports of press and court cupboards, and bed posts, in the late 16th and early 17th centuries. They were turned and carved. See also *Cup and cover*, and *Melon bulb*.

TABLE

BED

PRESS

CAPITAL: RAMPURVA

Bull: regarded in very early civilisations as a symbol of fertility and physical strength, and possessing mythological associations with Osiris, Zeus, and Cretan sun-worship, this animal, synonymous with the ox, was widely used as an ornamental motif in ancient sculpture and carving. In Egypt, *c.* 3000 BC, ivory chair legs simulated those of a bull: the head was used as a decorative mask and motif on Chinese ritual vessels of the 13th–10th centuries BC: winged bulls with bearded human heads, were dominating features in the architectural composition of royal palaces in Assyria: the capitals of columns in ancient Persian temples and palaces were in the form of a double-headed bull. In heraldry, the bull is sometimes shown with a nose-ring: the Black Bull of Clarence is one of the Queen's Beasts, *q.v.*, winged, it is the symbol of St Luke the Evangelist. See also *Bucranium*.

ST LUKE'S.
GOSPELS OF ST AUGUSTINE. ITALIAN. late 6th century

DOUBLE-BULL. SUSA 4th-Cent. BC

ASSYRIAN WINGED BULL

HERALDIC

Bullion or bull's eye: this circular distortion in the centre of a disc of crown glass, caused by the blowing process used in the early manufacturing methods, was originally considered a blemish, and glass thus distorted was used only in small, cheaply-built cottages, or for unimportant windows in larger houses. The Arts and Crafts movement in the late 19th century, and the 'Cottage style' that followed it, and was popular in the opening decade of the present century, favoured the use of the bull's eye as a decorative device: it was introduced in the glazed doors of cabinets in the New Art and 'Quaint' styles, and in small windows. In architecture, the term means a round or oval window, with a pattern formed by glazing bars radiating from the centre, sometimes called an *oeil-de-boeuf* or a roundel. See also *Eye*.

Bun foot: a foot used in the legs of stands, tables and chairs, shaped like a compressed ball: introduced from Holland in the late 17th century. An American term is onion foot. See *Ball turning*.

Bush of feathers: see *Plume*.

Byzantine ornament: the form of decoration that developed in the Eastern Roman Empire, after the Emperor Constantine established his new capital at the ancient Greek city of Byzantium in AD 330. Byzantine architecture and decoration united classical and oriental elements. Christian symbols, the cross, the monogram of Christ, surrounded by acanthus foliations and scrolls, were associated with a variety of motifs: fish, birds, the vine, the interlaced knot of eternity, and intricate arabesques, forming a dazzling composition, executed in sparkling mosaics. See *Amorini* and *Roundel*.

MARBLE RELIEF. RAVENNA. mid 6th century

THE ASCENT OF ALEXANDER.
CONSTANTINOPLE. 11th or 12th century

C

C-scroll: a C-shaped scroll; a characteristic ornamental element first introduced in rococo decoration in the early 18th century. Occasionally used on chair backs of the early Georgian period.

Cable moulding: a round convex moulding enriched with cable ornament, *q.v.* Also known as rope moulding.

Cable ornament: a moulding enrichment representing twisted ropes, originally used in Romanesque and Norman decoration, and sometimes called rope ornament.

Cabling: an architectural term, used in the 18th century, to describe a cable moulding, *q.v.*, that fills the flutes on the shaft of a column, for a third of the height from the base.

Cabochon: an ornamental device in carved decoration and jewellery, with a convex motif, round or oval, surmounted by acanthus foliations, scrolls, and shellwork. Sometimes used in conjunction with strapwork, *q.v.*, and on furniture in the early 18th century.

Cabriole profile: originally derived from the shape of a four-footed animal's leg, with a double curve, convex above, concave below, first used by the Greeks on the privileged seats of carved stone in theatres: the profile reappeared in Holland and France in the late 17th century, and in England in the early 18th, and was used on chair and table legs, and in the mid 18th century, on the angles of case furniture. Chair legs with these opposing curves were sometimes known as bandy legs. The term cabriole was not used to describe the double curve until the late 19th century. See also *Broken cabriole*.

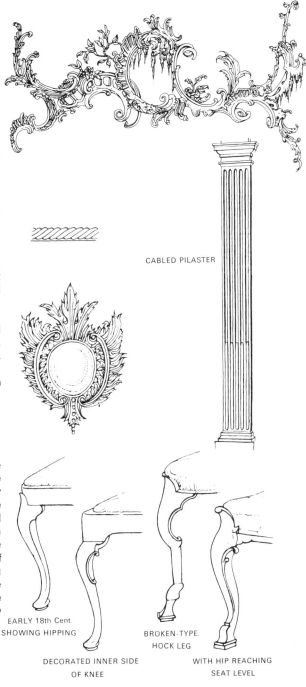

CABLED PILASTER

EARLY 18th Cent.
SHOWING HIPPING

DECORATED INNER SIDE
OF KNEE

BROKEN-TYPE.
HOCK LEG

WITH HIP REACHING
SEAT LEVEL

Cadency marks: an heraldic term, also called differences, for the devices that identify sons of the same family.

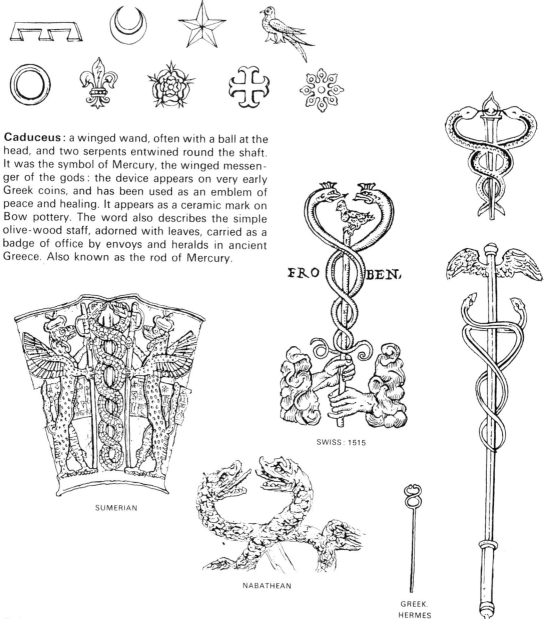

Caduceus: a winged wand, often with a ball at the head, and two serpents entwined round the shaft. It was the symbol of Mercury, the winged messenger of the gods: the device appears on very early Greek coins, and has been used as an emblem of peace and healing. It appears as a ceramic mark on Bow pottery. The word also describes the simple olive-wood staff, adorned with leaves, carried as a badge of office by envoys and heralds in ancient Greece. Also known as the rod of Mercury.

FRO BEN.

SWISS: 1515

SUMERIAN

NABATHEAN

GREEK.
HERMES

ITALIAN *circa* 1560

Calvary cross: a Latin cross, *q.v.*, resting on steps: sometimes called a Passion cross.

Cancer: the crab: the fourth sign of the Zodiac. See *Zodiacal devices*.

Canephora: a caryatid, *q.v.*, with a basket supported on the head : the word is derived from the sacred baskets borne by women in one of the great Athenian religious festivals.

COLUMN OF ACANTHUS 4th Cent. BC

Capricornus: the goat : the tenth sign of the Zodiac. See *Zodiacal devices*.

Carbuncle: an heraldic term describing an ornamental boss from which sceptre-shaped rods radiate : the device is derived from the strengthening of shields by similar iron members. Alternate names are charbocle and escarbuncle. The carbuncle is used as a motif in strapwork, *q.v.*, especially in that variety known as strap-and-jewel work, *q.v.*

Card-cut: a form of blind fret, *q.v.*, carved lattice work often used in the decoration of mid 18th century furniture in the 'Chinese Taste'.

Cards: see *Playing cards*.

Caricature: see *Grotesque* and *Mask*.

Cartouche: a small tablet, in a scrolled frame, bearing an inscription, monogram, or heraldic arms. In architecture the word also describes a modillion below a cornice. The cartouche as an ornamental device was used in the 16th century and later in the decorative treatment of Baroque, *q.v.*, buildings and interiors, especially on such features as chimney-pieces. In the early and mid 18th century, a cartouche was frequently used by cabinet-makers as a surmount above the cornice or in the centre of a broken pediment on case furniture. The word is also applied to the cartridge-shaped frame within which the hieroglyphic names of Egyptian kings of the Second Dynasty onwards, were inscribed : this frame was originally circular, but assumed the cylindrical shape in order to accommodate a larger number of hieroglyphs.

CLEOPATRA from OBELISK of PHILÆ

POTTERY. J. & R. CLEWS.

ORTELIUS'S THEATRUM. ANTWERP. 1570

ST MARTIN'S CHURCH. LONDON

CARTOUCHE MARKS

ENOCH WOOD & SONS. BURSLEM

RALPH HALL of TUNSTALL

HERCULANEUM POTTERY. LIVERPOOL

Caryatid: a sculptured female figure, sometimes used in place of a column, singly, or in series to support an entablature. It has been suggested that these figures represent the women of Caryae, in Laconia; they were enslaved by the Greeks, who also killed the men and destroyed the city, as an act of vengeance after the inhabitants had fought against them at Thermopylae: the word caryatid, however, was not used until after the Roman conquest of Greece. See also *Canephora*.

Castellated: a term that describes carved ornament in the form of a repeating pattern of miniature battlements and turrets, used on chimney-pieces and above the coping mouldings of 15th and 16th century panelling. See also *Brattishing* and *Embattled*.

from THE ERECHTHEUM

Cat: in ancient Egypt, a small figure of a cat often ornamented the top of the sistrum, a sacred musical instrument in the form of a rattle, used in the worship of the goddess Bast, to whom the cat was sacred. The animal usually appears in heraldic arms as the wild or mountain cat: a civet cat was an 18th century shop sign for an apothecary.

BRONZE, SAITE PERIOD

CHAVIN=CAT GOD.
PERUVIAN 1200–400 BC

COVENTRY (ct.-of-arms)

Cat's head: see *Beakhead*.

Catenary: a festoon composed of links, hanging like a chain from two points.

Catherine wheel: as an heraldic device this is usually shown with six or eight spokes that end in curved blades at the rim: as one of the emblems of St Catherine of Alexandria, it appears broken, and set with knives.

ST CATHERINE'S COLLEGE. CAMBRIDGE

HERALDIC

TURNER

Caulicoli: an architectural term for the eight small curled acanthus stalks that support the volutes on a Corinthian capital: two of these stalks appear on each face. An alternative term, now archaic, is urella.

THE OLYMPIEION, ATHENS

Cavetto: a concave moulding having the profile of a quarter circle. Sometimes called a gorge. See *Congé* and *Overdoor*.

Celtic Cross: a form of wheel cross, *q.v.*, common in Ireland, Scotland, the Isle of Man, and the Celtic areas of England, from the 6th to 12th centuries: the distinctive shape was characterised by intricate, interlaced, carved ornament, that often enclosed symbolic figures and devices: the carving was arranged in panels. A small sloping roof frequently surmounted the cross as a protection from rain. Sometimes runic inscriptions were carved on the surface, which originated the alternative term, runic cross.

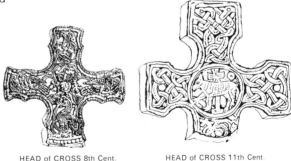

HEAD of CROSS 8th Cent.
YORKSHIRE

HEAD of CROSS 11th Cent.
DURHAM

Celtic fret: a curved diagonal fret, *q.v.*, which, in its simplest form, gives the effect of regularly entwined cords or ropes: intricate, interlacing patterns are also characteristic of this fret. See *Celtic cross* and *Interlacing*.

Centaur: a fabulous monster, male or female, with the body and legs of a horse, and the trunk, arms and head of a human being rising from the forepart. The centaur originated in Greece, and was used in carved decoration throughout the Graeco-Roman world. In heraldry, the centaur is usually shown holding a bow and drawing an arrow, and is called a sagittarius or sagittary. The origin of these creatures, represented in mythological fable as inhabitants of Mt Pelion in Thessaly, may be the fact that the wild and savage Thessalions were noted equestrians and exponents of bull-hunting on horseback: the word centaur is generally understood to mean a man-horse, but this hybrid is, strictly speaking, a hippocentaur: bucentauri and onocentauri were also devised, *q.v.*

from THE PARTHENON

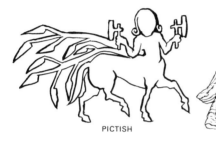

PICTISH

EXETER CATHEDRAL

PERSIAN 1400

Ceramic marks: the marking of pottery, in order to identify potter, time and place of manufacture, was practised by the Chinese and Romans, before its general introduction to Europe in the 16th century: imitations and frauds were common until the end of the 18th century when the first steps were taken to protect marks by law. The marks may consist of simple initials and numbers, but often include a device, *q.v.*, or rebus, *q.v.*, that may be changed from time to time.

1745–50

CHELSEA–DERBY 1784

MINTON 1822–36

1805–20

circa 1861

WEDGWOOD *circa* 1878

CHARLES MEIGH 1835–49

COPELAND

1851–85

circa 1890

1902

Johnson Bros. England.

1913 onwards

Spode FORTUNA England.

1950's

WALTER CRANE 1865–1915

BL.

1921

JOHN SHELLY 1949–56

VAN DER STRAETEN 1948

JOHN FISHER 1950

Chain band: a decorative band, *q.v.*, consisting of circles, squares, elliptical or lozenge shapes, all facing the same way, or in alternate profile.

Chaplet: an alternative term for a wreath or garland: as an heraldic device it is an ornamental wreath for the head: in architecture, a bagnette, *q.v.*, carved with small enrichments such as pearls and round beads, is sometimes called a chaplet.

Charbocle: see *Carbuncle*.

Charge: an heraldic term applied to any device or figure contained in an escutcheon.

Checker: see *Chequer*.

Cheniscus: a Greek word, meaning an ornamental ship's prow, in the form of the head and neck of a water bird, usually a goose: occasionally the figure was placed on the stern of the vessel: it was used throughout the Ancient world, and as late as the 12th century by Scandinavians and Saxons. See *Acrostolium*.

Chequer: a pattern of alternating dark and light squares, giving a chessboard effect, and used for surface decoration. Cabinet-makers in the 16th and 17th centuries used contrasting woods for inlaying this pattern on the horizontal members of joined furniture. Chequer work in architecture describes a wall faced with contrasting building materials, achieving the same decorative effect. In heraldry, the term checky or chequey, refers to a field covered with squares of alternating colours.

Cherub: a celestial being in the angelic hierarchy, appearing in many Old Testament stories, and having the attributes of wisdom and knowledge: depicted as a human figure with wings at each shoulder and to cover the feet. The word cherub also describes the winged head of a young child, a familiar religious motif: with puffed out cheeks it symbolises the wind. See also *Seraph*.

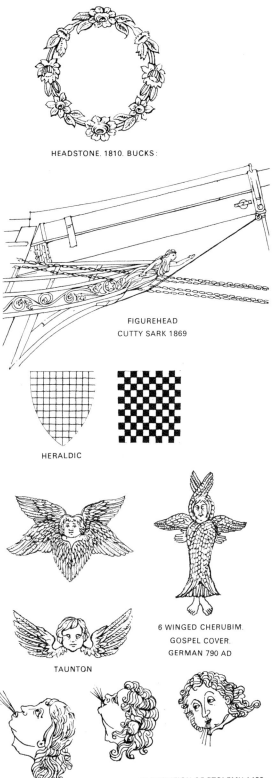

HEADSTONE. 1810. BUCKS:

FIGUREHEAD
CUTTY SARK 1869

HERALDIC

6 WINGED CHERUBIM.
GOSPEL COVER.
GERMAN 790 AD

TAUNTON

BERNARDUS SYLVANUS 1511 VENICE·

DIOGO RIBERO. 1529. SPANISH

ULM EDITION OF PTOLEMY 1482

Chessmen

BRĀHMĀNĀBĀD CHESSMEN

INDIAN

YAKUTAT

*MALAY

SIAMESE

ABYSSINIAN

KURDISH

LUCENA 15th Cent.

TURKISH

from PUBLICIUS. ARS ORATORIA 15th Cent.

from 'STUDIES OF CHESS' 1804

FRENCH. 18th Cent.

STAUNTON

from 'A HISTORY OF CHESS' by H. J. R. MURRAY by kind permission of THE CLARENDON PRESS. OXFORD

* by kind permission of the UNIVERSITY MUSEUM OF ARCHAEOLOGY AND ETHNOLOGY. CAMBRIDGE

Chessmen: the origins of chess, probably the oldest game in the world, lie in the remote past: the Hindu game of *chaturanga*, was played *c.* 2500 BC with four players who each controlled a king, elephant, horse, ship, and four foot soldiers: a version of the game known as *shatranj*, reached Europe from India, via the Middle East and Arabia, early in the 10th century. Arabian chesspieces were subject to the Mohammedan ban on the representation of living things, and Arab sets consisted of abstract geometrical shapes or barely recognisable symbols, but when the game reached Christian countries the pieces were given realistic forms that represented the powerful figures of the Church, royalty, and the nobility, as well as less exalted members of society. The popularity of the game encouraged the production of many cheap sets and simple pieces and these, combined with the elaborate and ornate Renaissance chessmen, eventually resulted in the familiar standard set with two kings, two queens, four bishops, four knights,

four castles and sixteen pawns. The Staunton set, named after the famous English player, Harold Staunton, designed by Nathaniel Cork in 1835, has remained the basic version, virtually unchallenged on its merits of simplicity, clarity, and stability in play.

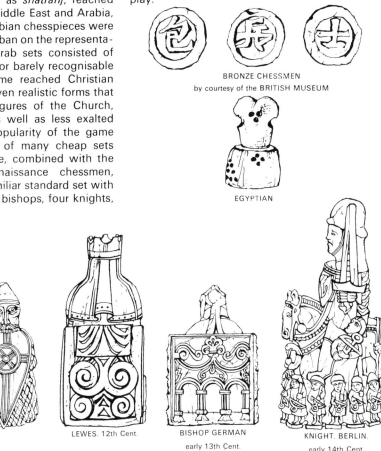

BRONZE CHESSMEN
by courtesy of the BRITISH MUSEUM

EGYPTIAN

LEWES. 12th Cent.

LEWES. 12th Cent.

BISHOP GERMAN
early 13th Cent.

KNIGHT. BERLIN.
early 14th Cent.

Chevron: probably the oldest ornamental motif, originating in Paleolithic and Neolithic line patterns, and used ubiquitously since. It is the basis of much conventional ornament, and among barbaric and ancient peoples has symbolized many natural forms, such as water, lightning, or a serpent. Formed like an inverted V, sometimes supposed to represent the gable rafters of a house, it is used in series as a running zigzag surface decoration; as an inlay

pattern; as an architectural moulding enrichment, characteristic of Romanesque and Norman work, when it is sometimes called a dancette. In heraldry, it is an ordinary, *q.v.*, in which it may point to the top of the shield or appear reversed: a half-sized chevron is called a chevronel, and three or more of these may be shown, one above the other, or interlaced. See also *Zigzag*.

 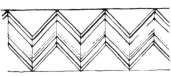 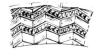

Chevronel

Chevronel: see *Chevron*.

Chi-Rho: see *Monogram*.

Chief: in heraldry, an ordinary, *q.v.*, consisting of a horizontal band covering the upper third of a shield. See also *Fillet*.

DURHAM CATHEDRAL 1110–33.

Chimera: in Greek mythology, a fabulous, fire-breathing monster, having a lion's head, goat's body, and dragon's tail, slain, according to legend, by Bellerophon, mounted on the winged horse, Pegasus: it has been suggested that the origin of this grotesque creature lay in the volcano named Chimaera, in Lycia. The chimera appeared as a sculptured and carved motif in classical times, and in architectural ornamentation in the 11th, 12th, 15th and 16th centuries, and became a symbol of cunning. In heraldry, the term chimerical figures is used to define all kinds of imaginary, grotesque monsters.

GREEK. mid 5th Cent. BC

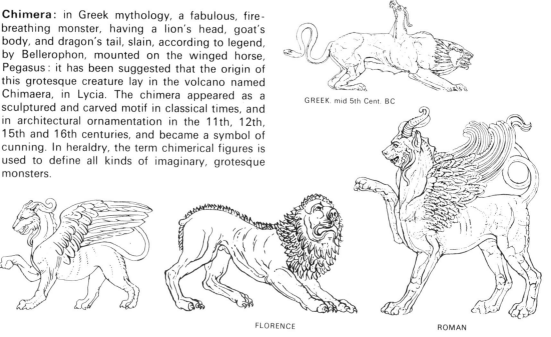

FLORENCE

ROMAN

Chinese fret: a variation of the fret motif, *q.v.*, that was used profusely in China as secondary or background ornamentation: generally right-angled, and having a much longer meander, *q.v.*, than the basic Greek fret: sometimes the frets appear as separate units; and with curved endings. A favourite form of decoration used by furniture makers for designs in the 'Chinese Taste', during the mid 18th century.

CHIPPENDALE. 'DIRECTOR' 3rd EDITION 1762

56

Chinese taste: see *Chinoiserie*.

Chinoiserie: a general descriptive term for Chinese ornament, decorative devices and motifs. Interest in Oriental, and especially Chinese, art, became modish in England after the Restoration, and the Chinese taste reached its zenith in the mid 18th century, concurrently with the rococo style. (There was an affinity between rococo and Chinese ornament.) Thomas Chippendale designed furniture in the Chinese taste, and in 1757 the publication of *Designs of Chinese Buildings, Furniture, Dresses, Machines, and Utensils*, by the architect, Sir William Chambers, expanded interest in the fashion.

PLATE XXVIII. CHIPPENDALE'S 'DIRECTOR' 3rd EDITION. 1762

Chrism: see *Monogram*.

Chrysanthemum: a typical Chinese and Japanese symbolic decorative motif. It originated in ancient China, where it appeared in highly conventional forms; its use spread to Japan, where the plant was extensively cultivated and the flower became a symbol of Japanese imperial power. See *Kikumon*.

ENGLISH TANKARD 1607–8

Cima: see *Cyma*.

Cincture: see *Annulet*.

Cinquecento: the culture, art, ornament, and decoration of 16th century Italy. In the opinion of many authorities, the Italian Renaissance achieved the highest degree of perfection at that time. The Cinquecento style was characterised by carved ornament, the use of classical motifs such as the acanthus and anthemion, arabesque scrolls and spirals, and conventional naturalistic forms. See also *Quattrocento* and *Trecento*.

Cinquefoil: an architectural and heraldic term for a figure of five equal arcs or lobes, separated by cusps, *q.v.*, used ornamentally in tracery, *q.v.*, and carving. In heraldry, when it is also called a quintfoil, it appears as a device formed by five formal leaves joined together at the centre. See also *Foil*.

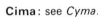

HERALDIC

QUINCY

ENCAUSTIC TILE

Cipher or Cypher: an ornamental arrangement of the initials or letters of the name of an individual or organisation, sometimes embellished with some small emblem such as a spray of leaves, or a coronet. As a personal or trading device, always appearing in the same form, it may be used on plate, signet rings, commercial productions, or works of art, as a form of private signature, seal, or guarantee of authorship. In heraldry, it means a monogram, *q.v.*

Circle: a geometrical figure. Closely linked with primitive sun worship, this ancient and universal symbol of eternity appears in such devices as the Egyptian hieroglyph of Ra, the sun god (a circle with a dot in the centre, still the astronomical sign for the sun): the serpent with tail in mouth, often used for rings and bracelets; the sacred wheel of Brahma: the Buddhist wheel of law; and the Christian nimbus and wheel cross: a combination of three, four, or five circles was a common form of cross in medieval times. See *Geometrical ornament, Tchakra* and *Wheel*.

Circlet: a small circle: the term often describes a circular ornamental band for the head.

from HOUSE OF CUPID AND PSYCHE. OSTIA

Clarion: a form of trumpet: as an heraldic device the name is misleading, for in heraldry the charge represents a lance rest, that closely resembles some kind of horn, or panpipes.

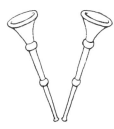

Classic orders: see *Order of architecture*.

Claw-and-ball: a ball, grasped by a large claw or talon, that forms an ornamental foot to the legs of chairs and tables. Possibly of Chinese origin, the claw-and-ball foot was in use in England in the 16th century, again for a time after the Restoration, and in the early and mid 18th century; also called talon-and-ball.

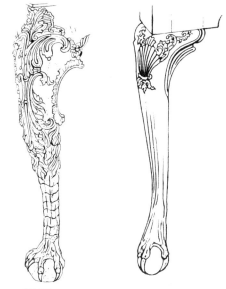

SIDE-TABLE.
ENGLISH. *circa* 1730–40

from STAND for CHEST or TALLBOY
ENGLISH 1715–30

Clock jacks: decorative carved and painted mechanical figures that strike the hours on the bell of a clock, usually that on a church tower or a civic building. Many of them are of 14th and 15th century origin. Also called jacks of the clock.

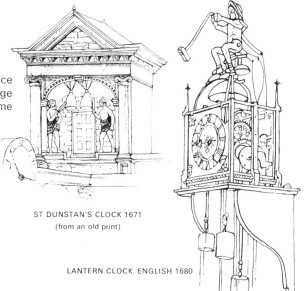

ST DUNSTAN'S CLOCK 1671
(from an old print)

LANTERN CLOCK. ENGLISH 1680

Closet: see *Bar*.

Cloud scroll: a characteristic Chinese motif of the Han Dynasty, (*c*. BC 206--AD 220). A long, convoluted, ribbon-like form, with deep curls and curves constantly changing direction, and at such points widening into grotesque shapes: within the loops thus formed were various symbols and marks. An older type of this device was a conventionalised dragon shape, long and straggling, with an embellished bird's head, and it is believed that the ribbon of the cloud scroll was a stylisation of some creature's remains, and the protuberances represented the tissues of its body.

Cloven foot: in Roman furniture a cabriole leg terminated in the cloven hoof of an animal: this ornamental foot, also called *pied de biche*, was revived in the 18th century. See also *Cabriole profile* and *Hoof*.

Clubs: the trefoil device used as one of the four suit signs on English playing cards: the French *trèfles* are identical: the device developed from the acorns (*eicheln*), clubs (*battoni*), and batons (*bastos*) of the German, Italian and Spanish packs respectively. This suit has been alleged to represent peasants, soldiers, violence and fortitude. See *Playing cards*, and *Suit signs*.

Cluster: a term sometimes used for a swag composed of flowers, foliage or fruit, or a combination of all these: suspended at each end it becomes a festoon, *q.v.*

MINTON & CO. 1951

Clustered column: a pier, composed of four or more much smaller columns around a central one; springing from a common base and ending in a common capital.

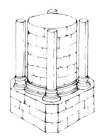

CLUSTERED COLUMN. 13th Cent. WESTMINSTER ABBEY

Coat of arms: see *Arms*.

Cobra de capello: see *Asp*.

Cock beading or cocked bead: an 18th century cabinet-maker's term for a small semi-circular bead moulding applied to the edge of a surface, often a drawer front. See *Astragal*.

Cockatrice: a fabulous two-legged creature, with the body, head, comb and wattles of a cock, and wings and tail of a dragon: an emblem of evil, and an attribute of St Vitus: used as a chimerical device in heraldry.

Cockshead: see *Trefoil*.

Cognizance: see *Badge*.

Coil: a continuous arrangement of concentric circles. See *Fret*.

HAGIAR KIM. MALTA

CONTINUOUS COIL. GREEK
TREASURY OF ATREUS, MYCENÆ

Coin devices: coins first appeared in the Far East, and in Greece *c.* 800–700 BC. They developed from pieces of metal, stamped with their weight and a guarantee of value, used as tokens in barter to represent goods: the guarantee was later assumed by religious, and then secular authorities, and early coins, as such, bore a recognisable symbol, often naturalistic, connected with pagan deities: the custom of representing the deities themselves followed, and led eventually to the use of the heads of states. All coin devices are symbolic, and have included every kind of naturalistic motif, gods, men, national and religious emblems, musical instruments, heraldic devices, and primitive signs like the swastika and triscele. See *Crown*.

SYRACUSIAN

GOLD OCTODRACHMA. PTOLEMAEUS I

SILVER TETRADRACHMA. ATHENS

STATER OF PAESTUM. GREEK. 530 BC

STATER FROM CORINTH. GREEK. 325–308 BC. HEAD OF ATHENA

4-DRACHMA PIECE. ATHENS. 530–520 BC. GORGON'S HEAD

Colonnade: in ornamentation, this term has been used to describe a series of continuous curves running in the same direction, serpentine rather than scroll-like, sometimes enriched with foliage, and applied as surface decoration.

Colonnette: a miniature column, which may reproduce the characteristics of an order.

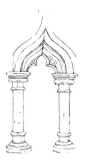

Colophon: a typographical term for a printer's imprint that, in the early days of printing, acted as a statement of his ability, a safeguard of his rights, and an identification of his work, and was the forerunner of the modern title page. Still a factual printed statement of names of publisher and printer, and date and place of printing, the colophon is not itself an ornament, but is often combined with decorative printers' devices, *q.v.*

This Foundery was begun in the Year 1720, and will be carried on, improved, and enlarged, BY WILLIAM CASLON, Letter-Founder, Chifwell-Street, LONDON.

from the 1785 SPECIMEN BOOK

COLOPHON from THE CATHOLICON 1460

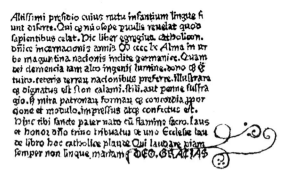

Altiſſimi prſidio cuius nutu infantium lingue fi
unt diſerte. Qui qᷓ nᷣ oſope puulis reuelat quod
ſapientibus celat. Dic liber egregiua catholicon.
dᷠice marmaconis anmis Oᷠ cccc lx Alma in ur
be maguntina nacionis indite germanice. Quam
dei clemencia tam alto ingenij lumine dono qᷓ ᷓ
tuirs. reteris terrau nacionibus preferre illuſtrara
qᷓ dignatus eſt ſuon calami ſtili aut penne ſuffra
gio. Aᷠ mira patronau formau qᷓ concordia ᵱpor
done et modulo impreſſus atqᷓ confectus eſt.
Dbic tibi ſancte pater nato cᷣ flamine ſacro. laus
et honoꝛ dᷠo trino tribuatuꝛ ct uno Ecleſie tau
de libro hoc catholice plauce Qui laudaꝛe piam
ſemper non linque maꝛiam ᶜDEO. GRACIAS

Column: a vertical member, circular in plan. In classic architecture it consists of a base, shaft and capital supporting an entablature and in such a form and designed in accordance with the rules of one of the five Orders of Architecture, a column denotes the Order. See *Order of Architecture, Lotus Palm, Queen's House.* When up to a quarter of the diameter of the shaft is incorporated with or concealed by the surface behind, the terms Attached Column or Engaged Column are used. See *Papyrus* and *Pediment.* A flat column, rectangular in plan, a long side and shaft (often part fluted or decorated) attached to a surface, and observing the character of an Order is a Pilaster. See *Cabling.*

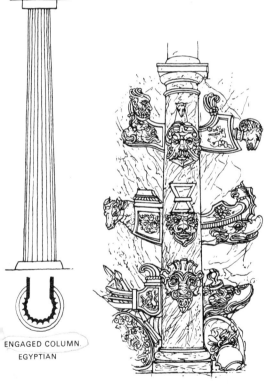

ENGAGED COLUMN
EGYPTIAN

Columna Rostrata or Rostral Column: a column decorated throughout the length of its shaft with projecting prows of ships (*rostra*): this form of ornament was common in Graeco-Roman times, when such columns commemorated naval personages or victories. The use of ships' prows to embellish the orator's stand in the ancient Roman Forum gave it the name of rostrum, used ever since for a structure used for public speaking.

Cone: a device, used singly or in the form of a double cone, joined at the apices, was used in Norman decoration.

DOUBLE-CONE

Congé: an architectural term for a cavetto moulding, *q.v.,* that joins the base or capital of a column to the shaft: sometimes called an apophyge.

CAVETTO-LARCHANT

Console: see *Corbel* and *Bracket.*

Constantine cross: a description sometimes applied to the seal used on Roman standards by the Emperor Constantine after his conversion to Christianity: this is the XP monogram of Christ, formed by the two first letters χ (*chi*) and ρ (*rho*) of the Greek word for Christ: the various forms of this cross arise from different combinations of the two letters. See *Monogram*.

Coquillage: derived from the French *coquille*, and characteristic of early and mid 18th century French ornament, the word is applied to rococo decoration in which a shell is often the central motif: used too, as a general term to describe crimped, shell-like ornamentation.

Corbel: a stone block, plain or carved with fruit, leaves, human heads or animals, projecting from a wall and supporting a weight, i.e. the beams or ribs of a roof or vault. Distinct from a bracket which is usually formed with scrolls or volutes: and when carrying the upper members of a cornice, brackets are termed Modillions or Consoles. See *Console, Order of Architecture*.

NORWICH CATHEDRAL

Corbel-table: a series of corbels supporting a projecting section of a wall.

NORMAN

Cornucopia: a goat's horn, filled and overflowing with ears of wheat and fruit, used since classical times as a decorative motif, and on coins; known as the horn of plenty, a description derived from the fable that the horn of the goat that suckled Jupiter was given a place among the stars as an emblem of plenty. The device was also based on primitive drinking horns, those of a bull or goat; the corn and fruit represent the basic foods necessary to man.

GOTHIC

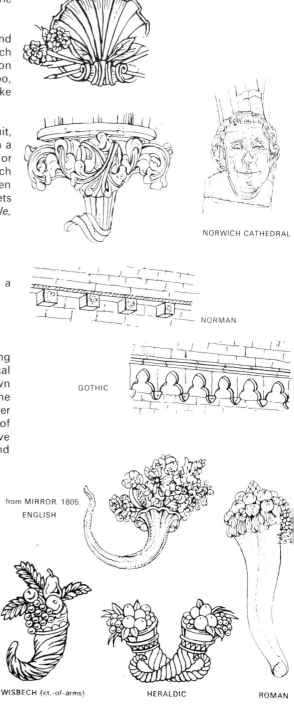

from MIRROR. 1805.
ENGLISH

ROMAN. ALTAR PANEL

WISBECH (ct.-of-arms)

HERALDIC

ROMAN

Cosse de pois: see *Pea pod*.

Cottage style: term applied to a binders' ornament *q.v.* the central motif resembles a roof-gable. Appearing in England late in the 17th century, sometimes associated with Samuel Mearne, bookbinder to Charles II. Also a mid 19th century furniture style, characterised by simple design, with natural woods, unpolished, or surfaces painted in pale colours. Originating in the United States of America, it was revived in England during the early part of the 20th century, as a popular, and far less costly, version of the work of artist-craftsmen who were followers of William Morris.

Counterchange: a pattern formed by repeating the same motif alternately in two different colours.

Course: a continuous horizontal layer of stone, or stones of differing lengths, bricks or tiles in a building's wall. When combined with a vertical course as in Anglo-Saxon buildings, is known as 'long and short work'.

Cove: an architectural term for a large concave moulding that may be a cavetto, *q.v.*, or scotia, *q.v.*, used mainly as a floor skirting, or at the junction of ceiling and cornice; and in cabinet-making on the cornices of case furniture. In general, the term describes any hollow or concavity; the word coving is sometimes used as an alternative, but this also means the extension of the upper floor of a house above the ground floor. See *Moulding*.

Cover fillet: a thin strip, either flat, or a bead moulding; a larger version is called a cover mould. This simple decorative device is used to conceal joints in panelling. Also called a cover strip.

Cover mould: see *Cover fillet*.

Cover strip: see *Cover fillet*.

Coving: see *Cove*.

Crescent: this symbol of the new moon had associations with Egyptian mythology, and with the Byzantine Empire, of which it was the emblem long before it was adopted by the Ottoman Empire after the capture of Constantinople by the Turks in 1453. The crescent appeared on old Byzantine coins: through its Ottoman adoption it has become an emblem of the Mohammedan faith: it was an important ceramic mark on Worcester porcelain from 1751 to 1840, and was also used on 18th century Caughley porcelain where it was eventually transformed into the letter C: as a cadency mark, *q.v.*, it signifies a second son, and usually appears with the points upwards.

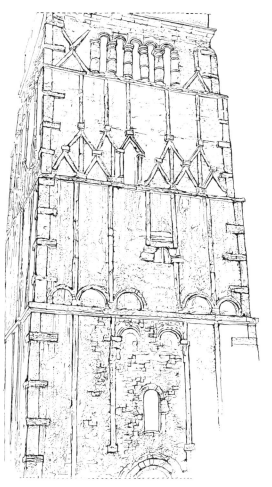

EARLS BARTON. CHURCH TOWER

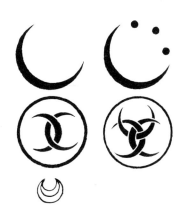

Crest: the heraldic device above the helmet in an achievement, often consisting of one of the charges of the shield. In medieval times it was worn on the helm or bascinet, to provide easy identification in battle, and took the form of a wooden or leather plate, bearing a device. Crests may be very elaborate, consisting of the figures or heads of animals, birds, or monsters, inanimate objects set in roundels, and the panache, *q.v.*

JAPANESE. CIRCULAR. BIRD and FLOWER

JAPANESE CIRCULAR BIRD

KIRI-MON. MON OF THE MIKADO

AWOÏ-MON MON OF THE HOUSE OF MINAMOTO

TOMOYE. MON OF THE HOUSE OF ARINA

Cresting: a line of ornament decorating a roof ridge, the uppermost moulding of a screen, the top-rail of a chair back, or surmounting the cornice of a cabinet, the upper member of a picture or looking-glass frame, or window architrave. Sometimes used for the ornamental railing of a window sill. See also *Brattishing* and *Surmount*.

GATEWAY. LATE 17th Cent.

GATEWAY. HAMPSHIRE. *circa* 1835

ITALIAN. 17th Cent. CUPBOARD

Crest-wreath: an heraldic ornament consisting of twisted coloured silks, worn between crest and helm, and securing them to each other: also called a torse. See *Banderolle*.

HERALDIC. ROCHDALE (ct.-of-arms)

Crio-sphinx: the Greek name for the Egyptian ram-headed sphinx, with the body of a lion. See *Sphinx*.

Crochet: see *Crocket*.

Crocket: sometimes called a crochet. An architectural term for a small carved ornamental projection, used in Gothic architecture to adorn sloping surfaces, such as pinnacles, the sides of spires, angles of roofs, canopies, gables, and the capitals of columns below the abacus, and sometimes as a decoration on medieval furniture and woodwork. The word is derived from the French *croc*, a hook, and the ornament is usually a hook-shaped leaf, arranged continuously at regular intervals: more elaborate variations of leaf appeared in later Gothic work, and occasionally animals and figures took its place.

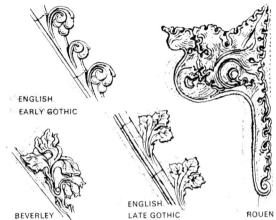

ENGLISH.
EARLY GOTHIC

BEVERLEY

ENGLISH
LATE GOTHIC

ROUEN

Croix cramponée: see *Swastika*.

Croix gammée: see *Swastika*.

Crope: see *Finial*.

Cross: a symbol of great antiquity, possibly originating in the swastika, a primitive sun sign, *q.v.* Since prehistoric times the equilateral cross has possessed religious and mythological significance, notably in relation to the spaces of the sky, the sun, weather, and rain. Of universal popularity, it has been an attribute of the deities of India, Assyria, Persia, Greece, and of the indigenous American Indian tribes. The Egyptian 'ankh, *q.v.*, the symbol of life, is a form of cross. The supreme importance of the cross as a Christian symbol, has led to its adoption as a religious device wherever Christianity is established, and it is an emblem of faith. In Byzantine decoration the cross constantly appears in conjunction with the circle, sometimes being composed of five circles, with two scrolls representing the serpent, at its foot, and with the vine and acanthus. In general, the Greek or equilateral cross, is used by the Eastern Church, the Latin cross (the actual form used by the Romans for crucifixions) by the Roman and Western communions. In heraldry, the religious importance and simple shape of the cross give it special significance; it is an ordinary, *q.v.*; the limbs may extend to the edge of a shield (see *Plain cross*), or terminate short of the edges, often with decorative ends. The frequency of its use in the early days of heraldry followed its adoption as an emblem by Crusaders, and many varieties of heraldic crosses exist. The number is so large that only a few are included among the illustrations, and brief definitions are given under their appropriate entries.

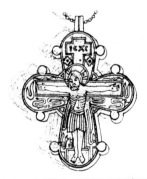

DAGMAR CROSS. (BYZANTINE DESIGN)

LUNATE

KNOBBED EXTREMITIES

Cross botonée or botonny: an heraldic cross, a variation of the crosslet, *q.v.*, in which each limb ends in three knobs.

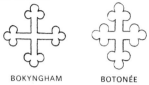

BOKYNGHAM   BOTONÉE

Cross fitchée or fitchy: an heraldic cross, with a shaft tapering to a point, the other limbs being splayed.

PATTÉE FITCHÉE

Cross fleurie or flory: an heraldic cross with the limbs terminated by fleur-de-lys, *q.v.* The cross floretty is a variation, with the limbs, straight or slightly splayed, squared off, before ending in fleur-de-lys.

STEWARD   FLEURETTE   SWINNERTON

Cross formée, or pattée: see *Cross pattée*.

Cross fourchée: an heraldic cross with forked ends to the limbs.

FOURCHÉE

Cross moline: an heraldic cross, with curved forked ends to the limbs, which takes its name from a mill-iron, also called a *fer-de-moline*, mill-rind or ink-moline, the piece of iron fixed to the centre of a millstone: in heraldry, this cross signifies an eighth son.

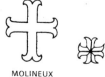

MOLINEUX

Cross of eight points: see *Maltese cross*.

Cross patence or patonce: an heraldic cross with slightly splayed limbs ending in three curved points.

COLVILE

Cross pattée or formée: an heraldic cross with splayed limbs of equal length. see *Iona cross*.

PATTÉE

Cross pommellé: an heraldic cross with a knob or roundel terminating the limbs.

JERUSALEM. EARLY FORM

Cross potent: an heraldic cross with crutch-shaped ends to the limbs: sometimes called a Jerusalem cross. Another form of cross potent, with one end of each crutch removed, resembles the ancient swastika, *q.v.* The border lines of these crosses are often decoratively treated, (see *Plain cross*).

JERUSALEM. LATER FORM

Cross urdée or urdy: a pointed cross, *q.v.*, with slightly splayed limbs.

URDÉE

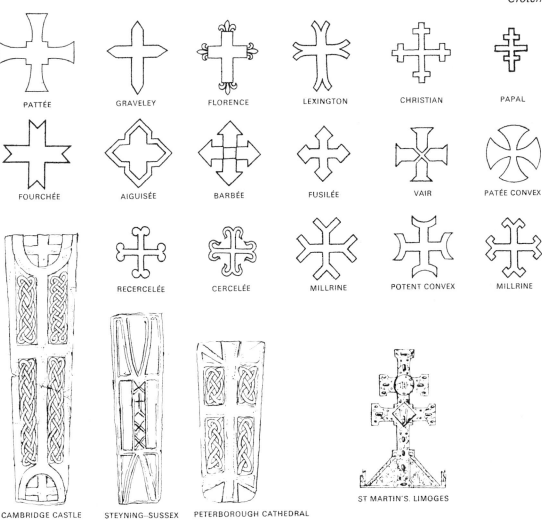

PATTÉE GRAVELEY FLORENCE LEXINGTON CHRISTIAN PAPAL

FOURCHÉE AIGUISÉE BARBÉE FUSILÉE VAIR PATÉE CONVEX

RECERCELÉE CERCELÉE MILLRINE POTENT CONVEX MILLRINE

CAMBRIDGE CASTLE STEYNING–SUSSEX PETERBOROUGH CATHEDRAL

ST MARTIN'S. LIMOGES

DOUBLE-HEADED CROSSES

Crossbones: the device of two arm or thigh bones, crossed, usually appears in conjunction with a skull, *q.v.* Used in heraldry, as a tombstone motif and to symbolise death. The pirate's flag, with a white skull and crossbones on a black ground, came into use *c.* 1700, and indicated that quarter was offered, as distinct from the red pirate flag that proclaimed no mercy. More recently, a yellow flag with black skull and crossbones and border, has been unofficially used to designate a ship undergoing fumigation.

Crosslet: an heraldic cross with a cross at the end of each limb. Known as St Julian's cross when it lies diagonally. The cross botonée, *q.v.*, is a variation.

Crotch or crotchet: see *Brackets*.

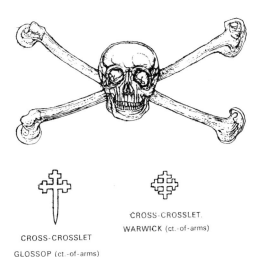

CROSS-CROSSLET
WARWICK (ct.-of-arms)

CROSS-CROSSLET
GLOSSOP (ct.-of-arms)

67

Crown: from earliest times a symbol of sovereignty, honour and victory. Pre-dynastic Egyptian royal crowns were like tall hats: those used later, the double crown of the Pharoahs, resembled a mitre: early Greek and Roman crowns, awarded for military and athletic prowess, were wreaths of leaves and berries: the Christian martyr's crown, signifying victory over sin and persecution, was at first a wreath of palm leaves, and later a golden, bejewelled coronet. The Oriental diadem, a band of embroidered silk or linen, was also used by Roman Emperors. The royal crown of gold or silver, studded with jewels, probably originated in the dark ages between the end of the Western Roman Empire and the rise of medieval civilisation.

The garland bestowed on a soldier who was the first to scale the walls of a besieged town was called a mural crown. In England, the crown is one of the oldest and most popular inn signs, alone, or in association with the sceptre or some other non-royal symbol: also used as a shop sign, where the crown and fan announced a fan-maker, the crown and rasp a snuffmaker, the crown and halberd a cutler, and so on: it was and is frequently used as a pottery mark, though it has now lost the original significance of royal patronage. In heraldry, the crown is used in conjunction with regal and religious coats of arms, and worn as an external ornament the variations in its appearance indicate royal and noble rank.

ASSYRIAN.
745–727 BC

PERSIAN.
DARIUS. 6th Cent. BC

BABYLONIAN.
MARDUK'S 7th–6th Centuries BC

WHITE CROWN of UPPER (SOUTH) EGYPT
RED CROWN of LOWER (NORTH) EGYPT
DOUBLE CROWN

DIADEM.
IRAN 4th Cent. AD

CORONA OBSIDIONALIS

CORONA TRIUMPHALIS

CORONA CIVICA

MURAL

WARWICKSHIRE (ct.-of-arms)

PADDINGTON (ct.-of-arms)

STAFFORDSHIRE (ct.-of-arms)

WORKSOP (ct.-of-arms)

MITRE

CAP OF DIGNITY.
HESSLE

ANCIENT

SAXON
BRENTFORD &
CHISWICK (ct.-of-arms)

SAXON

EASTERN

PALISADO

VALLARY.
CHORLEY (ct.-of-arms)

OLD.
BLYTH (ct.-of-arms)

DUCAL CORONET.
WOODSTOCK (ct.-of-arms)

SOUTHWOLD (ct.-of-arms)

DUCAL CORONET

CREST CORONET

CHARLES II (COIN)

IMPERIAL

NAVAL.
PLYMOUTH (ct.-of-arms)

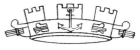

TOWERED and ROSTRAL or
CORONA TERRITA

Crozier: a Christian symbol of guidance, originating in the shepherd's crook: the pastoral staff of bishops and abbots, and widely used as an ecclesiastical heraldic device. See *Skull.*

HEAD OF TAU. early 11th Cent.

BARKING (ct.-of-arms)

Crux ansata: see *'Ankh.*

Cup and cover: the carved melon bulb on table legs and the supports of court and press cupboards in the late 16th and 17th centuries often resembled a goblet-shaped cup with a dome-like top over it, both sections often decorated with gadrooning, *q.v.* The term cup and cover for this ornamental form is of modern origin. See *Bulb* and *Melon bulb.*

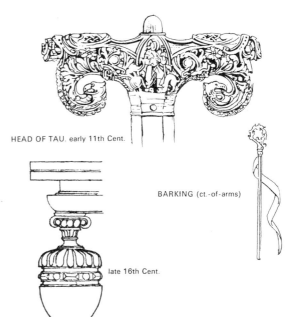

late 16th Cent.

Curl: decoration of an incurved or spiral form. See *Coil* and *Spiral.*

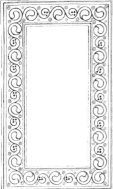

Curlicue: an ornamental curl, with exuberant and fantastic convolutions.

BOOK-COVER. leather

Arithmetick

Curvilinear tracery: a characteristic form in 14th century Gothic architecture, also known as flowing tracery, in which gently curving lines form oval or ogee shapes. See also *Flamboyant tracery, Mouchette, Reticulated tracery* and *Tracery*.

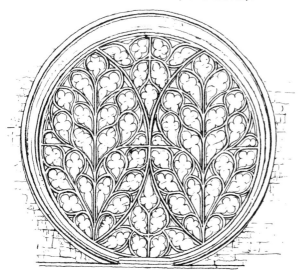

BISHOP'S EYE WINDOW. LINCOLN. *circa* 1330

Cusp: an architectural term for the projecting point that separates the foils, *q.v.*, in Gothic tracery, arches and panels: in the later Gothic period these points often ended in ornamental leaves, flowers, or human heads. See also *Foliation*.

EARLY–PRIMITIVE   MIDDLE–CHAMFER   LATE

CUSPS AND FOILS. ENGLISH 1860–70

Cusped quatrefoil: characteristic of Perpendicular Gothic tracery, this motif consisted of a quatrefoil with a trefoil within each of the four lobes.

Cyma recta: sometimes spelt cima (see also *Gola*). The architectural term for an ogee moulding, *q.v.* See *Moulding*.

Cyma reversa: sometimes spelt cima, gola or gula. The architectural term for a reverse ogee moulding, *q.v.*

Cypher: see *Cipher*.

D

Dagger: the architectural term for a lancet-shaped aperture or piercing used in Gothic tracery of the Decorated period. As a ceramic mark, the dagger appeared on late 18th century Bow porcelain: in typography it identifies an obsolete word, or the name of a deceased person. See also *Mouchette*.

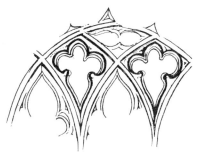

Dancette: see *Chevron* and *Dancetty*.

Dancetty: an heraldic term for an ornamental zigzag line formed by conjoined chevrons, *q.v.*; in the variation, known as dancetty floretty, the points of the zigzags are adorned with fleur-de-lys. See *Line*.

Danish knot: see *Runic knot*.

David's shield: composed of two equilateral triangles forming a hexagram, this motif is also known as the Star of David, and the Seal of Solomon; widely used as a Jewish religious symbol since *c*. AD 300, it signifies divine protection as epitomised by the alchemistic signs for fire and water, which were an upward and downward apexed triangle respectively.

Death symbols: the most common, found on gravestones, churchyard memorials, tombs, and sometimes on sundials, are a serpent with tail in mouth: a skull, alone or with crossbones: a scythe, or a figure of Time holding a scythe: an hourglass: an open book and quill pen: an urn: an escallop.

ENGLISH 1621

SERPENT OF ETERNITY. PENSHURST 1842

THE SOUL-BIRD. COPTIC early 6th Cent. AD

GRAVESTONE. ENGLISH 1763

PENSHURST 1830

GRAVESTONE. FRENCH 1826

SOUL-BIRD. COPTIC TOMBSTONE. 7th century AD

ANGEL OF SLEEP
VICTORIAN

POPPY OF SLEEP. PENSHURST 1842

SHERINGTON, BUCKS.

BLASTED TREE 1761

BURNING BUSH 1761

Death's head: see *Skull.*

Demi-figure: see *Half figure.*

Dentil: a small square block, used in series, as a projecting cornice ornament, on Ionic and Corinthian entablatures, and on the cornices of Georgian case furniture, to diversify the shadow cast by the cornice: dentils may have been derived originally from the ends of rafters supporting an arched roof and projecting beyond the cornice.

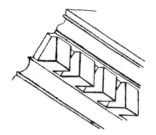

Device: in heraldry, a decorative personal badge or motto : it forms part of the armorial bearings, and originated as a distinguishing mark on shields and banners at medieval tournaments. During the Renaissance, the habit of adopting a personal device and motto, collectively called an imprese and usually allusive, was widespread among royalty and the nobility. As marks of identification, combined with ornamental qualities, devices have long been used by printers, shopkeepers and professional, commercial and industrial concerns. Also a generic term for ornamental motifs. See *Printers' devices*, and *Shop signs.*

Diamond ornament: see *Lozenge.*

Diamonds: the device used as one of the four suit signs on English playing cards: the French *carreaux* are identical: developed from the bells (*schellen*) coins (*denari* and *oros*) of the German, Italian and Spanish packs respectively. This sign has been alleged to represent merchants, the middle class, charity, and extravagance. See *Playing cards*, and *Suit signs.*

DIAMOND QUARTERED

Diaper: a form of ornamentation, consisting of an all-over pattern of small squares or lozenges made up of floreated or arabesque motifs, used as painted decoration on flat surfaces, for textile patterns, and in decorative carving and marquetry: in the 15th century a lozenge pattern was woven into the linen produced at Ypres, and the word may be a corruption of *linge d'Ypres*. In heraldry, the term describes a continuous all-over pattern forming the decorative background of an heraldic field, but distinct from any heraldic device.

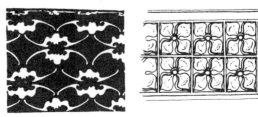

JAPANESE DIAPER OF BATS

Differences: see *Cadency marks.*

Diminutive: see *Ordinary.*

Diocletian window: an architectural term that describes an ornamental form of semi-circular window divided by upright mullions into a centre portion and two small side portions: used in 18th century Palladian design. Also known as a divided lunette. Such windows were used in the baths of Diocletian, in Rome, *c*. AD 302: also called a therm window.

Director style: sometimes used to describe rococo ornament of the type illustrated in Thomas Chippendale's *Gentleman and Cabinet-Maker's Director*, first published in 1754.

from CHIPPENDALE'S DIRECTOR. 1762

GIRANDOLE, from
'THE GENTLEMAN and CABINET-MAKER'S DIRECTOR'.
CHIPPENDALE. 1754

Divergent spiral: see *Trumpet pattern*.

Divided lunette: see *Diocletian window*.

Dog tooth ornament: the architectural term for a four-leaved motif, used in series to enrich hollow mouldings and break up shadow: characteristic of Romanesque and 13th century ornamentation: a form of this device appeared in Roman Britain: and it was sometimes used to decorate late 15th and early 16th century woodwork. Dog tooth ornament

developed from the nailhead, *q.v.* Sometimes called tooth moulding or tooth ornament, the origin of the name is obscure, though the pointed leaves of the motif might suggest a sharp canine tooth.

Dog's nose pattern: see *Trifid*.

Dolphin: this creature, not a true fish but a sea mammal, was used as an ornamental and symbolic motif in the ancient world, often combined with the Graeco-Roman sea deities: it has appeared on coins, utensils, furniture, and as an architectural and typographical ornament: the Japanese *shachikoko*, a large demon-headed dolphin, often crowned the top of a castle tower, its head resting on the roof ridge, its body and tail reared into the air. The dolphin was a popular motif for the decoration of furniture in the 17th, 18th and 19th centuries: the head was a terminal ornament for chair feet and table legs, and in the late 17th century as a motif on carved and gilded furniture, hence the terms dolphin foot and dolphin mask: a complete set of ceremonial furniture, each piece decorated with the dolphin motif, was presented to Greenwich Hospital for Seamen in 1813–15, by a Mrs Fish, in memory of Lord Nelson. In heraldry, the dolphin is a charge, shown bent into a curve, and the emblem of the Dauphin of France: it is often considered symbolic of affection and friendliness.

POOLE (ct.-of-arms)

WALLASEY (ct.-of-arms)

DOLPHIN STOOL. BRIGHTON PAVILION

Dolphin foot: see *Dolphin.*

Dolphin mask: see *Dolphin.*

Dot: in China, *c.* 1027–221 BC, a ritual gift by the emperor to his bride was the *ku kuei*, a flat, seven-inch tablet, bearing a pattern of dots, and sometimes called the tablet with grains; it was supposed that these represented fertility, and the pointed and square ends of the tablet the Chinese *Yang* and *Yin*, or male and female (see *Monad*). The dot or grain pattern also adorned bowls of the same era (see *Rice-grain*). Used singly or in interlaced patterns, and coloured, dots were an important embellishment to initial letters in early Celtic and Anglo-Saxon MSS. In heraldry, they sometimes indicate metals or colours. In the decoration of glass, the process known as stippling consists of the delicate mechanical engraving of small groups of graded dots on a glass surface, where they act as highlights. See *Pounced ornament.*

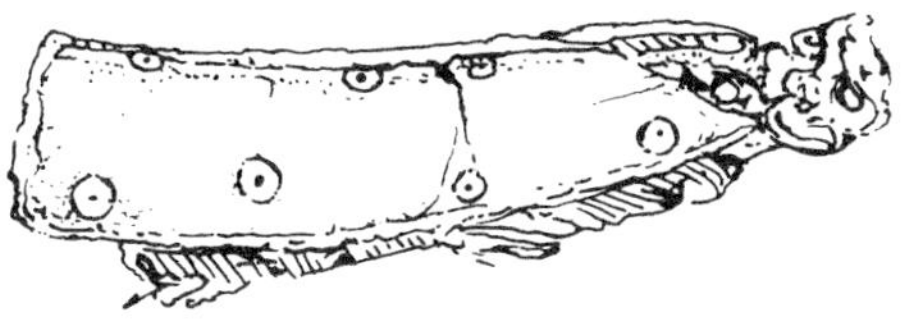

CIRCLE AND DOT. ROMAN PENKNIFE

Double cone: see *Cone.*

Double guilloche: see *Guilloche.*

Double ogee: see *Bracket moulding.*

Double open twist: see *Open twist.*

Double oval: a form of interlaced ribbon, often found in Roman tesselated pavement patterns, and sometimes as a decoration to early illuminated MSS.

Double rope: see *Barley sugar twist.*

Double sun snake: a multi-armed variation of the primitive sun sign known as a sun snake, *q.v.*

DOUBLE SUN-SNAKE OR SWASTIKA

Double twist: see *Barley sugar twist.*

Dove: used as a Christian religious motif, where it symbolises the Holy Spirit, love, and fidelity: it was also a pre-Christian decorative emblem, found on ancient Assyrian coins, and sculpture from the Eastern Mediterranean, and possibly associated with the goddess Astarte. Bearing an olive branch in its beak, the bird's representation as a messenger of peace and bringer of good news derives from the Biblical story of the Flood.

BLACKBURN (ct.-of-arms)

Dovetailed: in heraldry, the term for an ornamental, fan-shaped line. See *Line.*

Draggings: see *Loopings.*

Dragon: a fabulous creature of Chinese origin, that has been known as a decorative and symbolic device since the 6th century BC. In ancient China a dragon represented the spring solstice, possibly because a type of crocodile found in the lower Yangtze valley hibernated in mud during the winter and re-emerged in spring. The dragon has many variations, but the characteristics common to most are a long, scaly serpentine body, feline legs, fleshy mouth, and horns; wings, and a forked tongue, are other usual attributes. Most generally associated with Chinese and Japanese ornament, the draconic motif also appears in early Celtic and Scandinavian decoration, forming part of intricate interlacing designs: dragons' heads were carved on the prows of Viking ships. (They were sometimes called 'Dragon Ships'.) Until the late 15th century it appeared on Scandinavian jewellery, weapons and carved decoration. In Oriental mythology the dragon was a beneficient, life-giving creature: in Scandinavian and Graeco-Roman legend, as Fafni and Ladon, he guarded treasure, and later was transformed into a ravaging serpentine monster whose killing symbolised the triumph of right over wrong: in Christian symbolism he has become the epitome of evil, and with the serpent, *q.v.* the representation of Satan. In heraldry, the dragon was an early British tribal device, and retained his Celtic associations as a supporter of the Tudor Royal

Arms, as the badge of Wales, and as one of the Queen's Beasts.

HERALDIC

GOLDEN DRAGON. WESSEX

from THE WALL OF THE NINE DRAGONS. PEKING

CHINESE VERSION OF COSMIC DRAGON

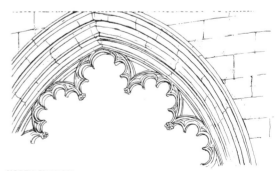

JAPANESE

Drop ornament: a pendant motif that decorates carved and other work.

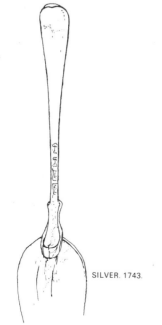

SILVER. 1743.

Drop tracery: an architectural term describing the adornment of the inner curve of an arch by tracery, *q.v.*, that appears to be suspended from it.

NORTH CHANCEL.
ST PETER. MAXEY NORTHAMPTONSHIRE. 14th Cent.

76

E

Eagle: in primitive Aztec and classical mythology, the bird has been linked with a serpent or hare, carried in its claws: it was sacred to Zeus, an emblem of victory and power, and was sometimes represented clasping a thunderbolt: in Christian symbolism, the emblem of St John the Evangelist, and associated with the Ascension. Used as a decorative motif by 18th century carvers, and as a symbolic device on coins, seals and flags, since Graeco-Roman times. It was an imperial and national emblem in the Roman republic and empire, and the standard of the legions: adopted by modern European nations, Napoleonic France, Germany, and the United States of America, where in 1782, it became the chief device on the Great Seal. The origin of the double-headed eagle motif is uncertain, but some authorities believe it to be the result of an inaccurate representation of two eagles standing back to back: it is of extreme antiquity, found in ancient Hittite sculpture, and was used by the Turks in Asia Minor, on coins and standards, and is believed to have been adopted by the Crusaders, to become the pre-eminent device in the arms of many European countries. It is the most important of heraldic birds, usually shown facing, the head turned, legs and wings outspread, and may be double-headed, crowned or collared. The slab that forms the top of early and mid 18th century console or bracket tables is often supported by an eagle with outspread wings, and an eagle often surmounted circular convex mirrors of the late 18th century. See also *Alerion* and *Aquila*.

ANCIENT MEXICAN

EAST RIDING, YORKSHIRE (ct.-of-arms)

TWO-HEADED EAGLE. FALMOUTH (ct.-of-arms)

MEXICAN

ROMAN

Early English leaf: see *Trefoil foliage.*

Echinus: an architectural term for the convex or ovolo moulding, *q.v.*, below the abacus on a Greek Doric capital: the word is derived from the fancied resemblance of such a moulding to a sea-urchin shell. The egg-and-tongue motif, *q.v.*, was consistently used to enrich an echinus, and the term has become synonymous with that device. See *Order of architecture.*

Edge moulding: a variation of roll moulding, *q.v.*, in which the centre of the curve is slightly edged; also called a scroll moulding.

Egg-and-tongue: also called egg-and-dart, egg-and-leaf, or egg-and-anchor, all variations of the basic pattern of a series of alternating eggs and points: the pointed shape may be sharp like an arrow, dart, or narrow tongue, or a leaf form, plain or serrated: both semi-oval members and points are sometimes decorated. The ornament was used as an enrichment for mouldings in architecture and on furniture, particularly on the Greek ovolo, and is often called an echinus, *q.v.* See also *Leaf-and-tongue* and *Waterleaf-and-tongue*.

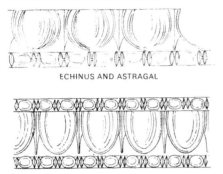

ECHINUS AND ASTRAGAL

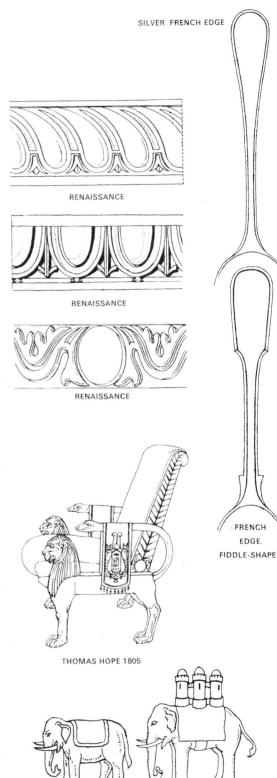

SILVER. FRENCH EDGE

RENAISSANCE

RENAISSANCE

RENAISSANCE

THOMAS HOPE 1805

FRENCH
EDGE.
FIDDLE-SHAPE

Egyptian style: a short-lived fashion for using Egyptian ornamentation and motifs existed in France during the reign of Louis XVI, but the true revival there of this style was the result of the researches made by the team of archaeologists who accompanied the French expedition to Egypt, under Napoleon, in 1798. Egyptian motifs such as the lotus, sphinx, winged globe, and bird- and animal-headed gods, combined with the military symbols favoured by Napoleon, became fashionable for surface decoration, especially on furniture. In early 19th century England, the Egyptian revival enjoyed a limited popularity, mainly due to the work of Thomas Hope (*c.* 1770–1831), a wealthy amateur architect and furniture designer, and the author of *Household Furniture and Interior Decoration*, published in 1807.

Elephant: an important motif in Oriental and Buddhist ornament. In heraldry, the animal was sometimes represented with a tower or castles on his back, and often appears thus on inn signs. See *Yakshi*.

HERALDIC   COVENTRY (ct.-of-arms)

Elizabethan style: a term that describes the architecture, furniture and ornament of late 16th century England. Interest in the period was revived in England and America during the 19th century, but 'Victorian Elizabethan' lacks the sense of style and the vitality of 16th century prototypes.

Embattled: crenellated or indented: heraldic term for an ornamental castellated line. See *Line*. Also used to describe some forms of mid 18th century case furniture, ornamented above the cornice with miniature battlements. See *Castellated*.

Embellishment: ornament applied purely as decoration.

from 'THE ETYMOLOGICON MAGNUM. VENICE 1499

from 'THE ARISTOTLE'
printed by ALDUS. VENICE 1495

from BOOK OF DURROW

ENGLISH 1535

from 'TEWERDANCK'.
NUREMBERG 1517

Emblem: a decorative device, often allegorical; a symbolic attribute of some figure or object.

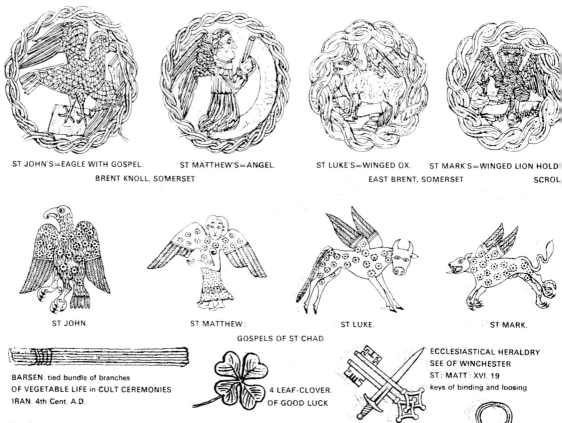

ST JOHN'S=EAGLE WITH GOSPEL.
BRENT KNOLL, SOMERSET

ST MATTHEW'S=ANGEL.

ST LUKE'S=WINGED OX.
EAST BRENT, SOMERSET

ST MARK'S=WINGED LION HOLD
SCROL

ST JOHN.

ST MATTHEW:
GOSPELS OF ST CHAD

ST LUKE.

ST MARK.

BARSEN. tied bundle of branches
OF VEGETABLE LIFE in CULT CEREMONIES
IRAN. 4th Cent. A.D.

4 LEAF-CLOVER.
OF GOOD LUCK

ECCLESIASTICAL HERALDRY
SEE OF WINCHESTER
ST: MATT: XVI. 19
keys of binding and loosing

EGYPTIAN.   GOLD

Embossment: sometimes used to describe a boss, *q.v.*, or decorative carving in relief.

Empire style: the revival of classical ornament, combined with Egyptian, imperial and military motifs, that characterised French furniture and interior decoration during the Empire of Napoleon I lasting throughout the first two decades of the 19th century, Gilt, brass and bronze mounts were used extensively. The style influenced design in the United States, but not in England, where so-called English Empire, *q.v.*, was not connected with it. A second Empire style arose in France after the mid 19th century, under Napoleon III, in which the imperial emblems reappeared, but the style was florid and over-burdened with luscious ornament.

Encarpa: a festoon of fruit and flowers, carved or painted, generally used on a frieze.

Endive scroll: a mid 18th century carved motif in the form of a conventional endive leaf.

Endorse: an heraldic term applied to a vertical line one-quarter the width of a pale, *q.v.*

English Empire: this is a modern and misleading term, wrongly applied to the furniture and decoration of the Regency period. Apart from the brief Peace of Amiens (1802–3), England was cut off from France during the Napoleonic wars, and uninfluenced by French fashions. See *Regency style*.

Engrailed: the heraldic term for an ornamental line with outward facing points or cusps. See *Line*.

Enrichment: the architectural and cabinet-maker's term for carved or inlaid ornament that decorates a moulding.

Ensign: originally a Roman military standard, consisting of a symbolic figure or emblem fixed to the top of a pole; the emblem, at first merely a scrap of straw, later took various animal forms, and eventually the eagle was adopted as characteristic of Roman military power. See *Labarum*. The word also means a special form of national, trading, or association flag, used on ships, in which the flag itself, reduced in size, occupies the top left hand corner of a white or coloured ground. Naval ensigns were first flown on British ships at the end of the 16th century.

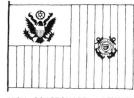

U.S.A. COASTGUARD and ENSIGN
EAGLE IN THE CANTON, DARK BLUE ON WHITE
SIGNIFIES FEDERAL SERVICE

WHITE ENSIGN. St. GEORGE'S CROSS
WITH UNION FLAG IN THE CANTON

CHILE. NATIONAL AND
MERCHANT FLAG AND
ENSIGN

Entrelac: a French word, sometimes used in typography, meaning ornament composed of interlacing figures, mostly used in borders. See *Printers' flowers*.

Ermine mark: a ceramic mark that has been used on Minton porcelain since the mid 19th century; the smaller variation indicates soft glaze ware, and this version is used as an heraldic device, to represent ermine fur.

Escallop or Scallop: this ornamental motif, derived from the rounded, ribbed shell of the mollusc *Pecten*, commonly called the cockle-shell or scallop, is of great antiquity. Its shape and fluting were imitated on drinking vessels and vases of the early Central and South American civilisations, and among these peoples it also had a symbolic and religious association with the god, Quetzalcoatl, and with burial. In Graeco-Roman times the device was a favourite symbolic and decorative motif, associated primarily with the sea, Aphrodite, and fertility: it was widely used in architecture as a niche-head; formed basins and drinking vessels; appeared in mosaic work; and in the decoration of sarcophagi and funerary monuments, and later, gravestones and coffins. In the late 17th century shell-hoods were a common adornment to porches, and from the early 18th century, the shell motif was extensively employed, particularly on the legs of furniture. Also an ancient heraldic charge: emblem of St James the Great, becoming the acknowledged badge of pilgrims, especially of palmers. See also *Coquillage* and *Shell*.

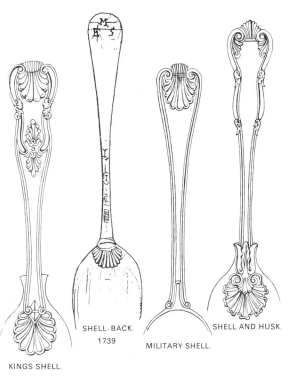

KINGS SHELL.

SHELL-BACK.
1739

MILITARY SHELL.

SHELL AND HUSK.

HERALDIC

Escarbuncle: see *Carbuncle*.

Escartelly: the heraldic term for an ornamental horizontal line embattled at long intervals. See *Line*.

Escroll: an heraldic term meaning a scroll or ribbon, more specifically the scroll on which a motto is inscribed.

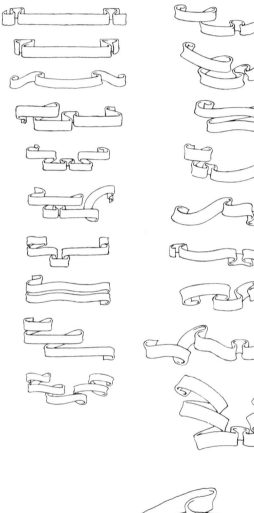

Escutcheon: sometimes called a scutcheon. An heraldic term meaning either a complete coat of arms, or the field on which the arms appear or, most usually, a painted shield used at a funeral. See *Orle*. Also applied to a carved armorial shield that decorates the pediment of a large piece of furniture. In architecture, the word describes an ornamental keyhole plate and pivot cover.

with SWAG. 17th century OVERDOOR. CHAPEL at FARNHAM CASTLE

Estoile: the heraldic term for a star with six or more straight or wavy rays. See also *Molet* and *Star*.

Etruscan style: a style introduced in England during the latter part of the 18th century by Robert Adam (1728–92), allegedly derived from the art and culture of the pre-Roman civilisation of Etruria in central Italy, and in which the use of black, terracotta and white colour schemes played a more important part than form and decorative motifs.

Evolute spiral band: a decorative band, consisting of a continuous undulating series of spirals, sometimes combined with leaf and flower motifs: this characteristic device flows along the centre of the band, so that the spirals lie equally above and below. See *Band*.

Eye: in architecture, the word is applied to a circular centre, or aperture such as the central part of a volute, the opening at the top of a cupola, and a small round or oval window in a pediment, also sometimes called a bullion, bull's eye, or oculus. As a symbol of a watching deity, the human eye has been associated with the religion of ancient Egypt (see *Udjat*) ; with Buddhism ; and in the 17th and 18th centuries with Christianity when it often appeared as the eye of God, in the centre of an equilateral triangle, representing the Trinity.

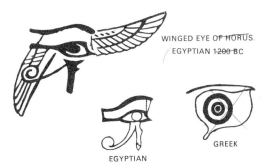

WINGED EYE OF HORUS. EGYPTIAN 1200 BC

EGYPTIAN

GREEK

BIREME WITH EYES.
GREEK 4th Cent.

GERMAN 1748

AZTEC
WEEPING EYE = WIDOWED

Eye ornament: a term for the concentric spiral and oval forms that represent a cross section of a human or animal joint in the symbolic decoration of primitive North-west American Indian tribes.

F

Fabulous monsters: representations of imaginary hybrid creatures, originating in ancient myths, folklore and nature worship, have been universally employed as symbolic, religious and decorative ornament. The transition of animals from reality to fable may have developed from the Chinese practice, in the Han era, of classifying animals according to four types of skin covering—shell, scales, feathers and hair—and these categories were associated with the elements of water, wood, fire and metal, the colours black, green, red and white, and the solstices, the dragon symbolising spring, the phoenix summer, the tiger autumn, the tortoise winter, these four creatures ruling the seasons and equinoxes: such symbolism would lead to the use of an animal or hybrid to represent some particular quality or attribute. The theriomorphism of ancient Egypt produced an array of animal- and bird-headed deities, precursors of the grotesque, semi-human monsters of Greek and Roman mythology. Many of these classical monsters are used as heraldic devices, as well as creatures of heraldic origin.

PICTISH 8th–9th Centuries

PERSIAN 1400 C

SCYLLA. GREEK

EGYPTIAN

from 12th Cent. BESTIARY

FIGURE. OXFORD. A. W. PUGIN

MONSTROUS SIMBURG BIRD

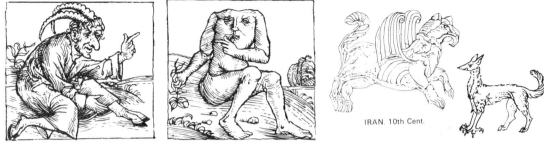

from NUREMBERG CHRONICLE 1493

IRAN. 10th Cent.

ENFIELD

CROCODYLUS from river NILE

ST GEORGE'S CHAPEL

Fan tracery: an architectural term sometimes used to describe the delicate spreading pattern of fan vaulting, formed by ribs rising from the same point and radiating outwards.

Fane: see *Weather vane*.

Fasces: used as an heraldic device, sometimes found in the armorials of the judiciary, a bound bundle of rods with an axe projecting from them, the insignia of Roman magistrates, symbolising their right of chastisement and execution. Also a symbol of sacrificial slaughter and, adorned with laurel leaves, of military victory.

HERALDIC

ROMAN

Fasces

SOUVENIR. CONTEMPORARY. NAPLES

Fascine pattern: a type of ornamentation used by prehistoric lake dwellers; an arrangement of horizontal and vertical lines, which may be derived from the bands of withy that fastened stone weapons to their hafts, or from a method of construction sometimes used in the lake dwellings, when the foundations were formed by interwoven horizontal layers of trees, with uprights driven in at intervals, known as fascine work.

Feathering: see *Foliation*.

Feathers: ostrich, swan and turkey feathers are used in heraldry, for crests, devices and badges, most usually ostrich feathers, that were favoured by Edward III for this purpose, and became increasingly popular in succeeding reigns. See also *Panache*, and *Prince of Wales's feathers*.

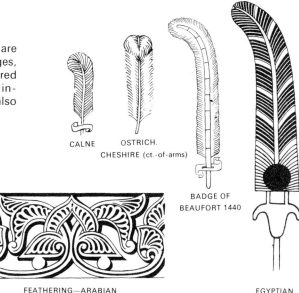

CALNE   OSTRICH.
CHESHIRE (ct.-of-arms)

BADGE OF
BEAUFORT 1440

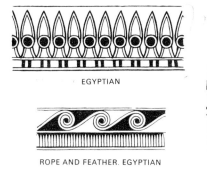

EGYPTIAN

ROPE AND FEATHER. EGYPTIAN

FEATHERING—ARABIAN

EGYPTIAN

Ferr: see *Horseshoe*.

Fertility symbols: the most commonly found in decoration are the bull, escallop, lily, pine cone, pomegranate, rice grains, Yang and Yin, Yakshi and water. See also *Dot and Monad*.

Fess: in heraldry, an ordinary, *q.v.*, consisting of two horizontal lines enclosing the third part of a shield at its centre.

Festoon: a carved or painted garland or wreath of flowers, fruit or foliage, suspended at each end, and used to adorn a frieze or panel. The device was employed by the Romans for the decorations used at sacrificial ceremonies and rituals, when the festoon was suspended from animals' skulls, rosettes or candelabra: in Renaissance ornament, the skulls were replaced by angels' heads, and the curved space between the supporters, *q.v.*, might be filled with rosettes, ribbons and masks. The term swag, though often used as an alternative, may also mean a festoon composed of draped folds of cloth. See also *Bucranium, Catenary, Cluster*, and *Encarpa*.

Fiddle back: see *Ladder back*.

Fiddlehead: a scroll in the form of a violin head, used by carvers; also applied to scrollwork on a ship's bow, or to heavy iron scroll-ends.

COUPED

Fillet: an alternative name for band, *q.v.*, sometimes called a listel. In heraldry, the diminutive of the ordinary, *q.v.*, known as a chief.

Fillet cross: a very narrow cross, used in heraldry to differentiate between, and at the same time unite, separate coats of arms appearing on a quartered shield.

Fimbriated cross: a plain cross, *q.v.*, in which the limbs are surrounded by a narrow border.

Finial

Finial: a carved or moulded ornament that terminates a pinnacle, gable, spire, or similar pointed architectural member, and also used to decorate pew ends and the back uprights of chairs. Usually the ornament consists of clustered foliage, fruit or flowers, and sometimes of human and animal figures, or of a knob, when it may be called a pommel; an obsolete name is crope. See *Spandril Piece*.

ENGLISH 16th–17th Centuries. STONE

FEDERAL FINIALS. FOR POST, PEDIMENT, AND INTER-SECTION

DESIGNS FOR WROUGHT IRON. A. W. PUGIN

TOLEDO

RENAISSANCE. BREMEN

OTTOMAN CUPOLAS

CHARTRES CATHEDRAL

NEW WALSINGHAM

AMIENS CATHEDRAL 1230

FOUNTAIN AT ROTTENBURG

ALL SOUL'S COLLEGE CHAPEL, C

Fir apple: see *Pine cone* and *Tree.*

Fir cone: see *Pine cone* and *Tree.*

Fire marks: metal plaques, first used after the Great Fire of London of 1666, fixed to houses by insurance companies, to identify their clients, and to ensure that they would be protected by the companies' private fire brigades. The plaque bore the device of the company, often a decorative rebus, *q.v.*, on its name, and the insurance policy number of the householder.

Fish: the fish had pagan religious associations in Mediterranean countries, but since the early days of Christianity it has been an important Christian device, symbolising baptism, St Peter the fisherman, and Christ, because the Greek word for fish ΙΧΘΥΣ), consists of the initial letters of the phrase 'Jesus Christ, the Son of God, the Saviour', in Greek. Engravings of the fish motif have been found on sarcophagi in the catacombs; it is a common decoration on fonts; and is the basis of the vesica piscis, *q.v.*, much used as an ornament on medieval ecclesiastical seals. As a Christian symbol, the fish may appear alone, or in conjunction with an anchor, dove, or ship, or two or three fishes may be entwined together. The device of two fish, tails downward, their heads almost joined, was one of the eight Buddhist Emblems of Happy Augury.

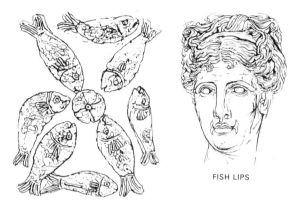

FISH LIPS

EIGHT FISH SYMBOLS OF THE DEAD ENCIRCLE
AND BITE AT A CENTRAL ROSETTE, SYMBOL OF LIFE
TOMB. GHIRZA

ANCIENT MEXICAN

VASE. EGYPTIAN. 1370 B.C.

EARLY CHRISTIAN. GRAVESTONE. SPANISH 13th Cent.

Flag: a national symbol, adorned with appropriate emblems, that developed from the wood, stone or metal device fixed to the top of a pole, and used as an identification badge by families, tribes, and then nations. Later, the device was transferred to a square or triangular cloth, hung from the crossbar of a lance; the Roman *vexillum*, and the Danish Viking flag with one vertical edge fastened to a pole, were early forms of the flag proper. The device itself was at first a sacred religious emblem, or the personal badge of a king or leader, but as nations emerged, it was replaced by appropriate national symbols or those of patron saints: during the Crusades the flag acquired much of its heraldic significance. Colour is important: red defines rebellion; black, death; green, a wreck; yellow, quarantine; white, goodwill. See also *Banner, Ensign, Gonfalon, Pirate flag*, and *Standard.*

BELGIAN.

GOLD SALTIRE BORDERED BY RED ABOVE AND BELOW
AND BY BLACK TOWARDS THE HOIST AND FLY.
WHITE FIELD. ABOVE THE SALTIRE A CROWN SURMOUNTS
TWO CROSSED CANNON IN BLACK.
BELOW A BLACK FOUL ANCHOR

Flamboyant tracery: a form of curvilinear tracery: *q.v.*, characteristic of late French Gothic ornament; the cusped conjoined cone shapes have a flame-like appearance.

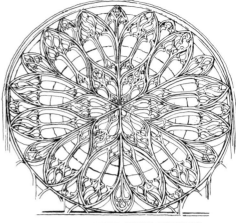

SOUTH TRANSEPT, AMIENS CATHEDRAL

Flames: formalised, they may appear as a decorative motif on finials (see *Auger flames*); and, as a symbol of renewal of life, have been used as a terminal ornament on sculptured urns: in heraldry, a twisted flame between two wings with diagonal darts of lightning behind, signifies a thunderbolt, and in more recent times, the forces of electricity. A conventional wheel, surrounded by flames, is one of the eight Buddhist Emblems of Happy Augury. See also *Linked flames*.

Flaunches: in heraldry an ordinary *q.v.*: segments of circles projecting into the field from two sides of an escutcheon: always in pairs; also known as Flasks or Voiders.

Fleur-de-lys: a decorative motif in the form of a stylised lily, usually with three curled petals, but occasionally with five. In architecture, it was used in 14th century tracery patterns, and as a carved and painted ornament in the 16th and 17th centuries. In heraldry, a familiar device, that signifies a sixth son: introduced in France, as the Bourbon heraldic bearing, by Louis VII (1137–80), possibly as a rebus, *q.v.*, symbolising the flower of Louis, it became emblematic of the country; the motif also appeared on the arms and coins of medieval Florence. It has been suggested that the device is adapted from the Egyptian lotus bud and flower, the iris, or the anthemion. An emblem of the Virgin Mary.

FORMS OF FLEUR-DE-LYS

VENETIAN 17th Cent.

FRENCH

FRENCH

MIDDLE AGES   late 15th Cent.   early 17th Cent.   late BOURBON KINGS

ENGLISH VERSIONS

Fleuron: a flower-shaped motif, used as an architectural ornament, a coin device, and a printers' flower, *q.v.* Occasionally called a floret.

CHIP-CARVED.
ALTAR-PEDESTAL 8th Cent.
VISIGOTHIC CHURCH

Floreation: ornamentation that consists of flowing lines of conventionalised floral and leaf devices. Floral motifs had Oriental origins, and were common in ancient Chinese, Indian and Persian ornament, and later, were freely used to decorate the borders of early illuminated MSS. Foliage—notably oak, vine and ivy—was a characteristic enrichment of capitals, corbels, crockets and finials in Gothic architecture and 14th and 15th century furniture.

CAPITAL. WELLS CATHEDRAL *circa* 1200

CATHEDRAL AT NEVERS

TENDRILS. COPTIC. 6th–8th Centuries

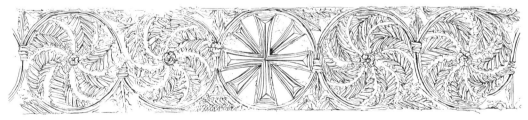

COPTIC. 6th–8th Centuries.

Floret: see *Fleuron*.

BYZANTINE. TEMPLE OF VENUS. APHRODISIAS

Florid style: a term occasionally used to describe the highly enriched architecture characteristic of the late Gothic period.

Flowing pattern: design of flowing, curved and smoothly continuous lines.

Flowing tracery: see *Curvilinear tracery*.

Flush bead: an astragal or bead moulding sunk to lie flush with the adjacent surfaces.

Flutes: see *Fluting*.

Fluting: ornamentation, by shallow rounded channels called flutes, flutings, or striges, cut vertically, and occasionally diagonally in a surface. The flutes may be separated by a sharp edge, or fillet, or may be partially filled by a convex moulding. See *Moulding* and *Stopped channel fluting*.

BAT'S WING FLUTING. silver

BRIDGE—FLUTING and PUNTS

RADIAL. FLUTING

FINIAL

CURVED FLUTING. ROMAN. early 3rd Cent. AD

Foil: the lobe lying between cusps, *q.v.*, in Gothic tracery. Three, four, or five foils usually pierce an opening. See *Foliation*.

TRE *FOIL*   QUATRE *FOIL*   CINQUE *FOIL*

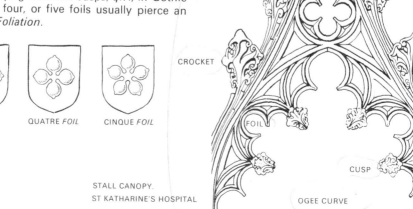

CROCKET

FOIL

CUSP

STALL CANOPY.
ST KATHARINE'S HOSPITAL

OGEE CURVE

Folded tape pattern: a term sometimes used to describe a continuous pattern of interlaced flat ribbons, used as a decorative band in medieval ornamentation.

Foliate head: a head wreathed in foliage, often oak or hawthorn, that also sprouts from the mouth, and sometimes from eyes, ears and nose, the face frowning, and expressive of pain and sorrow. This ancient ornamental motif, probably originating in tree worship and later associated with pagan rites of spring, appears to have acquired a symbolic connection with the Christian Easter and Resurrection. Used in Roman ornament, then widely in medieval church carving, on bosses, misericords, capitals, corbels and tombs. These heads are sometimes called Green Men.

WORMS CATHEDRAL

CROWCOMBE. SOMERSET. 1534

print. A. VERARD. PARIS 1503

HATCH BEAUCHAMP.
SOMERSET

Foliated band: a decorative band composed of a continuous pattern of stems, foliage, buds, flowers or fruit, or combinations of all these, used with characteristic variations, in Classical, Romanesque, Gothic and Renaissance ornament. See *Undulate* and *Vertebrate bands*.

Foliation: an architectural term for the arrangement of cusps and foils that form tracery: an alternate name is feathering. The term 'foliated' is applied to the use of foil- and leaf-shaped ornament, also to the convolutions of stylised plant forms, such as the acanthus.

Four-leaved or four-petalled flower: a favourite motif in Gothic ornament, often used for enriching mouldings. It sometimes alternated with a ball flower, *q.v.*, and consisted of a rose-like flower with an inner and outer set of four petals, placed obliquely to each other. The flower could be square or circular, and was often used alternately thus. See also *Tablet flower*.

Frame: in the ornamentation of Anglo-Saxon MSS, a frame of gold bars, often interlaced with decorative foliage, was sometimes used as a surround to a page.

GILL FLORIATED. type-face.
E. GILL 1882–1940

PSALTER. ANGLO-SAXON late 10th Cent.

French Empire style: see *Empire style*.

Fret: an ornamental geometrical pattern based on the rectangle, of horizontal and vertical straight lines, used in a continuous band for surface decoration in architecture, furniture, ceramics, textiles, and illuminated MSS. This device has appeared in numerous variations in the ornament of ancient Egypt and Assyria, Central America, China and Japan, but the term is generally understood to mean the Greek fret, one of the simplest motifs in classical decoration, also known as key pattern, labyrinth and meander. Some authorities believe that the fret may have evolved from the swastika, *q.v.*, or from the patterns used in the plaited straw mats of ancient Egypt. In heraldry, a fret is a device composed of a mascle, *q.v.*, interlaced with a saltire, *q.v.*

SIMPLE

DOUBLE

MEXICAN

SYMMETRICAL

YUCATAN

CHINESE

MEXICAN

CHINESE

CELTIC

ARABIAN

GREEK

ARABIAN

MORESQUE

RUNNING

GREEK

CHINESE

SIMPLE

EGYPTIAN FRET AND PATERAE

STEPPED WITH SPIRAL MOTIF. ANCIENT MEXICAN

TURKISH

TURKISH

STEPS AND HOOKS

YUCATAN

CHINESE

PUEBLO. FRET and INTERLOCKING COILS

Fret band: a decorative band consisting of a fret pattern, sometimes interlaced with plant motifs or stars.

CHINESE LATTICE-WORK FRIEZE. ENGLISH TALLBOY 1760

SCHEMES for FRETS:
CHIPPENDALE'S 'GENTLEMAN AND CABINET-MAKERS DIRECTOR' 1762

Fretty: an heraldic term describing a charge consisting of interlaced diagonal bands.

Frieze: in architecture the plain or decorated band which separates architrave and cornice on an entablature. The term also describes the upper part of an interior wall below the cornice, and the horizontal flat or convex surface below the cornice on a bookcase or cabinet. See *Spandril Piece, Bucranium* and *Moulding*.

LOUIS SEIZE STYLE. FAY

Funeral escutcheon: see *Hatchment*.

Fusil: in heraldry, an elongated lozenge, developed from the wharrow, a weaver's tool of the same shape, but with curved bulging sides.

Fylfot: see *Swastika*.

G

Gable stones: see *Shop signs*.

Gadrooning: an enrichment used in the decoration of furniture, and carved on curved surfaces, such as the edges of tables, cabinet stands, cabriole bracket feet, and the bulbs of table legs, bed posts, and cupboard supports, consisting of flutes or convex reeds in a repeating pattern. Occasionally used in architecture on the tops of pedestals. Also known as lobing and nulling.

PLAIN GADROONING. GLASS

SILVER

GADROON EDGE.
SILVER

Gammadion: see *Swastika*.

Garb: see *Wheat*.

Gargoyle: an ornamental rainwater spout that projects from a cornice or front of a buttress. Occasionally plain, in Gothic architecture usually carved in the form of a grotesque human, animal or bird's head, with an open mouth: the water flows out through this, or through a small spout above or below the head.

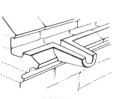

GOTHIC

NOTRE DAME DE PARIS

NOTRE DAME DE PARIS

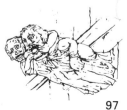

Garland: an alternate name for a festoon or wreath, *q.v.* In architecture, an archaic use of the word was to describe an ornamental band.

HERALDIC

CRANCELIN, a small GARLAND
[or termed : BEND TREFLÉ]
ARMS OF SAXONY

Gemel rings: see *Annulet.*

Gemini: the twins; the third sign of the Zodiac. See *Zodiacal devices.*

Genius: in Roman mythology, a symbolic figure (like a guardian angel) that accompanied each human being; generally shown as a winged naked boy. Roman genii included *lares* (spirits of the dead), *penates* (household gods), and locality guardians, represented in symbolic decoration and on coins by laurel-crowned youths, classical deities, or serpents. See *Serpent.*

Geometrical ornament: decorative patterns created on a basic network of straight lines, from which elaborate and intricate variations, inspired by geometric figures, are developed. Primitive peoples used this kind of ornament in arrangements of such simple figures as lines, squares, circles and stars, to decorate weapons, implements and skin and bark cloth, and for tattooing. Much Egyptian and Assyrian ornament was geometrical, and its subsequent development reached a zenith in the highly sophisticated and intricate ornament of the Byzantine and Arabian civilisations.

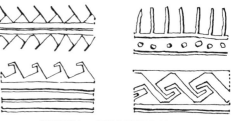

DESIGNS from EARLY PUEBLO POTTERY

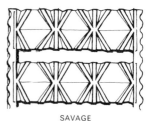

SAVAGE

NEOLITHIC PAINTED VASE.
circa 3000 BC SUR. PERSIA

MOSQUE SHEKHUN. 14th Cent.

PAINTED BALUSTRADE. HERCULES TOWER. SEGOVIA

Geometrical tracery: tracery composed largely of patterns of geometric figures, notably interlacing circles and varieties of foils, *q.v.* Characteristic of the Perpendicular period of English Gothic architecture. See *Pointed-and-cusped*.

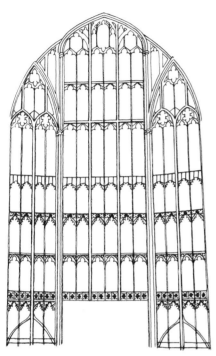

PERPENDICULAR. *circa* 1351. GLOUCESTER CATHEDRAL

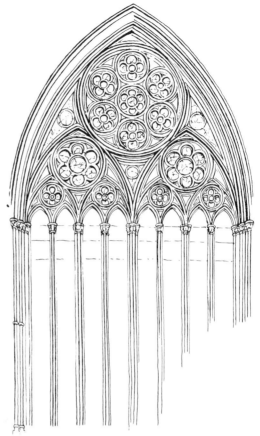

EAST WINDOW. LINCOLN CATHEDRAL. late 13th Cent.

Gibbet cross: see *Tau cross*.

Gigantes: see *Atlantes*.

Gimmel rings: see *Annulet*.

Gingko: a characteristic Japanese ornamental and heraldic motif in the form of two- and four-folded fan-shaped leaves, based on the foliage of a tree that has survived from prehistoric times, indigenous to the East, and known in Britain as the maidenhair tree (*gingko biloba*).

Glory: a radiation of light surrounding the head and figure of a deity or saint; the word is sometimes used to describe an aureole or nimbus, *q.v.*

Glyph: an architectural term for an ornamental groove cut vertically in a flat or curved surface.

Gola: sometimes spelt gula; an Italian form of the word cyma, *q.v.*

Gonfalon or Gonfanon: an ecclesiastical flag or banner, two- or three-tailed, fixed to a transverse bar on a pole, by a hinged frame that turns like a vane.

Goose-neck: an American alternative for swan-neck, *q.v.*

Gorge: In architecture, an alternate name for a cavetto, *q.v.* In heraldry, a gorge or gurge is a spiral device allegedly representing a whirlpool.

GORGE or WHIRLPOOL.
GORGES. (ct.-of-arms)

GURGE INTERLACING A CROSS ENGRAILED

Gorgon mask: grotesque and horrific, this represented the serpent-entwined head of Medusa. Also known as a gorgoneion or Medusa head.

ARCHAIC HEAD. BRONZE. FROM NEMI SHIP ROMAN GREEK. RONDANINI

Gothic revival: the name given to a movement in taste, that began early in the 18th century, when the founding of the Society of Antiquaries of London in 1707 fostered interest in medieval ruins, which later encouraged a fashion for incorporating fragments of Gothic ornament in furniture and interior decoration. By the mid 18th century Gothic taste had influenced architectural design, and until the end of the first quarter of the 19th century Gothic details and ornament were used with restraint within the discipline of classic rules and proportions that still governed architectural design. See *Strawberry Hill Gothic.* By the middle of the 19th century that discipline had weakened, and the revival of Gothic taste assumed more and more the character of an emotional, almost a religious movement: medieval designs and decoration were indiscriminately and often incongruously used in architecture and cabinet-making. See *Abbotsford period.* During the later 19th century imitation medieval Gothic forms, often misplaced, with inharmonious results, were applied to construction and decoration in the growing industrial society.

Gougework: an ornamental pattern, consisting of a regular series of shallow grooves made in a surface by a gouge. See also *Fluting* and *Nicking.*

Gouttes: an heraldic term meaning tear-drops, sometimes called guttae: a shield, described as gouttée, is sprinkled with drops that may be water, oil, blood, tears, gold, and so on, identified by different colours.

Grains of rice: see *Rice-grain.*

Grecque, à la: another term for labyrinth, *q.v.* Also used to describe the neo-classical style that captivated French taste in the 1760s, when everything modish in furniture, trinkets, and ornament was *à la Grecque.*

Greek cross: the basic form of heraldic cross, equilateral, with limbs all the same length.

Greek fret: a continuous rectilinear motif, also known as Greek key, key pattern, labyrinth, and meander. In its simplest form, the device consists of a single line, running in one direction, with right-angled keys at regular intervals: in a double fret, the basic line is interlaced by a second: among many variations are combinations of frets, placed back to back, enclosing squares, having a multiplicity of keys, and sometimes incorporating cross, circle, and plant motifs. The Greek fret was probably the most widely used form of surface decoration in the Graeco-Roman world, and adaptations of the device are recognisable in Byzantine, Celtic, Arabian and Renaissance ornament. See *Fret* and *Meander.*

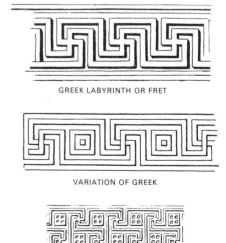

GREEK LABYRINTH OR FRET

VARIATION OF GREEK

GREEK FRET ORNAMENT

Greek key: see *Greek fret*.

Greek revival: in England the Grecian and neo-Greek revivals originated in the latter part of the 18th century, following the publication of *The Antiquities of Athens* by James Stuart (1713–88, 'Athenian' Stuart), and Nicholas Revett (1720–1804). This work, issued in four volumes, consolidated the interest aroused by antiquaries and archaeologists who had financed expeditions to Greece and Asia Minor, and the first volume, which appeared in 1762, became a source book for details of Greek ornament and architecture, that influenced the design of furniture and interior architecture. Later, the Greek revival was stimulated by such works as *Etchings of Ancient Ornamental Architecture*, published in 1799 by Charles Heathcote Tatham (1772–1842), and a second book by him, *Etchings representing fragments of Grecian and Roman Architectural Ornaments* (1806) and, most influential of all, Thomas Hope's *Household Furniture and Interior Decoration* (1807). The Greek revival affected the design of furniture until the mid 19th century.

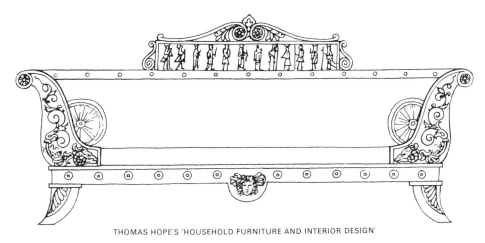

THOMAS HOPE'S 'HOUSEHOLD FURNITURE AND INTERIOR DESIGN'

Green men: see *Foliate head*.

Griffin: a fabulous monster, with the feathered head, wings, and front legs of an eagle, and the body and hind legs of a lion: a popular heraldic device, when it appears with ears, and a wingless version signifies a male creature. Used first as an ornamental motif by the Greeks and Romans, and later in Renaissance design, and as carved decoration on furniture in 18th century England. The griffin of Edward III is one of the Queen's Beasts, *q.v.* Variations on the name are griffon, gryphon, gryphos, gryps, gryphus.

SACRED GRYPHON. PALACE OF MINOS. CNOSSUS

ROMAN

IRAN. 10th–11th Centuries

Grotesque

Grotesque: an intricate and fantastic form of arabesque ornament, *q.v.* Also referred to as *grottesche*, a word derived from the grottoes, caverns, vaults and baths of ancient Rome, in which such ornamentation was discovered in the 16th century. Inspired by Raphael's use of this style of decoration for the Vatican loggias, its popularity expanded during the Renaissance, when it assumed a fanciful and fantastic character, embodying intricate patterns of animals, birds, festoons, tendrils, scrolls, and even landscapes. The term also describes a distorted, deformed or hideously grinning figure or mask, used as a carved device in medieval, Renaissance, baroque and rococo ornament: sometimes called a caricature. See *Initial* and *Mask*.

MANUSCRIPT, ENGLISH 1439

ARABESQUE. SIENA

DUTCH RENAISSANCE. OUDENARDE

from 'HOURS'

PUBLISHED BY
SIMON VOSTRE
SHOWING PAGAN DEVICES
AND DOTTED GROUND

Grottesche: see *Grotesque*.

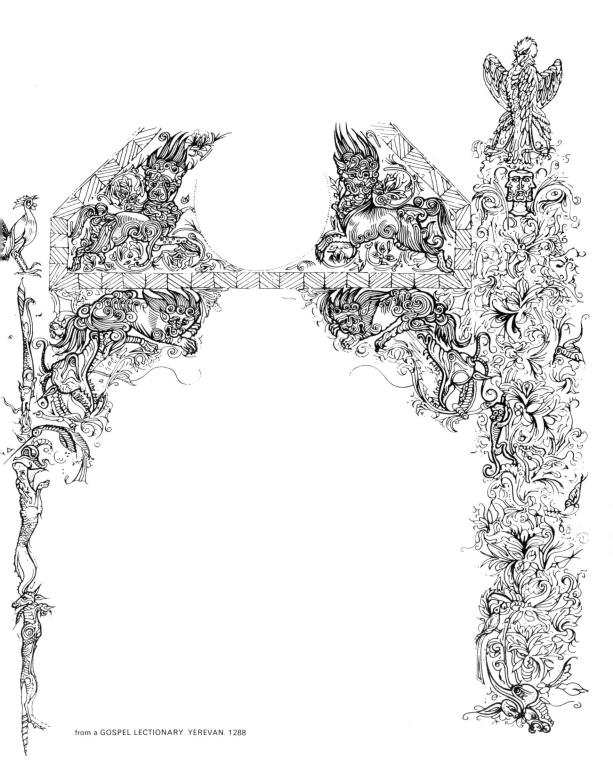

from a GOSPEL LECTIONARY. YEREVAN. 1288

Gryphon: see *Griffin*.

Guilloche

ARCTIC AMERICAN

PERUVIAN

Guilloche: an ornamental pattern of continuous interlaced curving bands, used to enrich mouldings or flat surfaces, in appearance like an orderly network. Two, or three, conjoined, are known as double and treble guilloche respectively. The device, common to Assyrian, Greek, Roman, medieval, and Renaissance decoration, has been described as a form of rounded fret, and is distinctly related to strapwork, *q.v.* Sometimes called snare-work, the motif may have been inspired by flower or leaf tendrils, or twisted ribbons.

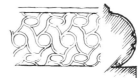

TORUS WITH GUILLOCHE

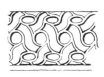

GREEK

ROMAN VERSION OF GREEK ORIGINAL

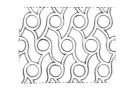

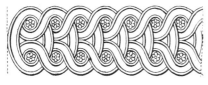

BASED ON INTERLACING CIRCLES

Gula: see *Gola.*

Gurge: see *Gorge.*

Guttae: small, wedge-shaped drop ornaments, used on the frieze of the Doric order of architecture, below the regula and mutules. Guttae appear on the feet of chairs, tables and case furniture by some mid 18th century makers, and were known as guttae feet. In heraldry, the word is sometimes used as an alternative to gouttes, *q.v.*

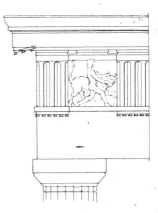

Half figure: a term sometimes used for the upper part of a human figure, rising from a bowl of foliage and scrolls, used ornamentally, i.e. as a door knocker, or as surface decoration, and sometimes on 16th and early 17th century bed-heads and chimney-pieces. Also known as a demi-figure.

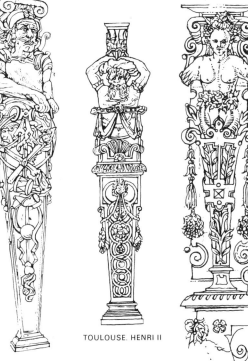

TOULOUSE. HENRI II

GERMAN RENAISSANCE. BRUNSWICK

Hallmark: the device used on silver, denoting the Assay office where it was tested: in the plural, the word is a generic description of all the marks on silver. The chief devices used as Assay marks are the heraldic lion, and its head: leopard's head; three wheatsheaves; crown; anchor; castle; thistle; harp; elephant.

STERLING STANDARD 1549–50

1565–66

1670–71

HIGH STANDARD 1711–12

NEWCASTLE 1672

NORWICH 1679

EXETER 1715

1730–31

1831–2

CHESTER 1733

BIRMINGHAM 1779

1785–86

SOVEREIGN'S HEAD DUTY MARK 1784 ONWARDS

SHEFFIELD 1822

DUBLIN 1737–8

EDINBURGH

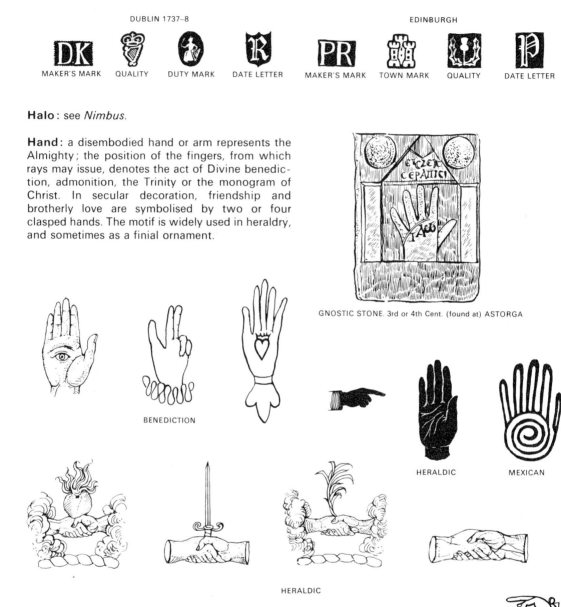

MAKER'S MARK   QUALITY   DUTY MARK   DATE LETTER   MAKER'S MARK   TOWN MARK   QUALITY   DATE LETTER

Halo: see *Nimbus*.

Hand: a disembodied hand or arm represents the Almighty; the position of the fingers, from which rays may issue, denotes the act of Divine benediction, admonition, the Trinity or the monogram of Christ. In secular decoration, friendship and brotherly love are symbolised by two or four clasped hands. The motif is widely used in heraldry, and sometimes as a finial ornament.

GNOSTIC STONE. 3rd or 4th Cent. (found at) ASTORGA

BENEDICTION

HERALDIC   MEXICAN

HERALDIC

Harp: this musical instrument, of great antiquity, known in ancient Egypt and the Graeco-Roman world, was used as a decorative device on vases, coins, sculpture and in painting. Early harps varied in size: some, rising above the performer, stood on the ground, others were small enough to be held in the player's hands: old harps had fewer strings, and those on the Irish instrument were of brass, plucked, not by the fingers, but by the fingernails. Introduced early to Britain, where it was chiefly associated with the Celtic races, it became the national symbol of Ireland, and appears as an heraldic device in the Royal Arms: an attribute of

CELTIC   WELSH   WINGED LADY

St Cecilia and the Jewish king, David. The name harp-back was applied to a late 18th century type of chair with a splat carved like a lyre, *q.v.*

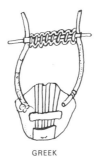

GREEK

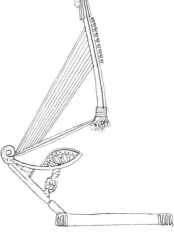

EGYPTIAN

Harpy: a fabulous monster of classical mythology, having the head and breast of a woman, and body, wings and clawed feet of a large bird of prey: legendarily associated with evil, the Furies, and as an instrument of punishment by the gods. Ornamentally, it is used almost exclusively as an heraldic device.

BRIT. MUSEUM

CLOISTER OF SILOS

Hatchment: heraldic term for the armorial bearings, *q.v.*, of a deceased person, painted on a black-framed lozenge and exhibited on his house front before the funeral procession left for the church; also called a funeral escutcheon.

WHITE ON SINISTER=SURVIVING WIFE
BLACK ON DEXTER=DEAD HUSBAND

Hawk: in ancient Egyptian mythology, the hawk-
or falcon-headed deities included Horus, Ra and
Seker, gods of sky, sun and the dead respectively;
and in the form of a funerary amulet, a man-headed
hawk, symbolic of the soul, was alleged to empower
a dead person to reunite his body, soul, and spirit.
Also associated with Apollo, the bird was believed
to be unique in its ability to stare unwaveringly at
the sun. As an heraldic device, it often appears
with the jesses and bells of falconry.

EGYPTIAN

EGYPTIAN. ROYAL GOD HORUS REPRESENTED AS
A HAWK [WITH A DOUBLE CROWN]

Heart: in ancient Egypt, the symbol for the heart
(*ib*) was an important funerary amulet. A highly
conventionalised human heart is used as a Christian
symbol; pierced, it signifies the sorrows of Christ
and the Virgin Mary: a flaming heart denotes
charity, Divine love and religious fervour; it is
the emblem of a number of saints, including St
Catherine of Siena. The heart-shape cut in the back
of wooden chairs made in America in the 18th
century originated the name, heart-back chair.
Heart-shaped apertures were also cut in surfaces
and chair backs of late 19th century furniture in the
Art Nouveau style. The device of a heart is one of the
four suit signs on English playing cards: the French
coeurs are identical: the device developed from the
hearts (*herzen*), cups (*coppe*), and chalices (*copas*)
of the German, Italian and Spanish packs respectively. As a suit sign it has symbolised the Church,
faith, and drunkenness. See *Playing cards* and *Suit
signs*.

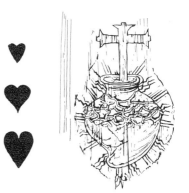

SACRED HEART.
DEVOTIONAL PLAQUE. MEXICO 1805–45

HERALDIC

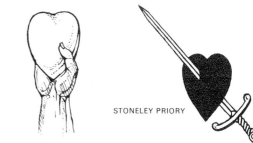

STONELEY PRIORY

Helix: architectural term for the small spiral ornament that lies beneath the abacus of a Corinthian
column; helices are arranged in pairs, that rise
together from one base in carved foliage, and curl
outwards, to meet under the abacus. See *Order of
Architecture*.

Heraldic ornament: the science of heraldry arose from the use of identity devices by knights totally enclosed in armour, to enable them to tell friend from foe. During the 12th century, this need was met by the adoption of personal devices that could be displayed and painted on shields, banners, equipment and seals: following this utilitarian beginning, the international character of the Crusades and the increase of military jousts and tournaments developed the use of innumerable symbolic and decorative emblems, often allegorical or based on a rebus, *q.v.*, appropriated by families as hereditary personal insignia, which, by the 13th century, had been transformed into an authentic heraldic code. As the need for identification receded, armorial bearings and devices were increasingly used by their owners as architectural ornaments, and for the decoration of furniture, plate, books, liveries, equestrian equipment, vehicles and seals. Ecclesiastical and educational establishments, livery companies and guilds and trading establishments, have long possessed armorial bearings, and such insignia are now owned by municipal bodies, professional and commercial associations and public institutions. See also *Armorial style*.

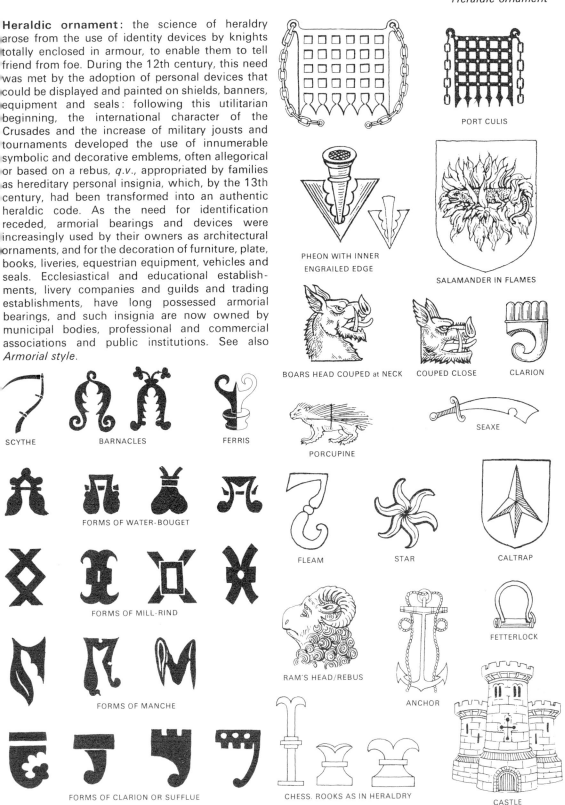

PORT CULIS

PHEON WITH INNER ENGRAILED EDGE

SALAMANDER IN FLAMES

BOARS HEAD COUPED at NECK COUPED CLOSE CLARION

SCYTHE BARNACLES FERRIS

PORCUPINE

SEAXE

FORMS OF WATER-BOUGET

FLEAM STAR CALTRAP

FORMS OF MILL-RIND

FETTERLOCK

FORMS OF MANCHE

RAM'S HEAD/REBUS

ANCHOR

FORMS OF CLARION OR SUFFLUE

CHESS. ROOKS AS IN HERALDRY

CASTLE

109

Heraldic supporters

ROYAL COAT OF ARMS HUNGARY

RUSSIA

ANTELOPE=MANCHESTER

HART=HERTFORDSH

UNITED GRAND LODGE of FREE and
ACCEPTED MASONS OF ENGLAND

ARMS OF DUBLIN

PIEBALD TALBOT=WALTHAMSTOW

RED DRAGON=SWANSE

ELEPHANT ERMINES=OXFORD

WINGED BULL=FINSBURY

GRIFFIN=HOLBORN

OWL=LEEDS

Heraldic ornament

NE LION=WESTMINSTER   ROYAL-STAG=NOTTINGHAM   TRITON LIVERPOOL   ANTELOPE=SALFORD

FIN=STAFFORDSHIRE   SEATED LION=DONCASTER   WINGED HORSE=EXETER   WYVERN=CARLISLE

T BUSTARD=CAMBRIDGE   DOLPHIN=FINSBURY   SEA-LION=PORT OF LONDON AUTHORITY   UNICORN=BRISTOL

Heraldic ornament

MERMAID=BOSTON

SEA-HORSE=CARDIFF

SEA-HORSE=CAMBRIDGE

GRIFFIN=BARNES

SWAN=BUCKINGHAMSHIRE

WOLF=CHESTER

OTTER=NEWARK-UPON-TRENT

GOAT=BRADFORD

LEOPARD=LORD, TENNYSON

WOLF=SALFORD

BEAVER=CITY OF OXFORD

RAM=LEICESTER

ANTELOPE
HERALDIC.

STAG
CABOSHED

OSPREY.
SWANSEA

WHITE HART.
RICHARD II. ENGLISH

SALAMANDER
APPLEBY

LEOPARD
GOVERNMENT OF NYASALAND.

SQUIRREL
WORKSOP

PIGEON
CHELTENHAM

OSPREY.
SUTTON-IN-ASHFIELD

Herm: see *Term*.

Herringbone: the zigzag pattern formed by two alternate courses of brick, stone, tiles or wood, in which the units are laid diagonally, giving the appearance of a herring spine. Although commonly used ornamentally on walls, floors, borders, and inlaid on furniture, this was basically a form of construction, which also had the practical advantage of achieving a level with the irregular shaped blocks used in Roman and medieval building. In the decoration of 19th century glasses, a circle of parallel mitres is known as a herringbone fringe. The name of a pattern in woven cloth; and type of stitch.

Hexagon: a figure of six equal sides and angles; occuring naturally as in mineral crystals, snow crystals and the honeycomb. Basis for all-over patterning when juxtaposed.

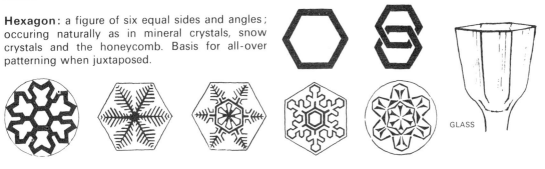

GLASS

Hieraco or Hierco-sphinx: the Greek name for the Egyptian hawk- or falcon-headed sphinx. See *Sphinx*.

113

Hieroglyph: a pictorial symbol representing a sound. The earliest form of Egyptian writing (in use *c.* 3000 BC) was hieroglyphic: after it had been supplanted by hieratic and demotic writing, the hieroglyphic pattern of objects and symbols that had been used for religious and instructive inscriptions became a form of decoration, and during the Ptolemaïc period that began *c.* 300 BC, persons of importance had their names inscribed in hieroglyphics and enclosed in cartouches, in imitation of Egyptian kings of the early dynasties.

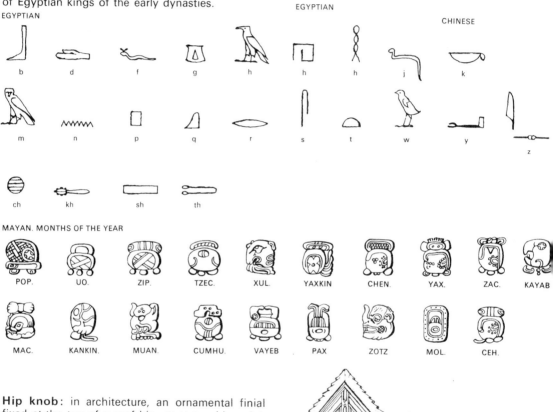

EGYPTIAN

BULL   RAM   BEAR   STAG

COW   EWE   EWE   SOW

CHINESE

EGYPTIAN

b   d   f   g   h   h   h   j   k

m   n   p   q   r   s   t   w   y   z

ch   kh   sh   th

MAYAN. MONTHS OF THE YEAR

POP.   UO.   ZIP.   TZEC.   XUL.   YAXKIN   CHEN.   YAX.   ZAC.   KAYAB

MAC.   KANKIN.   MUAN.   CUMHU.   VAYEB   PAX   ZOTZ   MOL.   CEH.

Hip knob: in architecture, an ornamental finial fixed at the top of a roof hip, or at a gable point, where bargeboards meet: in the latter position, often ending in a pendant. See *Finial*.

ELTHAM PALACE

Hippocamp: a fabulous marine monster, with the head, body and forelegs of a horse, and the tail of a fish, often a dolphin: the tail is tufted, the hooves tufted or webbed, and the creature may be winged. In classical mythology, Poseidon (Neptune) was believed to have created the horse, and to possess a stable under the sea: hence the representations of hippocamps drawing the chariots of sea deities. They also appear as motifs in arabesque decoration, and as emblematic ornaments on Venetian gondolas.

ROMAN MOSAIC. mid 2nd Cent. AD

Hippocentaur: see *Centaur*.

Hippogriff or hippogryph: a fabulous monster with the head and forepart of a griffin, and body and hindquarters of a horse: used as an heraldic device.

Hob nail: an ornamental device used in late 18th and early 19th century glass decoration, consisting of a deep cut diamond pattern with a four-pointed star cut in the face of each diamond-shaped compartment.

Hogarth capital: a jocular variation on the classical capital, by William Hogarth, with volutes and foliage replaced by wigs and tricorne hats, included in an engraving in his treatise, *The Analysis of Beauty* (1753).

Hom: the word sometimes describes the Persian version of the sacred tree, a religious and ornamental motif of remote antiquity and universal variation. The Persian tree was the *haoma* or *homa*, associated with the worship of the god, Assur, credited with the power to defy death and inculcate spiritual understanding, the sap producing a liquor used ritually: it usually appears as a kind of hybrid date palm, with branches ending in formalised leaves, cones or anthemion motifs, the central trunk with a palmette top, horns at the base, and flanked by a human or animal figure on each side. See *Sacred tree*.

from GOLD PLAQUE. ZIWIYE. 7th Cent. BC.

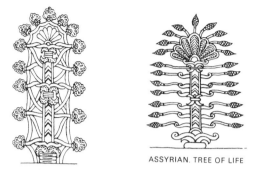

ASSYRIAN. TREE OF LIFE

ASSYRIAN. HOMA OR SACRED TREE (or HOM)

Honeycombed: as the term implies, it describes the ornamentation of a surface by an all-over pattern of small cell-like punctures.

Honeysuckle ornament: see *Anthemion*.

Hoof: the earliest movable pieces of furniture were supported by legs imitating those of animals, ending in an animal foot, a hoof, paw, or claw. Hoof feet first appeared on chairs during the earliest Egyptian dynasties, were used by the Romans, and became a fashionable decorative termination to furniture legs in the late 17th and 18th centuries.

from CHIPPENDALE'S 'DIRECTOR' 1762

Horns: in ancient China, a common symbolic device consisted of formalised rhinoceros horns crossed over one another, hollowed, and with small ball-shaped finials. Goat horns formed part of the Egyptian winged globe, *q.v.*, and of the widespread variations of this symbol: the Assyrian lion, *q.v.*, was adorned with horns. In the ancient world they represented power, strength, and protection, symbolised by their use on the crowns, helmets and headgear of gods, kings and leaders, and as funerary motifs. With Christianity, they acquired an evil reputation, possibly because of their association with the pagan Pan, and the dragon, both horned, and became an identification mark of Satan. In heraldry, the points of a crescent are described as horns, and horned animals appear as devices. Hunting horns, originally plain curved tubes, were semi-circular in medieval times, and the heraldic bugle or hunting horn appears thus, usually suspended from a knot of ribbons or strings.

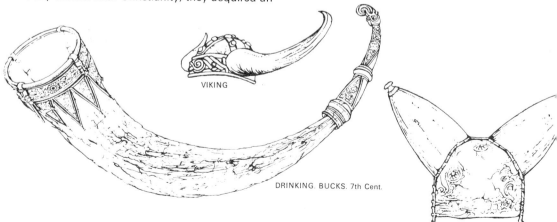

VIKING

DRINKING. BUCKS. 7th Cent.

BRONZE HELMET. 1st century AD

116

Horse: an important subject in monumental sculpture : as an heraldic device it may appear in various postures, and, when the head alone is used, is often called a nag's head, a familiar inn sign. A white horse was a tribal device of Saxons and Jutes, and is now an emblem of Kent. It appears cut in the turf of hills in many parts of England : one of the oldest examples, the White Horse of Uffington, in Berkshire, is believed to have been cut by the Belgae, and to have a link with early coins bearing horse designs, brought to pre-Roman Britain from Gaul. The White Horse of Hanover is one of the Queen's Beasts, *q.v.* Ancient beliefs about the animal included an association with the sun, its creation by Poseidon, and its function of trans-porting souls from this world to the next. Pegasus, the winged horse of Greek mythology, has been used as a supporter and emblem in heraldry, and is the device of the Inner Temple. See also *Centaur* and *Hippocamp*.

SHAMAN'S DRUM. SIBERIA

ROCK ENGRAVINGS. near TAGHIT

WARWICKSHIRE 1812.

in a MEDALLION. IRAN 10th–11th Cent.

STATER from CORINTH, 325–308 BC.

Horseshoe: in Moorish architecture, variations of arch based on a horseshoe shape were character-istic : in England, in the 18th and early 19th centuries, horseshoe tables (also called kidney tables) were made. As an heraldic device, the horseshoe, sometimes called a ferr, usually appears with curve upwards : it was used as a ceramic mark during the 19th century by Minton, and Smith & Ford.

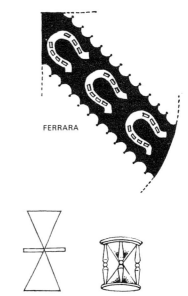

FERRARA

Hour-glass: a popular motif on tombstones and memorial tablets in the 17th and 18th centuries, symbolic of time passing, and sometimes accom-panied by a skull, wings, scythe, or figure of Time. The hour-glass also gave its name to a 19th century upholstered or straw seat, of that shape. A formal-ised representation of an hour-glass, consisting of two equilateral triangles joined at the apexes with a horizontal band crossing the junction, is an important Japanese heraldic family badge.

KENT early 18th Cent.   JAPANESE   GREENWICH

117

Husks

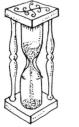

HERALDIC   LOUDON'S ENCYCLOPAEDIA 1833

Husks: a continuous carved pattern of flowers and buds, often used to decorate late 18th century furniture; the bellflower, *q.v.*, was an American variation of the device.

Husks

118

I

Icon or ikon: a mosaic, ivory, or painted wooden panel or image, portraying a religious subject or occurrence. These objects of worship, also possessing considerable ornamental value, and first produced in late medieval times, are characteristic of the sacred art of eastern European Christianity.

ST. LEONTIUS. late 16th Cent. POSSIBLY SCHOOL of TIVER

Ideograph: a development of the hieroglyph, *q.v.*: a formalised, easily recognisable drawing, that symbolised an idea, or condition of mind or body; a single object, such as a musical instrument, would mean joy or pleasure; a star suspended from a bar would indicate darkness or night.

Imbrication: an architectural term for a roof where the joints of the flat tiles are covered by overlapping semi-circular ridge tiles, known as *imbrices*, from the Latin *imber*, a shower of rain. Imbricated ornament consists of a similar pattern of carved overlapping segments like fish scales, and is also known as scale ornament: a common enrichment of surfaces and mouldings in Norman and Romanesque architecture. See also *Scaling*.

Imprese: a decorative badge consisting of personal device and motto: a popular adornment used in the Renaissance by royalty and nobility. See *Device*.

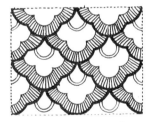

PILKINGTON 1914–38

Indented: the heraldic term for an ornamental, sharply serrated line. See *Line*.

Indian mask: motifs carved on late 17th and early 18th century furniture, representing a North American Indian mask with feathered headdress: sometimes used as a surmount on a looking glass frame, or the frieze of a side table.

Initial letters: decorative and interlaced initials, often enriched with flower motifs or geometric devices, were used to compose ciphers, *q.v.*, and to adorn personal possessions, first in France, then

SAXON. LETTER C

SAXON. LETTER J

in England, at the end of the 14th century. The highly ornamental and richly embellished initial letters of early illuminated MSS continued in use when printed books first appeared at the end of the 15th century, and were produced by hand by craftsmen known as rubricators. Later, when initials as well as text were printed, they retained the same decorative character, adorned with interlaced scrolls and conventional foliage and flower motifs that were sometimes so prolific that the letter was almost hidden.

QUEEN MELISSENDA'S PSALTER 1131–43. LETTER E

ENGLISH. 16th Cent. COPY-BOOK

TITLE OF THE YORK MISSAL. PRINTED AT ROUEN BY OLIVERI 1490

Ad vfum celeberrime ecclefie Eboracenfis

GROTESQUE INITIAL. GERMAN 12th Cent. MANUSCRIPT

ITALIAN

Inn signs: the inn signboard, a necessity when illiteracy was widespread, has survived as a decorative and often humorous publicity symbol. The forerunner of such signs was the bunch of ivy or vine leaves tied to a pole and exhibited outside Roman taverns: not only was the foliage an attribute of Bacchus, but it remained green for a long time. In England until the early 17th century, a bunch or bush of evergreen leaves was often the only indication of a tavern, and many inns still bear 'The Bush' as a sign. In the 14th century English publicans were compelled to exhibit a sign, and this often took the form of a red lattice window that provided ventilation and privacy in an age when glass was rare and costly. The armorial bearings of royalty, the nobility and local landed gentry, have probably contributed the majority of devices, notably the coloured Lions, Boars, Bears, Stags, Talbots and other heraldic creatures: the humbler animals and birds usually appeared in their natural hues. The Crown, Rose and Crown, individual sovereigns, and national and local heroes, are common, together with real and imaginary potentates, and pictorial representations of mythological and legendary figures such as Green Men (see *Foliate head*), and ships and maritime symbols.

MEDIEVAL EVER-GREEN-BUSH SIGN. 14th Cent. MSS.

OLD TRADE SIGN. GLOUCESTERSHIRE

ALTRINCHAM. CHESHIRE

OLD BATTERSEA

STRATFORD-ON-AVON   SHIPTON OLIFFE   NEWCASTLE. STAFFORDSHIRE

Interchange: a continuous pattern, divided into two different ground colours by a central line, so that each ornamental segment opposes one of the same form but alternate colour.

Interlacement band: a decorative band, *q.v.*, in which the pattern is formed by interlacing or plaited lines passing over and under each other alternately. See *Guilloche*, *Interlacing* and *Rope ornament*.

Interlacing: an ornamental arrangement of bands, woven or plaited together, and crossing each other to form variously intricate patterns. Curving ribbon-shapes in this type of decoration may have originated in primitive sun signs, *q.v.*, and with the gradual loss of religious significance these, and some animal forms, were used more and more as pure decoration. The patterns became extremely involved, and incorporated intertwined shapes of formalised lions, serpents and dragons, many of barbarous and hideous appearance, and indescribable complexity. Such interlacing occurs in Scandinavian, Celtic and Runic ornament. Byzantine and Arabian interlacing may be traced to the Greek fret, is inspired by geometrical figures, and appears as complicated arrangements of horizontal, perpendicular and diagonal straight lines: such motifs, as well as a more flowing variety, were characteristic of much Tudor ornament, and have a recognisable affinity to strapwork, *q.v.*

ARABIAN

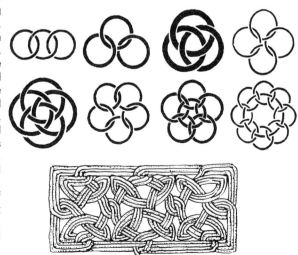

SCANDINAVIAN ROMANESQUE. WAL

121

Interlacing

BYZANTINE. SANTA SOPHIA

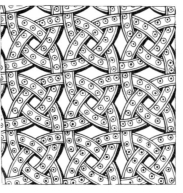

BYZANTINE

SPANISH ROMANESQUE: OVIEDO

MORESQUE

ALHAMBRA. GRANADA. 9th–14th Centuries

CELTIC

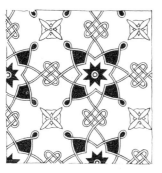

PERSIAN. FROM MSS. OF 17th Cent.

CELTIC. CROSS

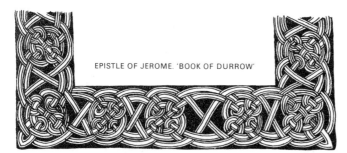

EPISTLE OF JEROME. 'BOOK OF DURROW'

CELTIC

CELTIC

122

TILE

MORESQUE

INTERLACED SPLAT. CHIPPENDALE'S 'DIRECTOR'. 3rd Edition

BRAIDED CIRCULAR PATTERN

DIAMOND PATTERN

EARLY CHRISTIAN

Intersected tracery: developed from the basic Y-tracery, *q.v.*, the arms of the mullions continue upwards to cross each other and form groups of lights.

EAST WINDOW. ALL SAINTS. SHARKINGTON. NORFOLK. 13th Cent.

Invected: the heraldic term for an ornamental line with outward convex curves. See *Line*.

Iona cross: a cross pattée, *q.v.*, in which the shaft is longer than the horizontal limbs, and the cross is superimposed on a circle.

Irminsul or Jeminsul: a pagan Germanic symbol, in the form of a stone or wooden pillar, sacred to the god Irmin: it may have been surmounted by a pine cone, *q.v.*, thyrsus, *q.v.*, or figure, and was one of many columnar devices associated with sacred tree rites and worship. See *Sacred tree*.

Ivy: used, with the vine and lotus, to decorate Egyptian columns, and Etruscan, Greek and Roman vases, where it often appeared as a continuous meander, *q.v.*: foliage, berries and branches formed decorative motifs on Roman drinking vessels. With the vine, ivy was an attribute of Dionysus or Bacchus, an association embodied in the bunch of ivy leaves that often identified a Roman tavern. (See *Inn signs*.) An emblem of friendship, fidelity and affection.

GREEK

GREEK

GREEK

J

Jacks of the clock: see *Clock jacks*.

Janus: Latin 'god of gates' and 'spirit of opening' who frustrated Tarpeia's plan for the city of Rome's betrayal to the Sabines. The commemorative archway built by Numa was always to be open in times of war so that he could come instantly to the aid of the Romans, and shut in times of peace. As the 'spirit of opening' he was invoked as patron of all enterprises; i.e. gates of buildings public and private; the beginning of the day, month and year (hence January). Generally represented with double profile: similar heads are found in Rococo decoration.

Japanese fret: the Japanese variation of the fret motif, usually right-angled and often disconnected and irregular, resembling the Chinese fret, *q.v.*, is lavishly used as background decoration for textiles, cloisonné and lacquered work, often in the form of medallions, but rarely in a border.

JAPANESE CORNER

Jeminsul: see *Irminsul*.

Jerusalem cross: see *Cross potent*.

Jesse or tree of Jesse: a pictorial genealogy of Christ, of which many 12th to 14th century examples exist, in sculpture, painting, stained glass, illuminated MSS, and embroidery. Jesse was the father of David, the Jewish shepherd boy who became king, and whose descendent, Joseph, was the husband of Mary, the mother of Jesus. The tree springs from the recumbent figure of Jesse, the branches, laden with leaves and grapes, support the kings and patriarchs named in St Matthew's record of Jesse's line, and the tree is crowned either by Christ upon the Cross, or as an Infant in the arms of His mother.

from a PSALTER AND HOURS OF THE VIRGIN.
MSS. ARRAS. FRANCE. 13th Cent.

MSS. WRITTEN IN VALLEY OF THE RHINE. FIRST HALF OF 12th Cent.

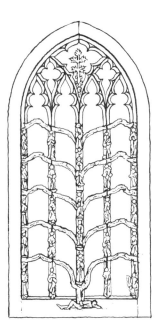

DORCHESTER ABBEY. OXON

from QUEEN ELIZABETH I's PRAYER BOOK 1578

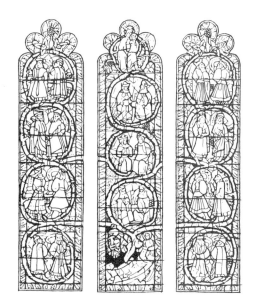

MARGARETTING. ESSEX. *circa* 1460. PERPENDICULAR TRACERY

K

Keel moulding: a moulding composed of two ogee, *q.v.,* curves joined in a sharp edge and resembling the keel of a ship.

Kent style: a term sometimes used to describe lavishly carved and gilded early Georgian furniture, with the baroque characteristics associated with the work of the architect, William Kent (*c.* 1686–1748).

from MR INIGO JONES and
MR Wm. KENT'S 'SOME DESIGNS'. 1744

Kentish tracery: divided cusps, *q.v.,* are characteristic of this type of tracery, which is most commonly found on church windows and woodwork in Kent.

EAST WINDOW. ST. MARY CHATHAM KENT

Key of life: see *'Ankh*.

GREEK VASE. MUSEUM OF FINE ART. BOSTON

Key pattern: a geometric motif of continuous straight lines arranged at right angles, developed from the Greek fret, *q.v.*; also used as an alternate name for this device.

by courtesy of the ASHMOLEAN MUSEUM

THE TOP AND BOTTOM BANDS OF DECORATION
OF AN OIL-FLASK.

Keys: as an heraldic device, keys may represent state office; they are included in the arms of religious establishments of which St Peter is the patron saint, and as his emblem are the insignia of the Papacy, when they appear crossed diagonally, one gold and one silver.

3-KEYS. SYMBOLISE LOVE,
HEALTH AND WEALTH

CROSSED KEYS.
WOLVERHAMPTON

ST. PETER'S KEYS.
HEMSWORTH (ct.-of-arms)

ST. PETER'S KEYS.
PETERBOROUGH. (ct.-of-arms)

Kikumon: a conventionalised chrysanthemum, *q.v.*, in the form of a wheel with sixteen petals; the symbol of Japanese imperial power.

Knop: a rounded protuberance, bulb, or knob, used as an ornament on turned work, and on the stems of drinking glasses. In the decoration of furniture it may form a repetitive motif in conjunction with cusps or rings: the term multiple knops describes its use in series on glasses.

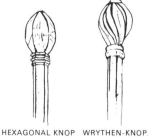

SILVER   DIAMOND KNOP.   KNOP   HEXAGONAL KNOP   WRYTHEN-KNOP.

15th Cent.   1565–6   1488

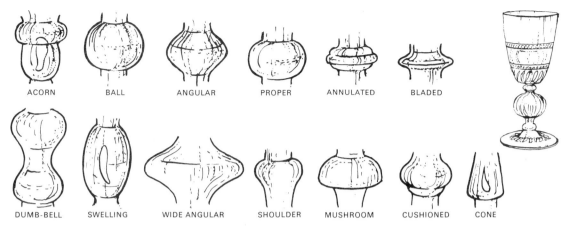

ACORN BALL ANGULAR PROPER ANNULATED BLADED

DUMB-BELL SWELLING WIDE ANGULAR SHOULDER MUSHROOM CUSHIONED CONE

Knop-and-flower: an ornamental border motif, Assyrian in origin, that consists of a series of lotus flowers alternating with lotus buds or fir cones; another version, used for the adornment of ceilings and sills, is a rosette of lotus flowers and buds, used singly or in squares.

Knorpelwork: see *Auricular ornament.*

Knot: in heraldry, a badge device of interlaced cords or ropes that may be combined with other motifs: the best known are the Stafford, Bourchier, Bowen, Harrington, Heneage and Ormonde knots. The endless knot (or entrails), signifying longevity, is one of the Buddhist Emblems of Happy Augury.

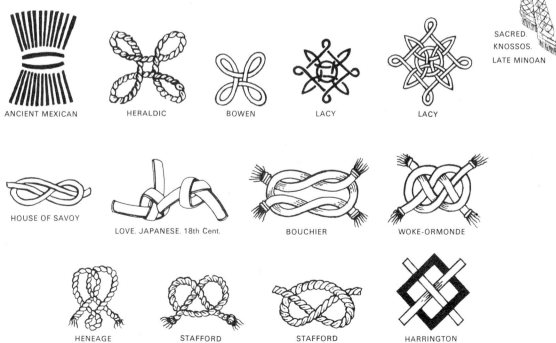

ANCIENT MEXICAN HERALDIC BOWEN LACY LACY SACRED. KNOSSOS. LATE MINOAN

HOUSE OF SAVOY LOVE. JAPANESE. 18th Cent. BOUCHIER WOKE-ORMONDE

HENEAGE STAFFORD STAFFORD HARRINGTON

Knotwork: a device of complicated interlacings of thin, wire-like links and knots, originating and based on 15th century Arabesque metalwork. Used in the 16th century for balustrades, mouldings, panels and friezes, it has a recognisable affinity with strapwork, *q.v.*

Knuckle: the scroll ending to the arms of certain kinds of Windsor chairs; occasionally called knuckle arms in America.

Knurl foot: a cabinet-making term for a whorl foot, *q.v.*, that ends in an inward-turning scroll.

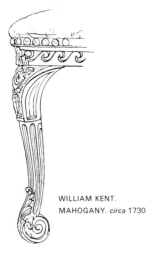

WILLIAM KENT.
MAHOGANY. *circa* 1730

L

Labarum: the Roman imperial standard. This long pole terminated in a short wooden member, fixed transversely, that bore the figure of an eagle. After Constantine had proclaimed Christianity the religion of the Empire, the eagle was replaced by the seal or monogram of Christ, also called the chrism. See *Monogram*.

from MEDALLION OF CONSTANTINE

Label: in architecture, a descriptive term for a rectangular dripstone or hood mould, a projecting moulding or canopy above an arch to throw off rainwater from the wall: sometimes called a weather moulding. A label also means a band or scroll bearing an inscription: in heraldry, it denotes a horizontal ribbon-shape, from which other straight, splayed or dovetailed ribbons hang. Used thus, with three pendant ribbons, it is the cadency mark, *q.v.*, of an eldest son.

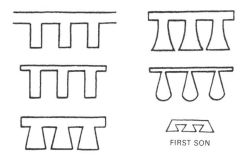

FIRST SON

Label stop: an architectural term for a decorative boss, sometimes in the form of a carved head, or ornamented with foliage, that terminates a dripstone. See *Label*.

Labyrinth: in ornamentation, this is a variety of fret, *q.v.*: sometimes called *à la Grecque*, and used in classical decoration in the form of an undulating ribbon-like continuous stripe: a simple labyrinth consists of a single stripe, a double labyrinth of two stripes twisted together.

GREEK. CNOSSUS 350 BC from a STATER

Lacunar or lequear: an architectural term for a panelled or coffered ceiling or soffit: such ornamental panels, coffers, or caissons, are sometimes called lacunaria, meaning sunken spaces: the edges might be decoratively carved, and the centre adorned with a painting.

Ladder back: a chair-making term for a chair-back with horizontal rails or slats: when these members are pierced by holes like those in a violin, the description fiddle-back is sometimes used.

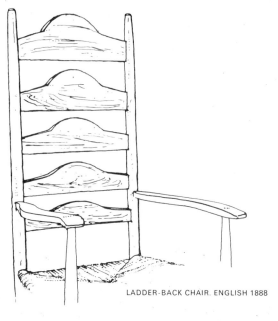

LADDER-BACK CHAIR. ENGLISH 1888

Lamb: associated with Hebrew sacrifice, it became an important Christian symbol, both sacrificially and as representative of gentleness and humility. Christ was for many centuries almost invariably portrayed as a lamb, and it is still symbolic of Him. Representations of the animal are common in the catacombs, and numbers of Biblical characters have been delineated in the guise of lambs: where the creature is related to passages in the Apocalypse it is shown with seven eyes and crowned with seven horns. In heraldry, it often appears as the Agnus Dei: *q.v.*: it was the badge of the Order of the Knights Templars, and the device of the Middle Temple: an emblem of St John the Baptist.

HOLY LAMB.
LAMBETH (ct.-of-arms)

HOLY LAMB. PRESTON (ct.-of-arms)

Lambrequin: see *Mantling*.

Latin cross: a cross with a vertical limb longer than the horizontal limbs: sometimes called a long cross. See *Cross*.

LONG or LATIN

Lattice work: a form of ornamental tracery consisting of a network of bands of varying width and spacing, crossing each other, either at right angles or diagonally, or in a curvilinear form. Lattice work in building originated in the lead glazing bars that framed the small diamond shaped panes of 16th and early 17th century windows, and subsequently became a decorative device. Also used by furniture makers for the doors of cabinets and bookcases, and in chair backs, which were called lattice backs.

ARAB. 13th Cent.

ARAB. 13th Cent.

SPANISH TRANSENNA
661 AD

ENGLISH TRANSENNA
10th Cent.

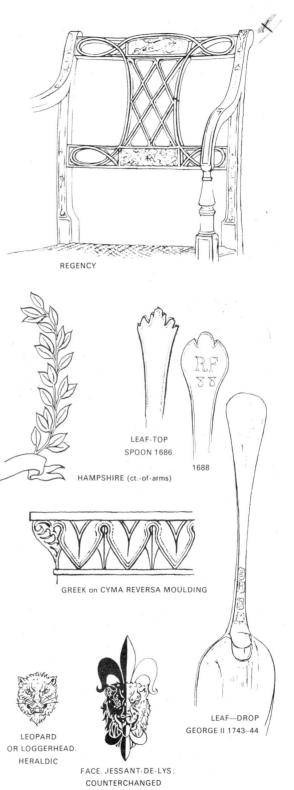

REGENCY

Laurel: a motif of classical origin, also used as an enrichment on early and mid-Georgian furniture. In ancient Greece, the laurel leaf, sacred to Apollo, signified artistic achievement, and in the form of a crown, victory at the Delphic games: it was the Roman symbol of victory, and laurel crowns were worn by the Emperors when celebrating triumphs. See *Bay leaf, Crown, Sword* and *Wreath*.

HAMPSHIRE (ct.-of-arms)

LEAF-TOP
SPOON 1686.

1688

Leaf-and-tongue: a variant of egg-and-tongue, *q.v.*, in which the oval form is replaced by foliage: occasionally the tongue is omitted altogether, and the enrichment consists of a series of leaves.

Leo: the lion: the fifth sign of the Zodiac. See *Zodiacal devices*.

GREEK on CYMA REVERSA MOULDING

Leopard: in early heraldry, the name was often given to a lion shown *passant guardant*, but later became a device in its own right: the head alone, full face, is usual: a fleur-de-lys sprouting from the top of the head and from the mouth is known as *jessant-de-lys*. In religious symbolism the animal acquired an evil reputation, derived from an alleged relationship to the beast of the Apocalypse.

Lequear: see *Lacunar*.

Libra: the scales: the seventh sign of the Zodiac. See *Zodiacal devices*.

LEOPARD
OR LOGGERHEAD.
HERALDIC

FACE. JESSANT-DE-LYS;
COUNTERCHANGED

LEAF—DROP
GEORGE II 1743–44

133

Lily: a Cretan ornamental motif of *c.* 1550 BC; in the classical world a symbol of purity, innocence and fruitfulness and an emblem of deities who protected hunters, fishermen and sailors. Later, as the Christian emblem of the Virgin Mary, chastity, and purity, it became as ubiquitous in Christian ornament as the lotus in Egyptian, and frequently appeared on the tombs of early Christian virgins. An heraldic flower, believed by some authorities to be the prototype of the fleur-de-lys, *q.v.*

CRETAN MURAL 1550 BC

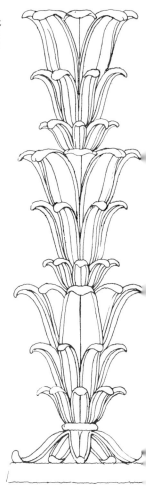

ROMAN FORMS

GREEK LILY-BASED DETAILS

HERALDIC

ASSYRIAN

ETRUSCAN AND GREEK

SAN MICHELI. VERONA

BAB-AL-HADID GATE.
DAMASCUS

ITALIAN 14th Cent.   INDIAN   INDIAN. STONE

ASSYRIAN FIR-CONE+HONEYSUCKLE+LILY MOTIFS

ART NOUVEAU

LILY OF FLORENCE.
printers mark. 1497

Line: a line is a projected dot: an increase in width transforms it into a band. Diagonal, parallel, and zigzag arrangements of angulated and curved lines formed the earliest type of decoration on primitive tools and utensils, by widely scattered communities, and were the source of such basic motifs as the chevron, fret and scroll (see these entries). In heraldry, the lines that divide a shield, and outline a device, may be plain or ornamental.

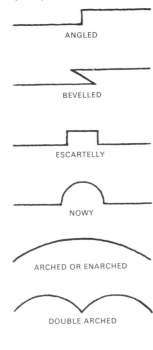

ANGLED

BEVELLED

ESCARTELLY

NOWY

ARCHED OR ENARCHED

DOUBLE ARCHED

SYMBOLS OF ELEMENTS :—

WATER

AIR

FIRE

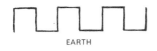

EARTH

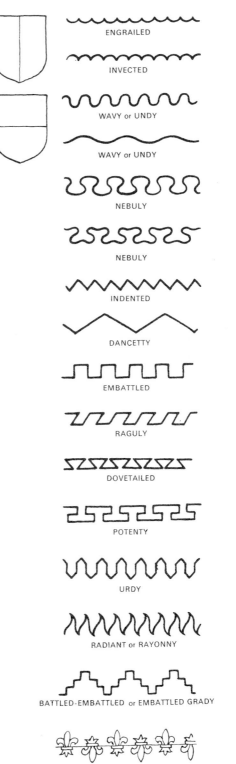

ENGRAILED

INVECTED

WAVY or UNDY

WAVY or UNDY

NEBULY

NEBULY

INDENTED

DANCETTY

EMBATTLED

RAGULY

DOVETAILED

POTENTY

URDY

RADIANT or RAYONNY

BATTLED-EMBATTLED or EMBATTLED GRADY

LINES OF PARTITION=FLORY AND COUNTER FLORY

Linenfold or linen-scroll: this motif, consisting of a series of highly stylised vertical folds of linen or possibly parchment scrolls, originated in 15th century Flanders, and was invented by carvers. Until the late 16th century, it was used with regional variations, throughout Europe, on wall and furniture panels, chimney-pieces, on chair backs, and the fronts of chests and cupboards. Occasionally known as napkin pattern.

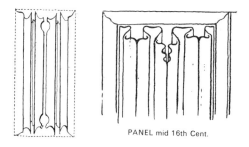

PANEL mid 16th Cent.

Linked flames: modern term for a series of flame-like shapes, as in Florentine stitch.

Lion: a solar emblem in primitive times and used since as an important symbolic and decorative motif. In ancient Egypt, where the annual flooding of the Nile coincided with the zodiacal sign of Leo, *q.v.*, it is found *couchant*, as the sphinx, which is a man-headed lion, and the feet of chairs and thrones were made in the form of lions' paws: in Assyria, where lion-hunting was a royal sport, the animal bore a more ferocious aspect, usually shown *rampant*: the head, often double, acted as a capital on columns in Persian architecture. As a religious ornament, the lion appeared on Buddhist edict columns, *c.* 250 BC in India, and has long been a national symbol in Ceylon, an established centre of Buddhism. In classical mythology, the lion was designated a guardian of gates, temples and springs: he represents the tribe of Judah, and in Christian symbolism winged, is the emblem of St Mark the Evangelist. The lion's head has been used as a gargoyle, vessel spout, mooring ring on quays,

with the ring gripped in the jaws, a device also used as a door knocker, rosette and boss, and, with the paws, as a support and ornament in furniture design. (See *Lion mahogany* and *Lion monopodium*.) Of supreme importance among heraldic beasts, probably associated with royal insignia before heraldry was established, and since included in the Royal Arms of England and of many other royal and noble families throughout Europe, the heraldic lion is a conventionalised figure, that has in some cases acquired fantastic and grotesque variations: he appears in certain clearly defined attitudes, described by such terms as *rampant, passant, couchant, reguardant*, and others: heraldic lions may be double-tailed, double-headed, collared, dismembered, three-bodied, and the heraldic sea-lion has a fish's tail. The Lion of England and the White Lion of Mortimer are two of the Queen's Beasts, *q.v.*

LION OF DJATTOU. PALAEOLITHIC

SAMSON AND THE LION. TYMPANUM STRETTON SUGWAS 1150

WINGED LION. SASSANIAN 6th–7th Cent. AD

WINGED LION WITH HUMAN HEAD. HITTITE

CAPITAL. CANTERBURY CATHEDRAL

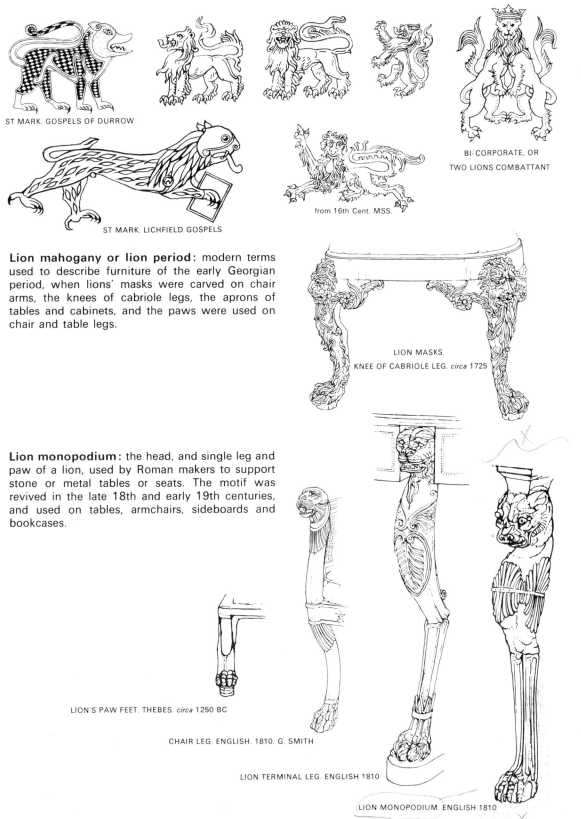

ST MARK. GOSPELS OF DURROW

ST MARK. LICHFIELD GOSPELS

from 16th Cent. MSS.

BI-CORPORATE, OR
TWO LIONS COMBATTANT

Lion mahogany or lion period: modern terms used to describe furniture of the early Georgian period, when lions' masks were carved on chair arms, the knees of cabriole legs, the aprons of tables and cabinets, and the paws were used on chair and table legs.

LION MASKS.
KNEE OF CABRIOLE LEG. *circa* 1725

Lion monopodium: the head, and single leg and paw of a lion, used by Roman makers to support stone or metal tables or seats. The motif was revived in the late 18th and early 19th centuries, and used on tables, armchairs, sideboards and bookcases.

LION'S PAW FEET. THEBES. *circa* 1250 BC

CHAIR LEG. ENGLISH. 1810. G. SMITH

LION TERMINAL LEG. ENGLISH 1810

LION MONOPODIUM. ENGLISH 1810

137

Listel: a narrow band or fillet, sometimes used as an alternative name for the latter.

Liver-bird: the name used for the fabulous bird (really a cormorant) that appears in the arms of Liverpool.

LIVER-BIRD AND SEAWEED

Lobing: see *Gadrooning*.

Long cross: see *Latin cross*.

Loopings: an ancient device used to ornament glassware, when festoons of coloured glass decorate the surface: also called draggings.

Lotus: the buds and flowers of this water plant were used ornamentally in ancient Egypt, Assyria, India and the Far East, and in classical times. It is probably the species *Nymphoea nelumbo*, whose leaves grow up out of the water and do not lie flat on the surface. Its appearance in the period between the ebbing of the Nile flood and the springing up of the crops, established it as a sacred emblem of plenty, goodness and of water, symbolising Osiris and Isis, the recurrent renewal of life, and of immortality. In Egyptian architecture, columns were designed as a complete plant, the root forming the base, a bundle of stalks the shaft, and the flower and buds the capital: as decoration on walls, ceilings, and pottery, the alternating flower and bud were sometimes combined with a zigzag motif, representing water. It is believed that the lotus flower and bud may have been the prototype of the Greek anthemion or palmate, egg-and-tongue, and fleur-de-lys motifs. The device was adopted by the Assyrians, and in India, China and Japan, and acquired a religious association with Buddha, who is often represented seated on a lotus: the flowering plant is one of the Eight Buddhist Emblems of Happy Augury. During the revival of interest in Egyptian ornament, that took place in the late 18th and early 19th centuries (see *Egyptian style*), the lotus motif was used for the decoration of furniture.

SYMBOLIC. LOTUS FLOWER EGYPTIAN.

EGYPTIAN PAINTED

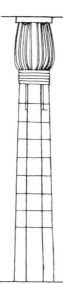

LOTUS CAPITAL COLUMN. BENIHASAN

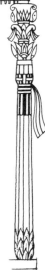

LOTUS COLUMN. TOMB OF PASER. THEBES *circa* 1300 BC

GREEK. LOTUS INSPIRED

GREEK

GREEK. LOTUS INSPIRED

ASSYRIAN

INDIAN

HINDU

MEDALLIONS IN STYLISED-LOTUS FORMS.
MATHURĀ. 2nd Cent. AD

Lozenge: basically, a square set at right angles, forming a diamond-shaped figure. It is a primitive decorative motif, used in Greece in the 5th century BC, and known in China *c*. 1500–1027 BC, where it was developed as a greatly varied ornamental form, notably the linked and zigzag lozenge, *q.v.*, a characteristic Chinese device. The lozenge appeared as an enrichment for mouldings in Romanesque and Norman architecture, as a panel in the 14th century, and as carved and inlaid ornament in the 16th and 17th centuries. In heraldry, the arms of a widow or spinster are displayed on a lozenge, and it is also used as a decorative border.

CROSS LOZENGY

LOZENGES IN CROSS

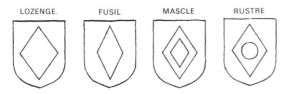

LOZENGE.   FUSIL   MASCLE   RUSTRE

DIAMOND PANELS.
BURGUNDIAN early 17th Cent.

Lunette: an architectural term for a semi-circular window. A type of early 19th century chair, in which the back consisted of two crescent shapes one inverted above the other, is known as a lunette back. Such a semi-circular motif appears in carved, *q.v.* sunburst, inlaid and printed work.

from ENGLISH OAK PRESS CUPBOARD 1610

LUNETTE-BACK CHAIR. ENGLISH

LUNAR SLICING
GLASS

Lyre: of great antiquity, probably of eastern origin, and of considerable importance in Greece, the lyre was the instrument associated with Apollo: the strings, four, seven or nine, were plucked like those of a harp, and the lyre was a form of miniature harp: the cithara, the ancestor of the modern guitar, was a large variety of lyre: the trigonum or triangular lyre had eleven strings. In the second half of the 18th century, the elegant shape and strings of the instrument attracted furniture designers and makers, and it was used as an ornamental motif by Robert Adam (1728–92), and in America by Duncan Phyfe (1768–1854). The lyre back chair with the back splat in the form of the instrument, and lyre-shaped supports for teapoys, bookstands, and various types of writing and work tables, and occasionally as tracery in the glass doors of cabinets, continued in favour throughout the Regency period, often with gilded brass or metal 'strings', and inlay.

LYRE-BACK CHAIR. ENGLISH 1767

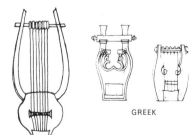

GREEK

MUSEUMS ASSOCIATION

M

Maenad: see *Bacchante*.

Maltese cross: a cross with each splayed limb ending in two points; occasionally called a cross of eight points. It was the badge of the Knights of St John of Jerusalem, or Hospitallers, when the Order was founded in the last decade of the 11th century.

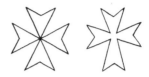

Mandorla: see *Aureole* and *Vesica piscis*.

Mandrake: this poisonous plant, a member of the potato family (*Solanaceae*), of great antiquity, and in ancient and medieval times alleged to possess various magical, sinister and mysterious powers, has a long, two-forked tap root resembling human legs: though not used ornamentally, it was depicted in medieval Europe as a tiny, macabre human figure.

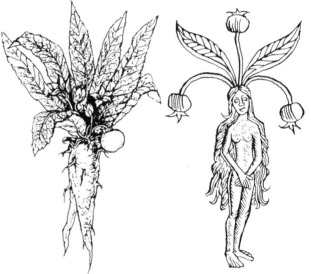

MANDRAGORA OFFICINARUM   from FRENCH MSS. 1498

Mantling: an heraldic term, also called the lambrequin, denoting the short mantle that hangs from a helm; its original purpose may have been as a protection against the sun. Formerly, mantlings often had scalloped edges; they were sometimes made of feathers, or of material that appears as a continuation of the crest, *q.v.* See *Banderolle*.

Mascaron or maskeroon: a grotesque face, carved in wood, gesso, or cast in metal. See also *Mask*.

Mascle: an heraldic term for a lozenge-shaped figure, voided or perforated within a narrow border. See *Lozenge*.

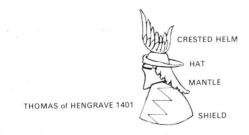

THOMAS of HENGRAVE 1401

CRESTED HELM

HAT

MANTLE

SHIELD

BLACK MASCLE

Martlet: in heraldry, this bird is the cadency mark, *q.v.*, of a fourth son.

Mask: originating with the artificial hollow faces worn in the ancient Greek theatre, and harvest games, the term in architecture and decoration means a carved human, animal, or grotesque face, used ornamentally. Bronze masks or heads often decorated the orifices of Roman fountains: masks were used as corbels in Romanesque and Gothic buildings, and in Early English churches the orna-mental corbel called a mask, notch-head or buckle, that resembled a severe human face, was often used in series as a corbel-table below a cornice. In Renaissance decoration the mask frequently appeared as a grotesque face, or caricature, such as the gorgoneion, or medusa head. See also *Grotesque* and *Satyr mask.*

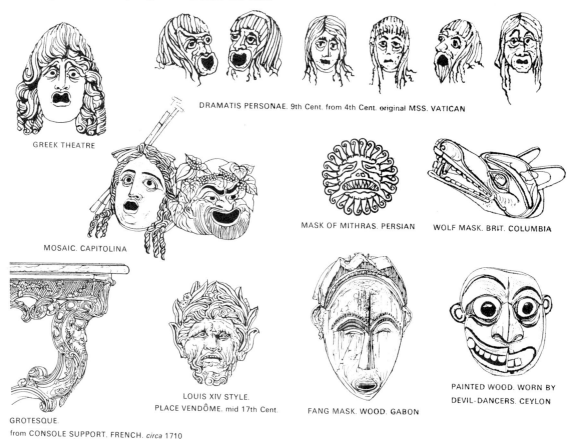

GREEK THEATRE

DRAMATIS PERSONAE. 9th Cent. from 4th Cent. original MSS. VATICAN

MOSAIC. CAPITOLINA

MASK OF MITHRAS. PERSIAN

WOLF MASK. BRIT. COLUMBIA

GROTESQUE.
from CONSOLE SUPPORT. FRENCH. *circa* 1710

LOUIS XIV STYLE.
PLACE VENDÔME. mid 17th Cent.

FANG MASK. WOOD. GABON

PAINTED WOOD. WORN BY
DEVIL-DANCERS. CEYLON

Mason's mark: an identification mark cut by a stonemason on blocks he had carved, a practice that continued in England up to the 19th century. The mark, that might be a circle, letter, arrow, cross, or other simple figure, was usually about two inches in height: succeeding generations of a family of masons, working on the same building, contributed to the basic mark to form a geometric pattern. Some authorities suggest that such marks were derived from the runic alphabet. See also *Merchant's mark.*

circa 1200

circa 1300

circa 1400

circa 1520–50

circa 1575

Mauresque: an alternate form of the word moresque. See *Arabesque*.

Meander: the continuous single line that is the basis of the Greek fret, *q.v.*, for which the word is sometimes used as an alternative. It may be derived from the convolutions of the river Menderes (formerly the Maender) in Asia Minor.

Medal: a medal or medallion, first used in ancient Greece and Rome, was an ornamental coin issued, not for currency, but to commemorate a person or event, or some united or individual action of importance, usually military. The earliest modern portrait medal (1438) is believed to have been the work of the Italian artist, Antonio Pisanello (*c.* 1395–1455 or 56). Renaissance medals, often bearing symbolic devices so complicated as to obscure the meaning, acted as family portraits: in modern times the medal fulfils its ancient function of commemoration, and reward for achievement, notably for valour in war. Medals are invaluable historical records, as they often bear inscriptions, dates, heads of important personages, and allegorical devices.

ORDER OF MERIT. AUSTRIA   ORDER OF GRATITUDE. IRAN

ORDER OF OLGA. GERMANY   ORDER OF CULTURAL MERIT. KOREA

Medallion: in the Graeco-Roman civilisation, a large medal, *q.v.* was usually the gift of a Roman emperor. Ornamentally, the term means a plaque, circular, oval, rectangular or square, enclosing a carved, inlaid or painted device. Decorative circular medallions were a common central ornament on

T'ang pottery in China (*c.* AD 618–906): these might consist of a rosette of formalised petals and leaves, or a circular stem-like shape enclosing a conventional pattern of buds or cones, springing from the inner side of the stem in regular spirals. As a decorative device within a plaque, the medallion was used on 16th to 18th century furniture: in late 18th century France it succeeded the cartouche, *q.v.*, becoming a characteristic ornamental device during the Empire period. The term 'medallion panel' describes an early 16th century carved panel framing a medallion, used on bedheads, chests, chair backs, chimney-pieces, and in series on a frieze.

Medusa head: see *Gorgoneion*.

Melon bulb: a modern term for a melon-shaped swelling, often carved with gadrooning, *q.v.*, used centrally on table legs, bedposts, and press cupboard supports, in the late 16th and early 17th centuries. See *Bulb*, and *Cup and cover*.

MELON BULB WITH GADROONING.

PRESS-CUPBOARD.
ENGLISH. early 17th Cent.

Melusine: the heraldic term for a double-tailed mermaid, *q.v.*

MERMAN
EXETER CATHEDRAL

143

Menorah: the Jewish name for the seven-armed candle-holder, which was an important symbol in the religious ornament of early Judaism.

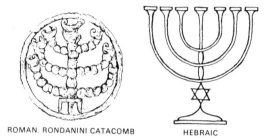

ROMAN. RONDANINI CATACOMB   HEBRAIC

from RELIEF on ARCH OF TITUS. ROME

CARMEL COLLEGE

Merchant's mark: the forerunner of the modern trademark: an identity device cut or stamped on goods by medieval merchants. It usually consisted of a monogram with initials, springing from a central vertical line, and embellished with signs that some authorities relate to the runic alphabet, the whole surmounted by a cross. Merchants used such marks also on their houses, tombstones, and in churches to which they contributed additions or adornments. See *Mason's mark*, and *Trademark*.

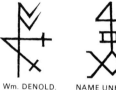

Wm. DENOLD.
CORDWAINER
NORWICH. 1506

NAME UNKNOWN.
CLOTHWORKER
NORWICH

JOHN BERIFFE.
SHIPOWNER AND MASTER MARIN
BRIGHTLINGSEA. ESSEX
1521.

ROBERT BROWN.
MERCER.
NORWICH

VALENTINE HARTNELL.
MERCHANT OF THE STAPLE 1400

Mercury, rod of: see *Caduceus.*

Mermaid: a fabulous sea creature, represented by a woman's body with a fish's tail. According to classical and medieval belief, singing mermaids seated on rocks and combing their long hair, charmed sailors to destruction, and they are often represented holding a mirror and comb. The mermaid has been identified with the sirens who attempted to lure Ulysses and Orpheus; with the legendary female monster who inhabited the rock Scylla; with seals, and with dugongs. She appears carved or painted in churches, as a symbol of worldly enticements, and is a favourite decorative motif on arabesques, *q.v.,* often with two tails. See *Melusine* and *Triton.*

POOLE (ct.-of-arms)

Mexican fret: a variation of the basic fret motif, *q.v.*: often resembling the Chinese version, in the use of separate units. The main characteristic is the long diagonal line that links the keys.

Millefleurs motif: a term sometimes used to describe a mass of scattered blossoms that form a background to some scene. Used in medieval decoration, revived by William Morris in the late 19th century, and used by artist-craftsmen and designers who followed the Morris tradition.

Mnemonic ornament: ornament or decoration deliberately designed to assist the memory. It includes inscriptions, hieroglyphics, texts, and natural forms, that may be enriched with other motifs, and while acting as records also have decorative qualities. The message such ornament recalls to the mind is not necessarily related to the object it adorns.

Molet or mullet: an heraldic term, derived from *molette*, a spur rowel. A star-shaped figure, usually five-pointed, with straight rays. The figure may be pierced centrally, and in Scottish heraldry, if unpierced, is known as a star: the cadency mark, *q.v.*, of a third son.

Monad: a geometric figure, of two arcs forming a circle, widely used in Far Eastern ornament. It represents the Chinese *Yang* and *Yin*, dual characteristics that oppose and complement each other: *Yang* may typify the sun, heaven, brightness, or virile masculinity, and *Yin* the moon, earth, darkness or passive femininity. See also *Dot*, and *Yang and Yin*.

Money-moulding or money pattern: a modern term for a series of overlapping discs or rosettes, resembling a continuous band of coins: sometimes called strung-coin.

Monogram: an ornamental arrangement of interwoven letters that may consist of initials, or of a complete name, often enriched with symbols denoting personal attributes: it is distinguished from a cipher, *q.v.*, because the arrangement of the letters may be varied at will, though the meaning remains the same. The sacred monogram, or monogram of Christ, sometimes known as the chrism, was one of the few early Christian religious symbols, limited in number because of the threat of persecution: the best known, adopted by the Emperor Constantine, to replace the eagle on the Roman labarum, *q.v.*, is probably the Chi-Rho, consisting of the Greek letters X (Chi) and P (Rho) —the first two letters of the name of Christ in Greek—superimposed: a simpler version shows a diagonal cross with a P placed between the upper members: another variation shows a Latin cross with the head ending in a P, and the first and last letters of the Greek alphabet (Alpha and Omega) beneath the arms. During the 12th century the Chi-Rho gave place to the more familiar IHS monogram, an abbreviation of the Greek word for Jesus. ($IH\Sigma OY\Sigma$). See *Book-plate.*

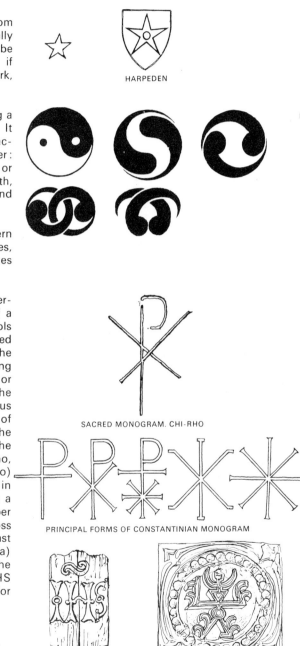

HARPEDEN

SACRED MONOGRAM. CHI-RHO

PRINCIPAL FORMS OF CONSTANTINIAN MONOGRAM

SACRED MONOGRAM. DEVON

SASSANIAN. STUCCO

A CHRISM AND A FISH

Monopodium: a support, in the form of an animal's head, with a leg immediately below: used on tables and seats of the ancient world. The device was revived in the late 18th and early 19th centuries, and widely used on Regency furniture. The lion, leopard and griffin, often winged, were used for monopodia. See *Lion monopodium*.

Moon: a planetary sign: as a religious symbol, a crescent moon was worn as an amulet by pre-historic peoples, or sometimes decorated with fascine pattern, *q.v.*, set up over an entrance as a magic talisman. It sometimes appears as a Christian emblem connected with the Virgin Mary, the Crucifixion, creation and last judgment. In heraldry, the moon may appear with a human face, and is known as crescent, increscent and decrescent when the horns point upwards, to the right, or to the left respectively.

Moresque: sometimes spelt mauresque. See *Arabesque*.

Motif: the basic unit in an ornamental composition.

Motto: derived from the French *mot*, and possibly originating in a war cry, this is a short phrase, in any language, embodying some meritorious sentiment, often allusive of the bearer's name, history or heraldic device. Except in Scotland, a motto is not part of armorial bearings, but usually appears within a scroll, below a shield or above a crest.

Mouchette: an architectural term for a motif in curvilinear tracery, *q.v.*, resembling a curved dagger.

Moulding: a continuous projecting or recessed band, horizontal, vertical or diagonal, carved on or applied to a surface, as ornamentation, and to diversify a plain surface by creating a shadow. A moulding may be plain, or enriched with natural or geometric motifs of all kinds.

CYMA RECTA or HOGARTHS LINE OF BEAUTY

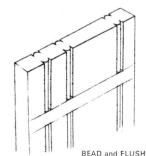

BEAD and BUTT

BEAD and FLUSH

BAND AND FILLET

ASTRAGAL or BEAD

FLUSH BEAD

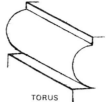

TORUS

CAVETTO

BEAD and QUIRK

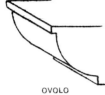

OVOLO

OGEE—CYMA RECTA

OGEE REVERSE

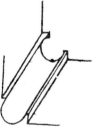

BOLECTION

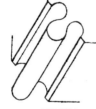

OGEE MOULDING

BIRD'S BEAK

SCOTIA

EDGE ROLL

BOWTELL

REEDING

FLUTING

TOAD-BACK-MOULDING

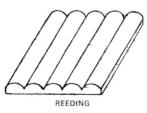

REEDING

REEDING

FLUTING

STRUCK MOULDING

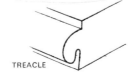

TREACLE

147

Mourners: see *Weepers*.

Mullet: see *Molet*.

Multiple knops: see *Knop*.

Musical symbols: instruments, such as bells, the harp, horn, lyre and trumpet, have been used as heraldic and ornamental motifs, and sometimes appear as the attributes of angels and saints. In the 18th century, carved and painted trophies often included violins, harps, and other instruments, in association with acanthus foliations, ribbons, and flowers.

PRINTERS VIGNETTES

N

Naga: a Buddhist religious symbol, in the form of a five-headed cobra.

INDIAN

Nailhead: in architecture, a characteristic Romanesque, Norman and Early English enrichment, used on mouldings, consisting of a series of small square or pyramidical projections like the heads of nails: dog tooth ornament, *q.v.*, was a development of this motif.

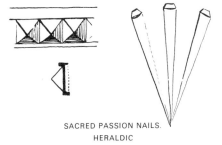

SACRED PASSION NAILS.
HERALDIC

Napkin pattern: see *Linenfold.*

Naturalistic ornament: the flora and fauna of the earth provided primitive man with many motifs at first used as religious and tribal symbols, or denoting powers, virtues and vices. The markings on butterflies' wings, the skins of animals, the scales on serpents, and the feathers of birds, all inspired ornament; animals such as the lion, tiger, elephant and horse, and plants, particularly the lotus, rose, hyacinth, iris, pink, pine and date palm, were used as decorative motifs in early Oriental and Mediterranean civilisations. In Europe, for some centuries after the fall of the Western Roman Empire, little attention was paid to natural forms: with the return of security and the rise of religious fervour, in the Middle Ages, ornamental devices, though conventional in appearance, reveal accurate observation of animals, birds and plants, that inspired the decoration of medieval psalters and bestiaries, sculpture, carved woodwork, and the pattern of fabrics. In heraldry, animals and birds were formally represented and, less frequently, fish, reptiles, insects, leaves and flowers.

PINK

ITALIAN   JAPANESE   PERSIAN

ART NOUVEAU   ITALIAN

IRIS

PERSIAN   INDIAN

ENGLISH HOLLY. GOTHIC

Naturalistic ornament

NUT WINCHESTER

MAPLE LEAVE

EGYPTIAN GRAPE

CHESTERFIELD (ct.-of-arms)

POMEGRANATE PERSIAN

OLD GERMAN

RENAISSANCE

THISTLE GLASS

DUTCH TILE. First half 17th Cent.

SEA-LION OR PANTHER. ROMAN MOSAIC mid 2nd Cent. AD

HEAD OF IBEX. PERSIAN
6th–5th Cent. BC. ACHAEMENID

SASSANID BOAR 5th–6th Cent. A.D.

PLAY-CARD
SWISS. contemporary. DEUCE of FLOWE

MINOAN:
from CLAY-SEAL

BURY (ct.-of-arms)

HERALDIC DOG

ANCIENT MEXICAN

CHINESE. ANTIQUE (PORCELAIN)

OTHERY–SOMERSET

Nautilus shell: the curved spiral shell of the mollusc, *Nautilus pompilius*, suitably mounted and supported on feet, was used as a drinking vessel in the ancient world, and an asymmetrical motif in 17th century ornament: the decorative character of its coiled shape is closely related to the ammonite and volute, *q.v.*

Nebule moulding: of heraldic origin (see *Nebuly*), in architecture this term describes an ornament with an undulating edge, generally a moulding enrichment on an arch or corbel-table.

Nebuly: an heraldic term for an ornamental line consisting of deeply curved undulations representing conventional cloud forms. See *Line*.

Neck mould: in architecture, a small convex moulding surrounding the neck or necking of a column, used between the capital and shaft.

Neo-classical style: an architectural style that influenced European taste during the last three decades of the 18th century, arising from a revival of interest in Greek and Roman antiquities, that followed the excavations, measurements, observations and publications carried out by archaeological expeditions organised by such bodies as the Society of Dilettanti, and by wealthy travellers. The work of Robert and James Adam (1728–92, and 1730–94), and the publication of *The Antiquities of Athens*, by James Stuart (1713–88), gave authority and direction to the growth of the style. See also *Greek revival*.

Nereid: See *Nymph*.

COPTIC 4th–5th Centuries

Network: an arrangement of lines or other geometrical outlines forming a pattern that covers a surface.

New art: see *Art Nouveau*.

Nicking: the most elementary kind of gougework, *q.v.*

Nimbus: a circle of light, or halo, surrounding the head in a representation of a divine or sacred figure. Originally connected with primitive sun worship, it became a religious symbol in Mithraism, the worship of Apollo, and in Buddhism; also used by the Romans as an emblem of divinity on statues of gods and deified emperors, and was not associated with Christianity until *c.* AD 400. It has since assumed various forms—a broad band behind the head; a disc above; a surrounding fillet; a triangle or square. The primitive relationship with light, beneficence and sanctity remains, though in early illuminated MSS, Satan appears with a nimbus, that represents power. See also *Aureole*.

CAROLINGIAN MANUSCRIPT 9th–10th centuries.
COLOGNE CATHEDRAL

Nonsuch: a name sometimes used to describe a type of chest, made in the late 16th and early 17th centuries, probably in Flanders or Germany, with inlaid panels, depicting architectural perspectives. Some authorities suggest that the buildings shown on such chests represented Nonsuch House, the wooden structure pre-fabricated in Holland, and erected on London Bridge in 1577.

REPRODUCED FROM 'GUIDE TO FURNITURE STYLES: ENGLISH AND FRENCH'
BY JOHN GLOAG AND MAUREEN STAFFORD, by kind permission of A. & C. BLACK LTD

Norman style: a development of Romanesque architecture, that came to England from Lombardy and France, in the 10th century: it was widely adopted after the Norman Conquest, and lasted until the end of the 12th century. Characterised at first by plain surfaces, massive circular pillars, round-headed arches, and an almost complete lack of ornamentation, it later became less ponderous, and mouldings were enriched by such decorative devices as the fret, chevron and lozenge. In the second and third decades of the 19th century there was a brief revival of the Norman style in furnishing and interior decoration, characterised by heavy, clumsy furniture, and crudely designed ornament.

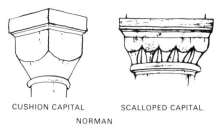

CUSHION CAPITAL   SCALLOPED CAPITAL.
NORMAN

Notch head: see *Mask*.

Nowy: heraldic term for an ornamental horizontal line, broken at long intervals by semi-circles. See *Line*.

Nulling: see *Gadrooning*.

Nymph: in Greek mythology, a female divinity of lower rank. Nymphae were divided into a number of classes, each representing various aspects of nature, i.e. the ocean (Oceanides), the Mediterranean (Nereides), fresh water (Naides), trees (Dryades), glens (Naphaeas) and mountains (Oreades).

ST BARTHOLOMEW THE GREAT. 1123-50

Oak: oak leaves have been used ornamentally and for symbolic wreaths since remote antiquity: formerly associated with Jupiter, and representing strength, power and valour, the leaves frequently adorned Greek and Roman coins and medals, and enriched columns, entablatures and cornices in classic and Gothic architecture: as an heraldic tree device, the oak is more widely used than others.

GOTHIC. ENGLISH. WESTMINSTER

OAK BORDER

ITALIAN RENAISSANCE. HERALDIC

Octofoil: in heraldry, a conventional eight-petalled flower or double quatrefoil: the cadency mark, *q.v.*, of a ninth son.

Oculus: see *Eye*.

Oeil-de-boeuf: see *Bullion*.

Ogee: a moulding that consists of a double curve, the upper concave, the lower convex: also called a talon moulding, and in classic architecture cyma recta. See *Keel Moulding*.

Ogive or ogyve: see *Ogee*.

Olive: the foliage and fruit frequently appear in classic ornament: in ancient Greece a crown of wild olive was the highest award of the Olympian games, the tree was sacred to Athene, and the olive branch symbolised peace.

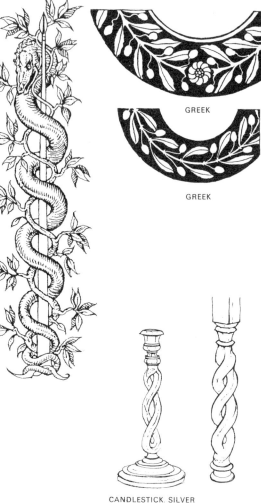

GREEK

GREEK

OLIVE-BRANCH and BASILISK coiled round pike mark of ROBERT ESTIENNE (printer) PARIS 1544

Onion foot: see *Bun foot*.

Onocentaur: a fabulous creature: a variation of the centaur, *q.v.*, half human, half ass.

CANDLESTICK. SILVER
QUEEN ANNE.

Open twist: woodworking term for a form of ornamental spiral turning (see *Turned ornament*), with separate curved members entwined to form balusters, or legs for chairs, tables, and cabinet stands. The terms double open twist and triple open twist describe the use of two or three spiral members in association.

Open zigzag lozenge: a variation of the Chinese zigzag lozenge, *q.v.* motif, used in China in the 3rd century BC.

Opinicus: a fabulous heraldic creature with the head, neck and wings of a dragon or griffin; the head beaked, and the ears pointed; the body of a lion, and a short tail.

Order of architecture: a column with a base (except in the Greek Doric order), shaft and capital, the columns used in series to support an entablature. Each order had its characteristic formalised ornament for the capitals of the columns, the enrichment of moulded detail, and the decoration of the frieze in the entablature. The Greeks invented three orders: Doric, Ionic, and Corinthian; these were adapted by the Romans, who added two others, Tuscan, a variation of Doric, and Composite, an ornate version of Corinthian.

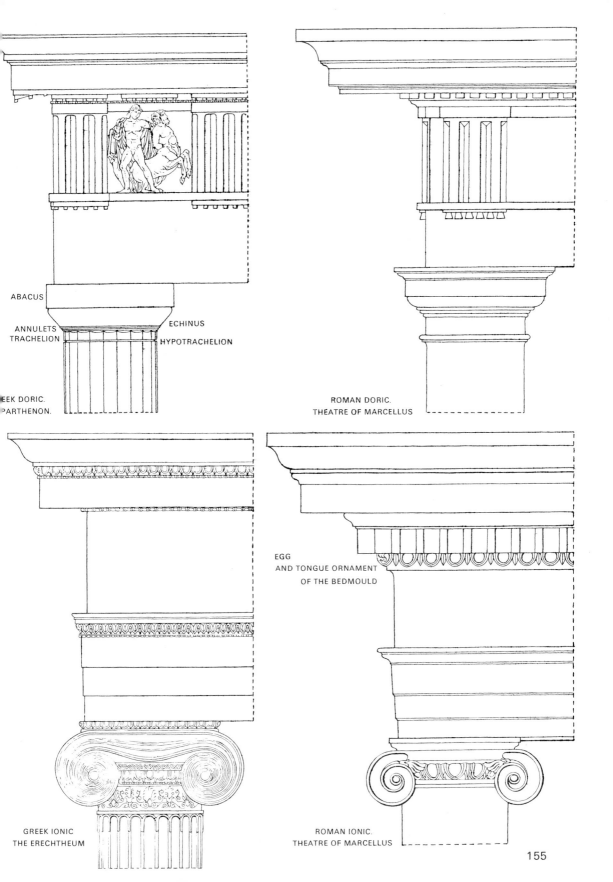

ABACUS

ANNULETS
TRACHELION

ECHINUS

HYPOTRACHELION

GREEK DORIC.
PARTHENON.

ROMAN DORIC.
THEATRE OF MARCELLUS

EGG
AND TONGUE ORNAMENT
OF THE BEDMOULD

GREEK IONIC
THE ERECHTHEUM

ROMAN IONIC.
THEATRE OF MARCELLUS

155

Order of architecture

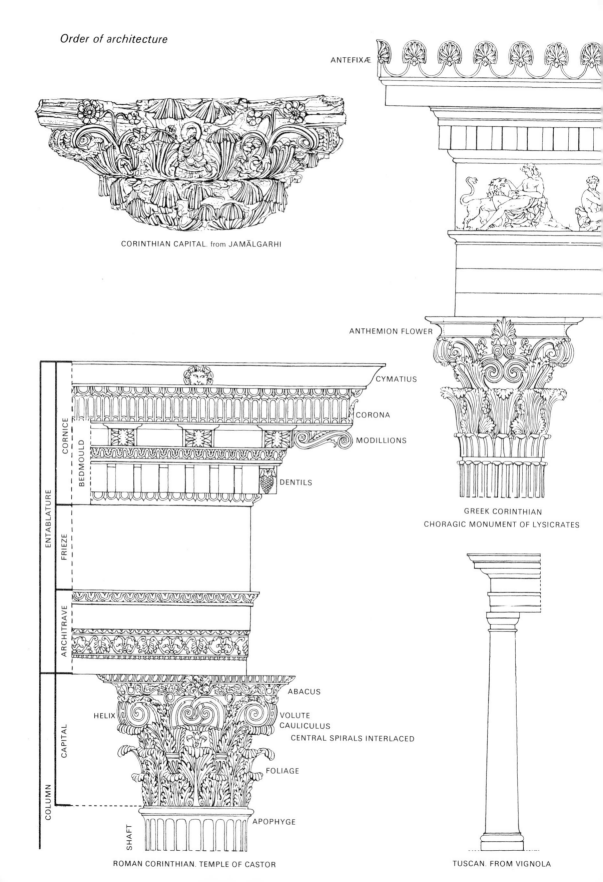

ANTEFIXÆ

CORINTHIAN CAPITAL. from JAMĀLGARHI

ANTHEMION FLOWER

CYMATIUS

CORONA

MODILLIONS

DENTILS

GREEK CORINTHIAN
CHORAGIC MONUMENT OF LYSICRATES

ENTABLATURE

CORNICE

BEDMOULD

FRIEZE

ARCHITRAVE

ABACUS

HELIX

VOLUTE
CAULICULUS
CENTRAL SPIRALS INTERLACED

CAPITAL

FOLIAGE

COLUMN

SHAFT

APOPHYGE

ROMAN CORINTHIAN. TEMPLE OF CASTOR

TUSCAN. FROM VIGNOLA

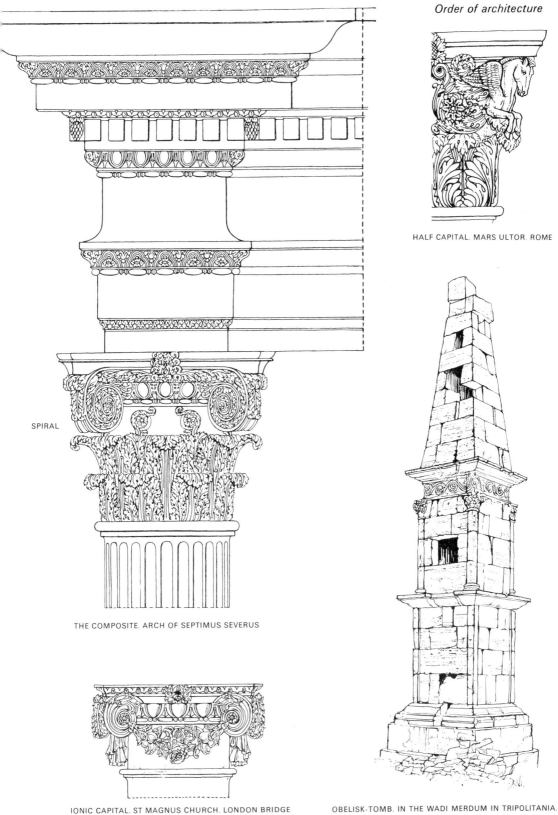

Order of architecture

HALF CAPITAL. MARS ULTOR. ROME

SPIRAL

THE COMPOSITE. ARCH OF SEPTIMUS SEVERUS

IONIC CAPITAL. ST MAGNUS CHURCH. LONDON BRIDGE

OBELISK-TOMB. IN THE WADI MERDUM IN TRIPOLITANIA.
with ENGAGED CORINTHIAN COLUMNS and FRIEZE with
RUNNING SCROLL

Ordinary: heraldic term for one of the simple geometric figures in common use on a shield, where it is frequently the predominant charge and sometimes the only device: probably originating with the metal bands that strengthened a wooden shield. Those known as honourable ordinaries, that occupy a specific place on a shield, include the bar, bend, bend sinister, chevron, chief, cross, fess, pale, pall, pile, and saltire (see these entries): their variations are known as diminutives and subordinaries.

Orle: the heraldic term for an escutcheon, *q.v.*, with the centre perforated or voided, leaving a narrow border.

Ornament: decoration in the form of moulded, carved, painted or inlaid adornment on buildings, furniture and objects, or as a pattern on a flat surface. Ornament has no utilitarian or practical purpose, although its character may have originally arisen from some structural form in building or woodworking. It satisfies one of the oldest human needs.

Osier pattern: a decorative pattern carved, sculpted or painted, consisting of simulated basket weave or wickerwork, in which narrow rods are interwoven with stouter upright rods; or the ornament may consist of a carved running pattern of willow branches.

COPTIC 7th or 8th Cent.

Overdoor: a decorative panel consisting of painting or bas-relief, above a door, and within the door case, or a carved surmount above the top member of the door architrave.

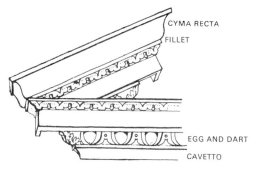

OVERDOOR, CHISWICK HOUSE *circa* 1725. [W. KENT]

Ovolo: a large convex moulding, with a quarter circle profile: also called a boultin, and an echinus *q.v.*

Ox bow: modern American cabinet-making term for bow-fronted case furniture.

Ox head: an ancient ornamental motif in the form of a mask or adorning the handles or stands of Chinese ritual vessels, of *c.* 1300–1000 BC. In the Graeco-Roman world, where the ox was a sacrificial animal, the skulls often appeared as supporters of a festoon in decoration on friezes, sarcophagi or sepulchral urns. (See also *Bucranium*). The device was frequently used by practitioners of the Neo-Classical revival in the late 18th century.

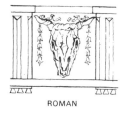

ROMAN

thus it possessed important religious and magical attributes, probably linked with the essential food, drink and shelter it provided: the motif has persisted as a decorative device in the Middle East. In ancient Egypt, Greece, Rome and Palestine, palm branches were symbolic of victory and were carried at games and triumphal processions: later they became a Christian emblem of Easter, martyrdom and victory over death, and appeared as a carved motif on tombs.

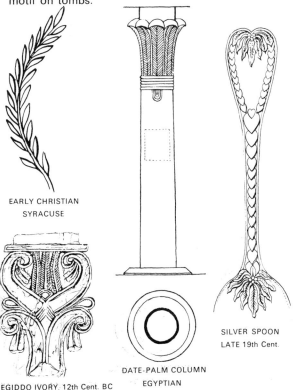

EARLY CHRISTIAN
SYRACUSE

EGIDDO IVORY. 12th Cent. BC

DATE-PALM COLUMN
EGYPTIAN

SILVER SPOON
LATE 19th Cent.

SHALLOW NICHE OR AEIDULA ROMAN MARBLE STELE.
Palm branch and dove

Palmette: of Assyrian origin, this motif has many variations: basically, it consists of an uneven number of narrow leaves springing from a tongue-like shape, the whole device resembling a palm leaf or the palm of a hand outspread: the central leaf is the largest, those on each side diminishing in size towards the outer edge. Much used in ancient Greece as a frieze, cornice, and border ornament, singly, in series, or in conjunction with some other motif. In Persia, palmate ornament was often in the form of a series of lotus-like flowers, joined by circles and a continuous band. The palmette is often called an anthemion, *q.v.*, which it closely resembles.

Palmette band: an ornamental band of continuous palmette, *q.v.*, motifs, usually joined or outlined by spiral lines, not always connected with each other. See *Spiral*.

Panache: a form of heraldic crest, *q.v.*, consisting of three or more tiers of feathers arranged like a pyramid at the top of a helm, or grouped together and fastened to the front of it.

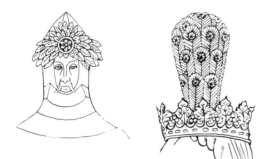

Panel tracery: a 15th century form of tracery, *q.v.*, formed by a series of straight-sided vertical panels that lie above the window lights and continue the line of the mullions that rise vertically from the base to the head of the window arch. Also called perpendicular or rectilinear tracery.

EAST WINDOW. ST JOHN BAPTIST. NOTTS. late 14th Cent.

Panther: as an heraldic beast it appears guardant —the head turned to show the full face—with flames issuing from mouth and ears.

Papyrus: conventionalised representations of the water plant, *Cyperus papyrus*, were widely used in Egypt as ornamental motifs, in painted decoration, sculpture and on such objects as wooden spoons: in architecture, the papyrus column represented the whole plant—the base was the root, the shaft the stalk, the capital the bud and flower, and a group of such columns would typify a grove of papyri. Often used in conjunction with the lotus and palm (see these entries) as a Nile fertility symbol.

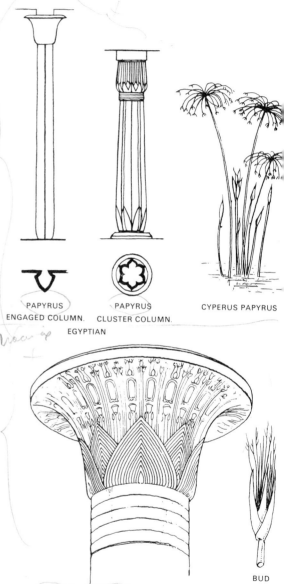

PAPYRUS ENGAGED COLUMN.
PAPYRUS CLUSTER COLUMN.
EGYPTIAN

CYPERUS PAPYRUS

BUD

BELL, or PAPYRUS-FLOWER CAPITAL, EGYPTIAN MIDDLE-KINGDOM

Parchment or parchemin panel: an ornamental device of late 15th and early 16th century origin, that consisted of two curved ribs, placed back to back, the ogee shaped spaces above and below and the oblong side spaces being filled with carved bunches of grapes, vine leaves, or fleur-de-lys. Used on wall panelling, chimney-pieces and joined chests. See also *Rib pattern*.

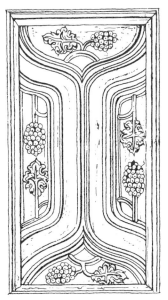

PARCHEMIN PANEL *circa* 1530

Passion cross: see *Calvary cross*.

Patera: a flat, circular or oval ornament, with carved decoration, often formalised flower petals or leaves: the word is derived from the *patera*, a shallow saucer, sometimes with a handle, used as a drinking and sacrificial vessel in Roman times.

GREEK

PATRÆ—EARLY 19th Cent. examples USED, ON FURNITURE

Paternoster: architectural term for a circular or oval bead, used as an enrichment on mouldings. See *Chaplet*.

Patriarchal cross: Latin cross, *q.v.*, with two horizontal limbs, the upper shorter than the lower: sometimes called an Archbishop's cross.

Paw: carved representations of animals' paws were used on the feet of thrones, chairs and stools in ancient Egypt, Assyria, Greece and Rome, and later in Norman and medieval England: the fashion was revived in the late 17th and 18th centuries, the paws of lions and bears being the most popular. See *Lion mahogany*.

Pawnbroker's sign: the three golden balls still used by pawnbrokers, originated in the byzant, the standard Byzantine gold coin, current throughout medieval Europe, and incorporated in an heraldic device brought to England by the Lombard bankers and merchants who settled in London in the 13th century.

LONDON S.W.3

Pawne: see *Peacock*.

Pea pod: a 16th century development of arabesque, *q.v.*, ornament, also known as *cosse de pois*. Characterised by formalised naturalistic motifs, curving twining stems, bouquets, groups of flowers and foliage, and small ovoid shapes, this style of decoration when used for jewellery and enamelwork achieved considerable popularity, but by the 17th century its individuality had been lost.

ITALIAN RENAISSANCE

...k: a motif of great antiquity: in early ... and Persian representations of the tree of ... (see *Sacred tree*) two peacocks faced each ..., often holding serpents, which they were alleged to attack, in their beaks. In ancient Rome the bird was sacred to Juno, and emblematic of the deification of empresses: it appeared on coins and in association with the vine and acanthus, and the belief that its flesh was incorruptible transformed it into a symbol of immortality: as such it was adopted by the early Christians, and it is possible that the much earlier pagan association with serpents also played a part. As a Christian symbol, peacocks became a characteristic Byzantine motif, used in conjunction with the cross, circle, dove and vine, usually in pairs, placed one on each side of a chalice, pedestal or column: again the pagan link with the sacred tree is evident. This motif appears constantly in the sculpture, mosaics and paintings of early Christian art, and in the catacombs: it symbolises the drinking of living water, the Eucharist, immortality and the Resurrection. In heraldry, where the peacock is sometimes called a pawne, the bird is usually shown with the tail displayed. See *Byzantine ornament*.

TAUNTON (ct.-of-arms)

INDIAN

COPTIC PEACOCK FEATHERS

TURKISH PEACOCK FEATHERS

PERSIAN

ITALIAN PEACOCK FEATHERS

Peardrop: the small brass pear-shaped handle, hinged to and hanging from a brass plate, on late 17th and early 18th century drawer fronts and cupboard doors: a series of continous inverted pear shapes sometimes found below a late 18th century bookcase cornice, is known as a peardrop moulding.

Pearling or beading: a form of enrichment on Norman columns, consisting of diagonal lines made up of small circles, enclosed by continuous borders, twined round the entire column.

Pediment: in classical architecture the triangular portion of wall, enclosed by raked cornices above an entablature and which supports the roof. In Renaissance architecture also featured broken-triangular, semicircular and broken: the wall ending for any roof. In Gothic architecture known as a gable. Introduced in 17th century as termination for case-furniture, and by 18th century used frequently for tallboys, cabinets and long-case clock hoods. The term also applied to a similar ornamental feature above a door or window opening.

BOOKCASE *circa* 1730

semi-circular-broken

broken-triangular

known as 'a pelican in its piety': in heraldry, a symbol of the Eucharist, and a device in the arms of Corpus Christi Colleges at Oxford and Cambridge.

KINGS LYNN   TYLDESLEY-WITH-SHAKERLEY

Pelta ornament: used in Early English decoration, mostly in friezes and on walls, this is a three-dimensional pattern of flowing, overlapping circular scales. The word, and in botany the term peltate leaf, are derived from the pelta, a small, light leather shield.

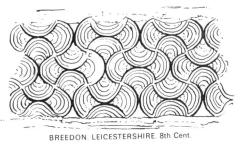

BREEDON. LEICESTERSHIRE. 8th Cent.

Pendant: an architectural term for an ornamental projection suspended from a canopy, ceiling or roof vault. A characteristic decoration of hammerbeam timber roofs and Perpendicular Gothic stone vaulting, when the pendant is generally large and elaborately carved with ornamental panels, foliage, figures and other devices: a smaller, more delicate type was used later on plaster ceilings. In cabinet-making the term describes any hanging or drop ornament. In heraldry, the word is occasionally used as an alternative for pennant. See *Pennon.*

AMERICAN. from ROOF OVERHANG   ENGLISH. from NEWEL POSTS

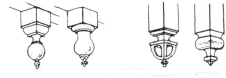

ROMAN MAUSOLEUM. SANTA MARIA CAPUA VETERA

pediment and engaged columns

Pegasus: see *Horse.*

Pelican: a Christian religious symbol of redemption, sacrifice, atonement, and the Resurrection. Widely used in medieval ecclesiastical ornament, on fonts, occasionally replacing the eagle on lecterns or pulpits, on MSS and seals. The legend that the bird feeds its young on blood from a self-inflicted wound in its breast, may have arisen from early confusion with the flamingo that does eject blood from its mouth: this is the most usual pelican representation in ornament and heraldry, and is

Pennant

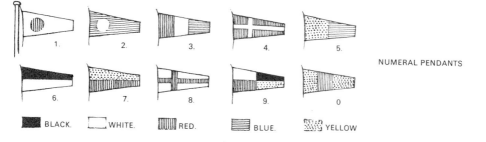

NUMERAL PENDANTS

▮ BLACK. ▯ WHITE. ▥ RED. ▤ BLUE. ▦ YELLOW

Pennant: see *Pennon*.

Pennon: an heraldic term for a small narrow flag, that could be forked or swallow-tailed, attached to a lance, and bearing the armorial device of a knight: the pennoncelle or pencel is a diminutive pennon that adorned the helmet or horse armour. The pennant is a longer, narrower version of the pennon, ending in a point, with no restriction on its length other than avoidance of entanglements, and flown from a height: occasionally called a pendant and known in the 16th century as a streamer. Pennants have become important naval flags: British examples now in use are the Broad Pennant of a Commodore: the Broad Pennant of a Commodore of the Royal Fleet Auxiliaries: the Masthead Pennant, sometimes called a coach-whip pennant; at first flown as an adornment, and in the 17th century to distinguish a man-of-war from a merchantman, it now denotes a naval vessel in commission: the Church Pennant, showing that Divine Service is taking place on board: the Paying-Off Pennant, of exceptional length, flown by a home-coming ship.

Pennoncelle: see *Pennon*.

Pentacle or pentagram: a five-pointed star: an important symbol in medieval alchemy, magic and witchcraft: the device of Marguerite of Valois. See also *Star*.

Pentagon: a figure of five equal sides and angles. Forms with five points are frequently found in Nature; and is the basis for several designs.

Perces: see *Atlantes*.

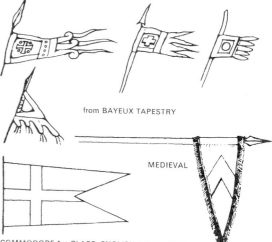

from BAYEUX TAPESTRY

MEDIEVAL

COMMODORE 1st CLASS. ENGLISH ROYAL NAVY

Perpendicular tracery: see *Panel tracery*.

Phalerae: decorative bosses, often with pendant drops or crescents attached, on which devices were carved, usually the heads of deities or emperors: worn on the cuirass of a Roman soldier, and sometimes as equestrian ornaments, as a mark of distinction or good service.

BELONGING TO GAIUS FLAVIUS FESTUS

ROMAN. BUST OF PSYCHE. BERLIN

Pheon: see *Arrow*.

Phoenix: a fabulous bird, believed by the ancients to live for five hundred years before self-immolation on an altar; from the ashes of the pyre a young phoenix arose, destined to repeat the cycle. The bird and its legend belonged to the mythology of ancient India, the Far East, Egypt and Rome; it was adopted by the early Christians as a symbol of the Resurrection, and was used as a funerary motif in the catacombs, and on sarcophagi: it is also found in mosaics and early MSS. An important heraldic bird, often used as a crest, and shown rising from flames: a badge of the Tudor monarchs Henry VII and Elizabeth I.

BRENTFORD AND CHISWICK (ct.-of-arms)

CIRENCESTER (ct.-of-arms)

WEARING CROWN OF OSIRIS
EGYPTIAN. XX dynasty.

Piecrust: a slightly raised, scalloped edging, like the decorative pastry edge of a pie, often used as an ornamental border to the tops of mid and late 18th century circular tables, now called piecrust tables, which was not a contemporary term. Pottery pie dishes with covers simulating pastry crust are known as piecrust ware.

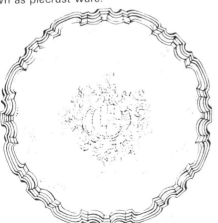

PIE-CRUST BORDER. SILVER WAITER. LONDON 1738

Pied de biche: see *Cloven foot*.

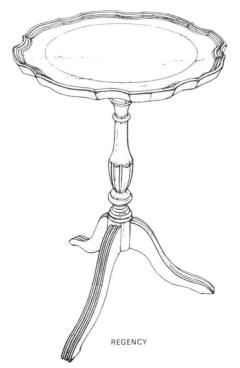

REGENCY

167

Pile: an ordinary, *q.v.*, in heraldry, consisting of a triangular wedge that may issue from the top, either side, or base of a shield, the point towards the centre.

Pincer motif: a Roman motif, rarely found, consisting of a series of conventionalised pincers, normally used as frieze decoration in sculpture, and occasionally in metalwork.

THEODORIC'S MAUSOLEUM 526 AD

Pineapple: an ornamental motif of the ancient world, notably in the Middle East civilisations, where it was an important fertility symbol and had affinities with the fir cones often found on the Sacred Tree, *q.v.* In 17th century England it was frequently used as a finial.

ASSYRIAN

GRAVESTONE. ENGLISH 1826

Pine cone and tree: originating in primitive tree worship, and possessing qualities and a shape that linked it with fire and fertility rites, the pine or fir cone was an ornamental and symbolic motif among the ancient civilisations of Egypt, India, Assyria, Greece and Rome: the prophylactic and evergreen properties of the tree were probably responsible for the use of both tree and cone as emblems of fertility and regeneration. In ancient Egypt, the tree was used as a motif in coffin decoration, and the cones on monuments: the branches of the Assyrian sacred tree, *q.v.* often terminated in pine cones, sometimes combined with buds: in India and Persia the tree was a popular motif, a highly formalised elongated flame or pear shape with a spiral twist at the top. (See *Paisley motif.*) In ancient Greece and Rome, where pine cones were used to flavour wine, and were burnt on sacrificial altars for the fragrance of their pungent scent, they adorned the thyrsus, *q.v.* carried by Dionysus and his votaries, and the tree was sacred to him. As a regenerative symbol, the cone decorated Etruscan tombs and urns: it appears only occasionally in Norman and Renaissance ornament, and is sometimes called a fir apple.

from KINGS ROBE. BABYLONIAN

FRENCH 1800

Pinnacle: in architecture, the pointed termination of a spire, or small turret-shaped ending on a buttress or parapet, sometimes decorated with crockets.

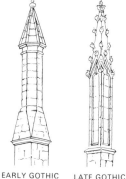

EARLY GOTHIC   LATE GOTHIC

Pirate flag: the device of skull and crossbones on a black flag probably became the recognisable emblem of pirates and buccaneers at the end of the 17th or beginning of the 18th century. The message it conveyed was that reasonable treatment would be given to the victims, but a plain red flag, also called the Bloody Flag, was also a pirate flag, and his announced no quarter and no mercy. The names Jolly Roger, the Black Flag, the Roger, or Old Roger, were all current for the pirate flag: the device, though usually in white, was sometimes found in yellow or red. See also *Crossbones* and *Flag*.

Pisces: the fishes: the twelfth sign of the Zodiac: see *Zodiacal devices*.

Pistris: a fabulous sea monster, with a dragon's head, animal's neck and breast, fish's body and tail, and fins instead of forelegs. This was the creature sent to carry away Andromeda: it was thus represented in classic ornament, and later, as the whale that swallowed Jonah.

Plain cross: in heraldry, this is a cross in the centre of a shield, the limbs extending to the edges of the shield. The border lines of the limbs may be ornamented with one of the heraldic decorative treatments applied to lines. *q.v.* See also *Fimbriated, Quarter pierced* and *Voided cross*.

Plait: three strands of material, interwoven one across the other to produce one rope-like strand whose decorative character lies in the regular crossed entwinement.

GREEK. ATTIC 480 BC

ANCIENT MEXICAN

HINDOO

ANCIENT MEXICAN

Planetary signs: the names and symbols for most of the planets are very ancient. Those for the *Sun* and *Moon* were probably based on old symbols for gold and silver: *Mercury*, the messenger, is represented by a stylised winged helmet: *Mars* and *Venus* by the traditional male and female symbols, an arrow and a mirror: the *Earth* by a cross within a circle, probably of medieval origin: *Jupiter* by a lightning bolt: *Saturn* by a stylised K (it was once called Kronos): the symbol for *Uranus*, discovered in 1781, was chosen arbitrarily: *Neptune*, discovered in 1876, is represented by a trident: and *Pluto*, discovered in 1930, is shown as a single symbol combining the first two letters of the name.

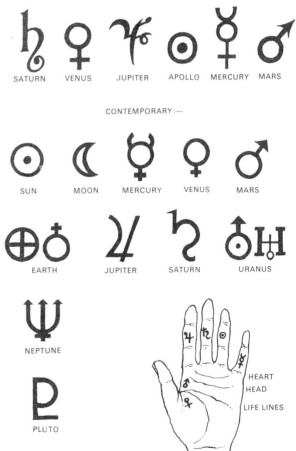

SATURN VENUS JUPITER APOLLO MERCURY MARS

CONTEMPORARY:—

SUN MOON MERCURY VENUS MARS

EARTH JUPITER SATURN URANUS

NEPTUNE

PLUTO

HEART
HEAD
LIFE LINES

Planted moulding: a moulding cut separately, and affixed to a surface: the term stuck moulding is sometimes used. See also *Struck moulding*.

Plaque: a flat plate, rectangular or circular, made of metal, porcelain, or lacquer, inserted in or fixed to a surface, as an adornment: usually carved, engraved, or painted with some decorative device, plaques occur in Georgian and Regency furniture.

Platband: an architectural term for a plain flat moulding of greater height than projection: it also describes the fillets that separate flutes (see *Fluting*) and is occasionally applied to a door lintel.

Plate tracery: the earliest form of tracery, *q.v.*, found in Norman and Early English architecture: at first, the stone surface above a window head and within the window surround was pierced by circular openings to form simple decoration: later, the openings assumed more complicated geometrical shapes and the ornamental effect became richer and more delicate. See *Bar tracery*.

Plateresque style: a term that describes the architecture and ornament of early 16th century Spain, when Moorish influence imparted an exotic richness of detail to decoration, comparable to the work of jewellers and designers in precious metals: the word is derived from the Spanish *platero*, a silversmith.

Playing cards: many authorities believe that these were first used in 12th century China, possibly before, and that they evolved from the practice by early man, of throwing an arrow into a magic circle so that he could determine, according to his primitive beliefs, to which of the four directions of the universe some object or event belonged. By the 14th century playing cards were well known in Europe, brought there by way of India, Persia, and the eastern Mediterranean countries, probably by Crusaders and the Arabs who invaded Spain. The close association of early cards with divination, sorcery, and occult practices is strongly indicated by the tarot pack, and still survives in conjuring and fortune-telling. It is believed that from the pictorial devices of the tarot, *q.v.*, are derived the court cards, king, queen and knave (formerly a valet or marshal), that have persisted, with national variations, and in

WINCHESTER CASTLE

spite of many attempts to displace them by figures of a political, religious or historical character. The patterns on the backs of cards, often complex arabesques, interlacements, geometrical designs, pictures or scenes, originally met the need to hide flaws in the paper. The ornamental suit signs, believed to have originated in value symbols or ancient Chinese paper money, were used on the old Chinese cards: in Europe, their true meaning was lost, and they were eventually transformed into the familiar spades, hearts, diamonds and clubs. See these entries, *Suit signs*, and *Tarot*.

GERMAN 1588

CHINESE

THE FIVE BLESSINGS

SHAU = long life

LUK = promotion   HI = posterity

FUK = happiness   T,S'OI = wealth

COPPE=CUPS   BASTONI=BATONS or CLUBS   DENARI=MONEY   SPADE=SWORDS

TAROT

Without Concern he from his Coach alights,
To stand a Tryal which its Hearers frights.

The D_r and his Friends in Consultation,
How to reply to Commons. Accusation

SACHEVERELL CARDS. from PACK ILLUSTRATING REIGN OF QUEEN ANNE

Plume: in heraldry, a variation of the panache, *q.v.*, in which feathers—usually ostrich—were arranged in one or two rows; sometimes called a bush of feathers. The testers of late 17th and early 18th century state beds sometimes had finials crowned with plumes, and they were also used as a decorative device in some late 18th century shield-back chairs. See also *Prince of Wales's feathers*.

Pointed-and-cusped: a form of geometrical tracery, *q.v.*, in which a pointed arch contains a two-cusped figure.

Pointed cross: a cross with pointed limbs.

Pomel or pommel: a finial, *q.v.*, in the form of a knob: the term is used particularly for a decorative finial at the top of a pointed or domed turret roof; or a pair of finials on state chairs: also applied to any globe-shaped ornament. In heraldry, a pommel is the ball that terminates a sword hilt.

Pope's cross: a Latin cross, *q.v.*, having three sets of horizontal limbs, each set shorter than the one below.

Poppyhead: a 15th century finial on pew ends, in the form of an intricately carved poppy seed head surrounded by flowing, formalised foliage; also used as a generic term for richly ornamented pew-end finials adorned with figures, flowers or foliage.

GHIBERTI   INDIAN

Portuguese swell: see *Baluster*.

Potency: heraldic term for an ornamental line of T-shaped blocks, joined horizontally. See *Line*.

Pounced ornament: a form of decoration, used on the ground surfaces of sunk carving on 16th and 17th century furniture, consisting of a close irregular pattern of small dots or punctures pricked in the wood.

Powdered: heraldic term for a field strewn with small devices such as stars, hearts or fleur-de-lys. The term powdering is sometimes used to describe a favourite form of medieval and Japanese decoration, when flowers, leaves and other small motifs were sprinkled over a background. See also *Millefleurs motif* and *Spotting*.

Prince of Wales's feathers: the heraldic badge of the Heir Apparent to the English throne, consisting of three ostrich feathers issuing from a coronet with a scroll under, bearing the words 'Ich Dien': this form, used today, is believed to have been devised by Edward Tudor, later Edward VI. Though other versions of the ostrich feather badge had been popular with the Kings of England since its introduction by Edward III, it did not acquire its special association with the heir to the throne until Tudor times. There is no evidence to support the tradition that this device was worn by the blind king, John of Bohemia, and assumed by the Black Prince after the Battle of Crecy. At the end of the 18th century the device was sometimes used to ornament oval and shield shaped chair backs, or as a surmount to or decoration of, the central splat. See also *Feathers* and *Plume*.

Printers' device: a decorative pictorial, heraldic or allegorical embellishment to the title page of a book, often combined with the colophon, *q.v.*, that acted as a trademark, a safeguard against the common danger of the pirated edition, a guarantee of quality, and an embryonic form of copyright, in the first printed books: the earliest is probably the motif of two shields suspended from a branch used by John Fust and Peter Schoeffer in 1462. Italian and French printers used devices of great ornamental beauty; many of these, as well as English examples, took the form of a rebus, *q.v.*, on the name of the printer: some embodied a portrait of the printer: the 16th century French printer, Badius Ascensius, used as his device a printing press in operation: the dolphin and anchor (*c.* 1502), of Aldus Manutius, is one of the best known. In England, the Copyright Act of 1709 reduced the use of such devices, and it was not until a mid 19th century printer, Charles Whittingham the younger, revived interest in them, that they began to reappear: since then recognisable devices have been employed by many printing and publishing houses. See *Lily* and *Olive*.

RICHARD PYNSON 1487

Printers' flowers: known also as *fleurons*, *vignettes de fonts*, and *roslein*, these small ornamental units have been used by printers and typographers since the early days of printing. Arabesque and geometric motifs such as stars, florets and leaves, originally employed by Persian and Moorish craftsmen in fabric design and on metal, pottery and leather bindings, were adapted as decoration in illuminated 14th century MSS: from the Moorish state of Spain, Egypt, and the Middle East, they reached Venice, where the first printing press had been established in the mid 15th century. Among the Venetian printers who pioneered the use of these small motifs to decorate borders, initial letters, and paragraph marks, were Erhard Ratdolt, Aldus Manutius, and Gabriele Giolito, all working there in the late 15th and early 16th centuries. Aldus Manutius invented the diminutive metal tools known as *piccoli ferri*, cut with a small motif, which could be used like type on covers and bindings to form regular patterns of ornament: these eventually came into use all over Europe, where other printers famous for the production and use of printers' ornaments were Bernard Salomon (1508–51 or 62), Geoffrey Tory (d. 1533), Peter Flötner, Jean de Tournes, Robert Granjon (all mid 16th century), Simon Gribelin (1662–1733) and John Johnson (1777–1848). During the 17th and early 18th centuries, baroque designs replaced many of the arabesques, and in the 19th century there was a revival of the popularity of flower and foliage motifs. Printers' flowers are now produced in a large, though often standardised range that includes many of the motifs of past centuries, cast in metal, as ordinary type, in varying sizes, and used singly or assembled to form decorative patterns. See also *Aldine leaf, Asterisk, Binders' ornaments, Borders, Entrelac, Fleuron* and *Rules.*

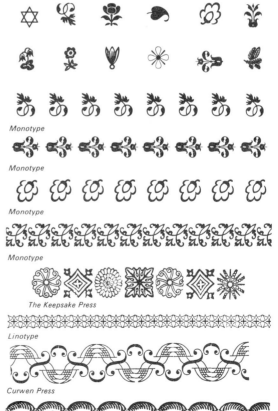

Monotype

Monotype

Monotype

Monotype

The Keepsake Press

Linotype

Curwen Press

Monotype

Stephenson Blake

Monotype

Monotype

Monotype

Monotype

Stephenson Blake

Monotype

Stephenson Blake

Monotype

Monotype

Monotype

Stephenson Blake

Prismatic ornament: see *Strapwork*.

Profile: in architecture and cabinet-making, the contour or section of a moulding.

Purled ornament: a decorative pattern on glass vessels, made by a continuous all-over design of small circular or oval depressions.

Putti: see *Amorini*.

Quadrant bead: see *Boultin*.

Quadrate cross: a cross with a square centre from which the limbs project.

Quadriga: a sculptured group that often surmounts a triumphal arch or monument, consisting of a chariot or car drawn by four horses, generally with a charioteer.

from CORINTHIAN KRAKER. 560 BC. BERLIN

Quaint style: trade term used to describe furniture based on Art Nouveau, *q.v.*, ornament. Popular in the late 19th and early 20th centuries, with decoration incorporating naturalistic trees and foliage, and pierced with heart-shaped apertures.

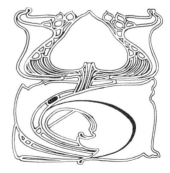

TILE ENGLISH 1896

Quarter: in heraldry, a square panel placed at the top dexter (see *Bend*) side of a shield. In architecture, an archaic term for a square panel.

Quarter column: a cabinet-making term for a plain or fluted column, with moulded base and carved capital, a quarter of a circle in diameter; sometimes used on angles of 18th century case furniture. See *Spandril piece*.

Quarter pierced cross: a plain cross, *q.v.*, with the rectangle formed by the intersection of the limbs left open.

Quarter round: see *Boultin*.

Quartering: an heraldic term for the division of a shield into four quarters in order to include additional coats of arms, acquired by marriage: each quarter may be further quartered as necessary. Also a cabinet-making term for the decorative pattern formed by the symmetrical arrangement of similarly figured veneers.

Quatrefoil: an architectural and heraldic term for a figure of four equal arcs or lobes, separated by cusps, *q.v.* A characteristic device in Byzantine decoration and Gothic tracery and carving, that regained popularity during the Gothic Revival, *q.v.* Sometimes stated to be based on the four-leaved clover; reliable authorities believe the quatrefoil to be a strictly Christian religious motif—a form of the Greek cross with rounded ends, or of the nimbus with the four arcs representing the four Evangelists. The word is also applied to a motif that was widely used in the lacquer work, textiles and inlay produced during the Han dynasty period (*c.* 206 BC— AD 220) in China: here the device takes the form of a flat heart-shaped leaf, probably that of a water chestnut. See also *Foil*.

Quattrocento: Italian Renaissance art and ornament of the 15th century. In contrast to the Trecento, *q.v.*, that preceded it, naturalistic rather than conventional motifs were used, and were no longer symbolic representations of animals, birds, fruit or foliage, but realistic, picturesque, and highly decorative. The introduction of devices like the cartouche and scrolled shield showed the growing influence of heraldry on ornament. Trecento interlacing patterns persisted, though less complex and bolder in form. See also *Cinquecento* and *Trecento*.

Queen Anne style: the style of architecture, decoration and cabinet-making practised during the first two decades of the 18th century: in architecture, characterised by modified baroque, *q.v.*, a sparing use of classical ornament, sliding sash windows, and bold, emphatic moulded detail: in furniture, by the introduction of curvilinear design, the cabriole leg (see *Cabriole profile*), and an increased use of decorative woods and veneers.

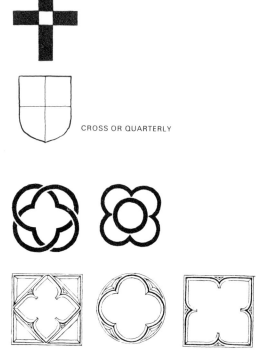

CROSS OR QUARTERLY

LATE GOTHIC EXAMPLES

WALNUT.
PLAIN BACK SPLAT.
1710

CARVED WALNUT. *circa* 1715

Queen's beasts: among the heraldic beasts that are supporters of the shield in the Royal Arms, ten are now known as the Queen's beasts, and are used as ornamental sculptured figures in large public parks and gardens. They are the Lion of England; the White Lion of Mortimer; the Unicorn of Scotland; the Griffin of Edward III; the Black Bull of Clarence; the Falcon of the Plantagenets; the White Greyhound of Richmond; the Yale of Beaufort; the Red Dragon of Wales; and the White Horse of Hanover.

SCULPTURED FOR CORONATION OF QUEEN ELIZABETH II 1953 BY JAMES WOODFORD O.B.E.

RED DRAGON OF WALES

BLACK BULL OF CLARENCE

WHITE GREYHOUND OF RICHMOND

YALE OF BEAUFORT

GRIFFIN OF EDWARD III

LION OF ENGLAND

WHITE HORSE OF HANOVER

WHITE LION OF MORTIMER

UNICORN OF SCOTLAND

FALCON OF PLANTAGENETS

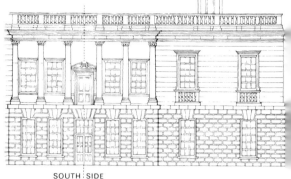

Queen's House, The: at Greenwich built 1616–35. Designed by Inigo Jones (1573–1652). The rusticated ground storey, baluster parapet, the façade to the south with central Ionic columns, loggia flanked by plain wings, balconies to the windows and broken-pediment above the door of the first floor—show the influence of Palladian architecture; and was the prototype of many later houses.

SOUTH SIDE

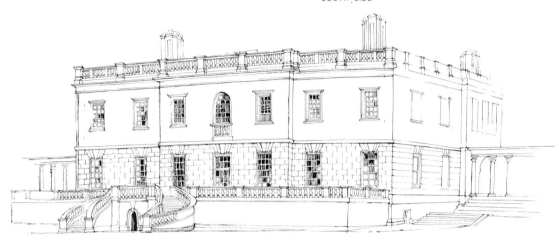

Quintfoil: see *Cinquefoil.*

Quirk: a deeply incised groove running between mouldings or separating a convex moulding and a flat surface: often used to cast a shadow.

Quirked bead: an astragal or bead separated from an adjoining flat surface by a quirk, *q.v.* Also called bead and quirk.

Quoin block: an architectural term for a block of stone, wood or brick, used in series on the corners of a building for ornamental effect. In cabinet-making, this form of decoration was sometimes applied to 18th century case furniture, such as tallboys.

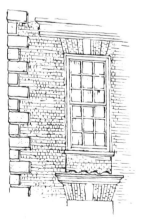

R

Radiant or rayonny: heraldic term for a series of formalised rays, used as an ornamental line. See *Line* and *Linked flames*.

Raguly: heraldic term for a slanting, castellated ornamental line. See *Line*.

Raking fret: a variation of the Greek fret, *q.v.*, with the keys slanted in the same direction.

Ram's head: the head or skull of this animal, also called an aegicrane, was used in Graeco-Roman times—when the ram was a sacrificial animal—as a corner ornament, on altar cornices, friezes, or tripods, and as a holder for a festoon: the same motif occurs in Renaissance ornament, and in the late 18th century it was widely used as a decorative motif by the brothers Adam. The iron head of the *aries* (the battering ram used by the Greeks and Romans) was moulded in the form of a ram's head. See also *Ammonite* and *Crio-sphinx*.

Rat tail: a V-shaped tongue that first appeared on late 17th century spoons, at the junction between stem and bowl, continuing down the back of the bowl. Intended primarily to strengthen the junction, it became an ornamental feature.

EXTERIOR PILASTER. CHAPEL OF ST SATURNIN

ASSYRIAN

MARBLE ALTAR. CAPITOLINE MUSEUM

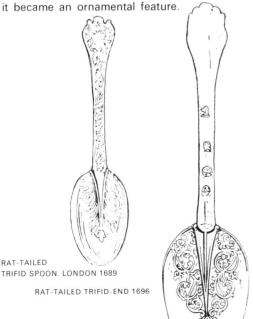

RAT-TAILED
TRIFID SPOON. LONDON 1689

RAT-TAILED TRIFID-END 1696

Rayonny: see *Radiant*.

Rebus: pictorial representation of a name, word or phrase, with a device, figures or letters. Rebuses were first used in the Middle Ages, when carved or painted animals and birds provided a pictorial pun on the proper name of an ecclesiastic or benefactor: a famous example was the recumbent hart carved on a vaulting shaft in Norwich Cathedral, where Bishop Lyhart built the nave vault *c*. 1460–70. The medieval practice of composing heraldic devices and mottoes in the form of a rebus on the name of the bearer became popular. Artists, artisans, shop-keepers and innkeepers adopted the rebus to identify their work, or advertise their trades.

Rectilinear tracery: see *Panel tracery*.

179

Reeding: a series of parallel convex mouldings, or inverted flutes, used as surface decoration. See *Fluting*.

Regency style: the decorative style largely derived from the Greek Revival in England, that began in the early 19th century and continued throughout the Regency period and the reign of George IV: characterised by the elegant use of classical Greek motifs, it influenced the form and ornamentation of furniture especially and appeared in the designs of Thomas Hope (*c.* 1770–1831) and Thomas Sheraton (1751–1806). The style was in no way connected with the French Empire style. See *Empire style* and *English Empire*.

Renaissance ornament: the use of classical decoration and motifs resulted from the renewal of interest in Graeco-Roman art and architecture that began in 15th century Italy, and spread throughout Europe, where, with national variations, it remained as a background of style until the mid 19th century. Byzantine and Saracenic influences can also be discerned in the arabesques, scrolls and strapwork, *q.v.*, that were characteristic of 16th century Renaissance ornament. See also *Cinquecento*, *Quattrocento*, and *Trecento*.

Reticulated tracery: a development of curvilinear tracery, *q.v.*, in which the ogee or oval shapes are conjoined in rows, creating a net-like effect.

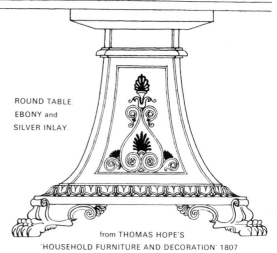

ROUND TABLE.
EBONY and
SILVER INLAY.

from THOMAS HOPE'S
'HOUSEHOLD FURNITURE AND DECORATION' 1807

Reverse ogee: a moulding with a double curve, the upper convex, the lower concave: known in classic architecture as cyma reversa. See *Ogee*.

Rib: a continuous structural member projecting from and appearing as a band or ridge on the surface.

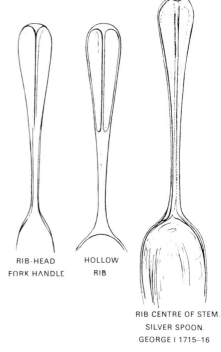

RIB-HEAD
FORK HANDLE

HOLLOW
RIB

RIB CENTRE OF STEM.
SILVER SPOON.
GEORGE I 1715–16

Rib pattern: a variation of the parchment panel, *q.v.*, in which the two curved ribs are sometimes interlaced.

Ribband: see *Ribbon ornament*.

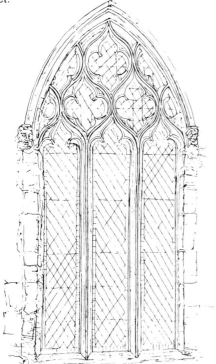

GILT GIRANDOLE. ENGLISH. 1790

Ribbon-and-knot: characteristic of Celtic ribbon ornament, *q.v.*, this term is used when the ribbon device is knotted or tied in a bow.

Ribbon-and-label: a variation of a ribbon device with a plain surface on part of the ribbon, on which a date or motto may be inscribed. See *Ribbon ornament.*

Ribbon-and-rosette: an ornamental ribbon device, used in the mid 18th century, and carved on the moulded edges of tables, with formalised roses entwined with ribbons; also called rose-and-ribbon. See *Ribbon ornament.*

Ribbon-and-stick: a ribbon spiralling around a stick or rod. A device that originated in France during the Louis XVI period, used as an enrichment on mouldings, generally on a bead.

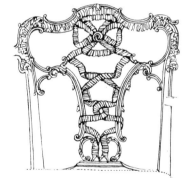

DESIGN for a CARD-TABLE TOP
3rd EDIT: of HEPPLEWHITE'S 'GUIDE'

Section from RIBBON-BACK SETTEE. ENGLISH *circa* 1755

Ribbon ornament: the ribbon was a motif used in Graeco-Roman decoration, either alone or as an ancillary to swags, festoons and garlands, or interlaced by laying one ribbon over another. The ribbon would often end in a ball or acorn-shaped knob. In 5th, 6th and 7th century Celtic ornament arrangements of knotted and intricately interlaced ribbons characterised the decoration of surfaces and illuminated MSS. Ribbon motifs played an important part in rococo, *q.v.*, decoration, where they often appeared elaborately crinkled, curled and flowing, with ends divided like a pennon. In the mid 18th century, carved ribbon decoration was widely used in England, and the ribbon or ribband back chairs made by Thomas Chippendale the elder, had interwoven splats in the form of intricate convolutions, sometimes called interlaced chair backs, a form so fragile that few examples have survived. See also *Ribbon-and-knot, Ribbon-and-label, Ribbon-and-rosette,* and *Ribbon-and-stick.*

HERALDIC

RIBBON-BACK CHAIR. ENGLISH. 1754

Rice-grain: also known as grains of rice, this term describes a decorative treatment applied to early Chinese and Persian pottery and porcelain; the surface was covered with small perforations that were afterwards filled with transparent glaze. See also *Dot.*

Ring: see *Annulet.*

Ring cross: a cross with splayed or crutch-shaped limbs (see *Cross potent*) superimposed on a circle: frequently found in Celtic and medieval memorial or sepulchral crosses.

Rocaille: see *Rococo.*

Rococo or rococco: derived from the French *rocaille.* An ornate, asymmetrical style of decoration originating in France and Italy, in the late 17th and early 18th centuries, spreading throughout Europe, and reaching England in the mid 18th century. The word 'rocaille' meant rockwork, and the style was first inspired by the shell-encrusted artificial fountains and grottoes at Versailles, that were imitated in parks and gardens in the early 18th century. Characterised by an exuberant intermingling of shells, C-scrolls, rocks, seaweed, ribbons and curving and irregular acanthus foliations, the style also had an affinity with Chinese art. Rococo enjoyed a short revival in mid 19th century England and America, when the term 'rococo' became popular as a description of excessively ornamental furniture.

GERMAN

FRENCH

Rod of Aesculapius: see *Aesculapius, rod of.*

Rod of Mercury: see *Caduceus.*

Roll-and-fillet: a variation of roll moulding, *q.v.,* with a square fillet projecting from the convex face.

Roll moulding: a plain round moulding of semi-circular section, found in medieval architecture, on string courses and dripstones. See also *Bowtell, Roll-and-fillet* and *Edge moulding.*

Romanesque: the architectural style that developed in the Eastern Roman Empire after the decline of the Western Empire. The style spread westwards in the 9th and 10th centuries. Romanesque ornament shows strong Byzantine influence, especially in geometrical mosaic designs, and interlaced foliage. In architecture, the rounded arch is an outstanding characteristic.

Romayne-carving: a form of early 16th century carved decoration consisting of small profile heads in medallions.

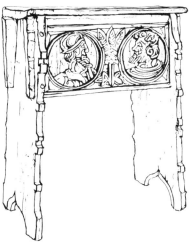

ROMAYNE OAK STOOL. ENGLISH. *circa* 1535

Rope moulding: see *Cable moulding*.

Rope ornament: alternative term for cable ornament, *q.v.* A primitive form of rope motif impressed on the surface of lake dwellers' pottery vessels, believed to have originated in the impression left in the wet clay by strings tied round the pots in order to keep them together.

ROPE AND SPIRAL. EGYPTIAN

ROPE AND PATERÆ. EGYPTIAN

Rose: in ancient Rome, roses were an obligatory decoration at ceremonies and feasts. Occasionally used as an ornamental motif in Norman architecture. In heraldry, it is a conventional five-petalled flower, with sepals or barbs between the petals, sometimes with an inner circle of five more petals: the cadency mark, *q.v.*, of a seventh son. The heraldic Tudor rose, *q.v.*, was a combination of the red and white roses of Lancaster and York, and the rose remains the Royal Badge of England. In early and medieval Christianity, it symbolised the Virgin Mary and Paradise. See also *Rosette*.

UNITED RED AND WHITE

FORMS OF HERALDIC ROSE

IRONWORK. GERMAN

PERSIAN. CERAMIC

WHITE

UNION

ROSE AND THISTLE

GERMAN. GOTHIC

ROSE WINDOW. WEST FRONT. CHARTRES

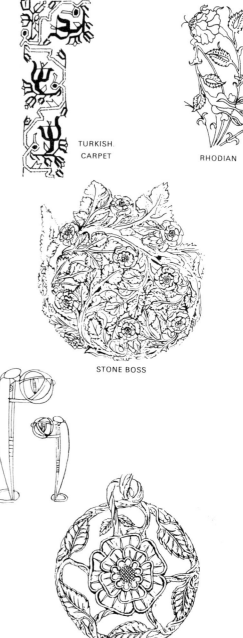

TURKISH. CARPET

RHODIAN

STONE BOSS

TUDOR. CHOIR STALL. HENRY VII's CHAPEL. WESTMINSTER

Rose-and-ribbon: see *Ribbon-and-rosette*.

Roseball: an Art Nouveau, *q.v.*, motif, in the form of a highly stylised tight-petalled rose, used as a personal device by the architect and designer, Charles Rennie Mackintosh (1869–1928), and as a distinguishing mark by the Glasgow school of designers.

Rosette: a formalised rose, with petals radiating outwards in zones from the centre, the rosette was a primitive solar symbol, and a religious and decorative motif among the peoples of ancient India, Assyria and Persia; it became a characteristic classical motif, used by the Greeks as an architectural, funerary and ceramic ornament, and by the Romans as the central motif in the panels of coffered ceilings. Rosettes have continued in use as ceiling ornaments and, carved singly on a patera, *q.v.*, or in series, may adorn furniture and metalwork. A pattern of overlapping rosettes is sometimes known as money-moulding, money pattern or strung coin. The word is also used as a generic description for any circular ornament radiating from a centre.

ROSE-SHAPED PATERÆ OR DISC ORNAMENTS FOR FURNITURE

WOODEN ROSETTES. GERMAN GOTHIC. COBURG CASTLE

Rosette band: a decorative band with a rosette, *q.v.*, as the chief motif, though sprays and tendrils may also appear.

Rostral column: see *Columna rostrata*.

Rouelle: an early solar symbol in mythology in the Middle East, believed to be associated with the primitive wheel cross, *q.v.* and, much later, with the Christian monogram (see *Monogram*).

Round: see *Torus*.

Roundel or roundle: any circular panel that adorns a surface, such as a decorative patera, medallion or plaque (see those entries), or an ornamental circular inset of stained glass in a window: occasionally used as an alternative for astragal, *q.v.*, and bullion, *q.v.* In heraldry, it denotes a circular shape that may represent such devices as an apple, coin, cake, or plate: it may appear alone, in series, or as a decorative termination to a figure. Carved roundels were a favourite form of ornament on medieval boarded chests, and glass roundels bearing heraldic devices, set in lead-glazed windows, were known from the 15th to the 19th centuries.

ROUNDEL DECORATION. BYZANTINE.
BASED ON TREE OF PARADISE THEME. 9th Cent.

CHIP-CARVING ROUNDELS 13th Cent. BOARDED CHESTS

Rule: in typography, this is a line, used to separate headings or columns, or as a punctuation dash: the thin strip of metal used by a printer to reproduce a rule may be of various widths, straight or wavy, or when thick enough, can be engraved with a design so that it becomes a decorative embellishment to a page. See also *Swelled rule*.

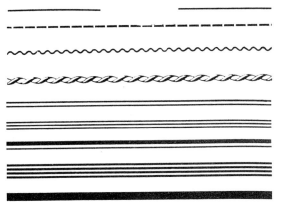

Runic cross: see *Celtic cross*.

Runic knot: sometimes called a Danish knot, this is a thick, closely-twined rope or serpentine motif, a Scandinavian version of the Byzantine symbol that showed the serpent, representing the fall of man, crushed and coiled around the cross. See *Serpent*.

WHALE'S BONE CASKET. FRANKS: *circa* 700 AD

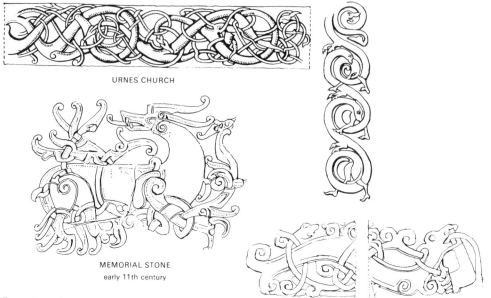

URNES CHURCH

MEMORIAL STONE.
early 11th century

Running dog: see *Vitruvian scroll*.

Running fret: a simple fret, *q.v.*, formed by a series of continuous keys running in the same direction. See *Fret*.

Running scroll: see *Vitruvian scroll*.

Rustication: architectural term for masonry or brickwork in which the joints between the units or courses are deeply recessed (banded), or chamfered. The term also describes a masonry surface that has been artificially roughened, so that it appears weathered (rock-faced), worm-eaten (vermiculated), or harsh (frosted).

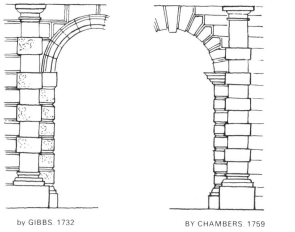

by GIBBS. 1732

BY CHAMBERS. 1759

Rustre: heraldic term for a lozenge pierced with a circular hole. See *Lozenge*.

S

Sacred tree: the mythology of the Sacred Tree, or Tree of Life, is found, with local variations, throughout the ancient world: the idea of a divine, miraculous tree providing food that would rejuvenate, restore and prolong life fulfilled an old human desire that has played an important part in religious practices. The species of tree thus venerated varied according to its local importance as a producer of food, drink and shelter, and this accounts for the many versions of the motif, its foliage, flowers, fruits, and attendants. Subject to these variations, the tree is always highly stylised: leaves, fruits and flowers are strictly symmetrical: two figures—monsters, reptiles, birds, animals or humans, according to their local and religious affinities—regard each other from either side of the trunk: and the whole form has a geometrical rigidity. The earliest sacred tree motifs are probably those found engraved on Chaldean stones of *c.* 3500 BC: throughout subsequent ages widely different versions continued to adorn sculpture, painting, mosaics and textiles; the fundamental principle of the life-sustaining tree and its attendant figures is discernible in the symbolic tree motifs of all religions. See also *Hom*.

PRE-INCA

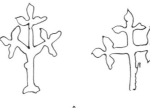

ASSYRIAN. TREE OF LIFE

ASSYRIAN. SACRED TREE

SASSANIAN. SACRED TREE WITH IBEXES.
LOUVRE

EGYPTIAN SACRED SYCAMORE OR TREE OF LIFE

APOSTOLIC TREE OF LIFE
WITH THE CROSS EMBLEM

187

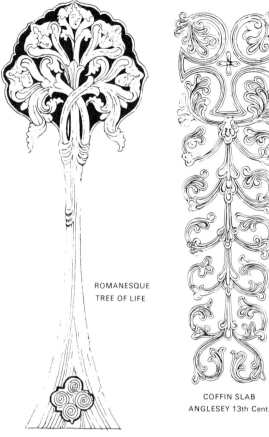

ROMANESQUE
TREE OF LIFE

COFFIN SLAB
ANGLESEY 13th Cent.

DESIGNS SHOWING ASSOCIATION OF
THE CROSS AND SACRED TREE OF LIFE.

from 'ENGLISH CHURCHYARD MEMORIALS' by FREDERICK BURGESS
by kind permission of THE LUTTERWORTH PRESS.
Also illustrations to DEATH'S HEAD.

Sagittarius or sagittary: the archer: the ninth sign of the Zodiac. (See *Zodiacal devices*.) The heraldic name for a centaur, *q.v.* is a sagittarius or sagittary.

St Andrew's cross: see *Saltire*.

St Anthony's cross: a tau cross, *q.v.* The crutch-like appearance of this T-shaped figure, occasionally called a tace, was supposedly emblematic of the old age and infirmities of the saint.

St Julian's cross: see *Crosslet*.

St Patrick's cross: see *Saltire*.

Salamander: a fabulous monster, often used as an heraldic device and badge, when it appears as a green newt or lizard surrounded with flames in which the creature was supposed to breed: the emblem of François I of France. It also appears on fonts, where it symbolises baptism by fire and water. See *Heraldic ornament*.

Saltire: in heraldry, an ordinary, *q.v.*: the heraldic term for a diagonal cross, often called a St Andrew's or St Patrick's cross.

Saracenic ornament: a style of decoration that arose in the 7th century AD, when the Arab conquest of the Mediterranean provinces of the Eastern Roman Empire, Syria, Egypt and North Africa brought the conquerors into contact with Christian culture. Although the Mohammedan faith prohibited pictorial representation of living creatures, the geometrical patterns, complicated curves and interlacings, usually combined with sacred inscriptions, of Arab ornament, were adapted by Byzantine designers to act as symbols and disguises for forbidden natural objects: classic architectural ornament was also incorporated, and the resulting forms were intricate and often involved patterns of tracery, strapwork, diapers, and interlaced curves. The origin of certain characteristic features of Norman decoration may be identified with Saracenic influence in Sicily between *c.*

AD 827 and the conquest and occupation of the island by the Normans at the end of the 11th century.

Satyr mask: a carved motif decorating the knees of chair and table legs, or as a central feature on a frieze, during the early and mid 18th century. See *Mask.*

Scale ornament: see *Imbrication.*

Scaling: a pattern of fish-like scales, lightly carved, as surface decoration on the legs, arms and frames of early 18th century furniture. See also *Imbrication.*

SCALE-CUTTING.
GLASS

Scallop: see *Escallop.*

Scalloping or scolloping: a series of continuous semi-circles, convex side outwards, used as a decorative edging.

Scarab: in ancient Egypt, the winged beetle, *Scarabaeus sacer,* was the emblem of the god Khopri, and symbolised the sun, life, generative power, and resurrection. The beetle is represented with outstretched wings, and raised upper claws, holding a disc. As a religious motif, it was widely used in Egypt, on tombs, mummy-cases and ceilings, and later on seals and amulets, becoming eventually a token of good fortune in other Mediterranean countries, and losing its religious significance.

EGYPTIAN SCARABÆUS

Sciapod or sciapode: a fabulous creature in the form of a man with only one immense foot: when recumbent, and the leg raised, the foot was large enough to shelter the whole body of the sciapod. Very rarely this creature has been used as a medieval carved ornament: probably the only English example is on a bench end in the 15th century church of St Mary, at Dennington, Suffolk.

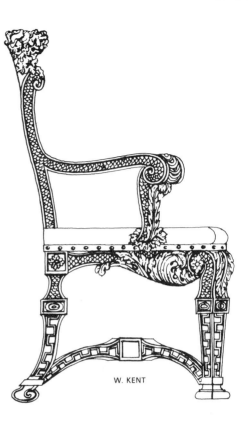

W. KENT

SUN-GOD. HYBRID form. EGYPTIAN. *circa* 1340 BC

NUREMBERG CHRONICLE 1493

189

Scorpio: the scorpion: the eighth sign of the Zodiac. See *Zodiacal devices*.

Scotia: a concave moulding: often used between two torus mouldings, *q.v.*, at the base of a column, where it casts a deep shadow. See *Moulding*.

Scroll or scrowl: a curvilinear motif, based on a C-curve, the ends terminating in tiny circles: of Graeco-Roman origin, the word is sometimes used to describe an Ionic volute. Used singly, or in series when a pattern of continuous scrolls forms an undulating band of spirals, each flowing from and into its neighbour: the scrolls may all run in the same direction, or be reversed, and embellished with a continuous curving meander, *q.v.*, or ornamental foliage, notably the acanthus, *q.v.*, when the points at which the spirals join are concealed by the stalk sheaths and leaves: presented thus, it occurs frequently in Roman ornament. Because it was identified with pagan design, the scroll was precluded from early Byzantine decoration, but it gradually assumed great importance, acquiring much Christian symbolism. The scroll motif has been widely used in the decoration of furniture, for example in a scroll chair back, a scroll foot, and a scrolled leg. See also *Braganza toe, Spiral, Swan-neck, Vitruvian scroll* and *Volute*.

GREEK: CHORAGIC MONUMENT of LYSICRATES

GREEK

'INHABITED SCROLL' WITH IBEX. NABATAEAN 200 BC

GREEK

SCROLL PATTERN DERIVED FROM COILED-WIRE. ROMAN.

GREEK

SCROLL-WORK. 2nd HALF 3rd Cent. AD. SASSANIAN

ROMAN

PERSIAN FAIENCE SCROLL-WORK

ROMAN MOSAIC SCROLL

SCROLL-WORK. NEOLITHIC TEMPLES. HAL TARXIEN. MALTA

ACANTHUS-LEAF SCROLL.   POMPEIAN. INTERLACED WITH LEAVES, FLOWERS AND ANIMALS

GOTHIC.   GERMAN.   THISTLE SCRO

'PEOPLED SCROLL' ROMAN
PAINTED WALL FRIEZE. VERULAMIUM. 2nd Cent. AD

CHINESE SCROLL-WORK

BYZANTINE.   ST SERGIUS.   CONSTANTINOPLE

LATE GOTHIC.   GERMAN.   THISTLE-SCROLL

ABBEY ST DENIS.   PARIS

SCROLL-LIKE.   HERALDIC MANTLING

PRINTED
SCROLL MARK.
circa 1825

VINE-SCROLL. LOMBARD VALLEY

PRINTED SCROLL MARK.
CAMBRIAN POTTERY

LATE GOTHIC. GERMAN SCROLLWORK

CHINESE PLANT SCROLL. 8th Cent.

RIBBON END

FISHTAIL SNUB-END　　SNUB-END　　HALF-PENNY SNUB-END　　BOLT-END　　LEAF-END　　FISHTAIL

[SCROLL—METAL :—*WROUGHT IRON*]

SCROLL LEGS. ENGLISH. *circa* 1685

SCROLLED FEET. CANDLE-STAND

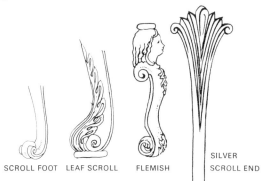

SCROLL FOOT   LEAF SCROLL   FLEMISH

SILVER
SCROLL END

Scroll moulding: see *Edge moulding.*

Scrolled pediment: see *Swan-neck.*

Scutcheon: see *Escutcheon.*

Seal of Solomon: see *David's shield.*

Seals: engraved seals were in use in ancient Egypt and the Middle East, and early forms were probably primitive trademarks. As a symbol of ownership and a form of signature, the seal remained in common use for centuries and still exercises these functions. In 12th century England, when it was generally employed to authenticate documents, the *secretum*, a personal as distinct from an official seal, owned by persons of high rank, was introduced. Seal devices were often complex, as a protection against imitation, and included naturalistic, religious and symbolic motifs, emblems of sovereignty, trade and commerce, and allegorical figures: with the development of heraldry, seals were increasingly engraved with personal and family armorial devices.

GUDEA of LAGASH'S. early BABYLONIAN
IMPRESSION from CYLINDER-SEAL

SEAL OF BOW CHURCH

GREAT SEAL OF UNITED STATES OF AMERICA 1782

INCOMPLETE PYRAMID SYMBOLIZES POSSIBILITIES
OF FURTHER DEVELOPMENT

EYE of PROVIDENCE and LIGHT of UNIVERSE

Seraph: like the cherub, *q.v.,* a member of the celestial hierarchy, particularly associated with love, purity and light. Usually shown with wings—in heraldry with six—and with a flaming heart or covered with eyes.

Serlian motif or serliana: see *Venetian window*.

Serpent: closely linked with dracontine legend, the serpent in the ancient world was an object of veneration, as a repository of great wisdom and power: prominent in Egyptian, Oriental, and Graeco-Roman mythology, and in South America, where the Toltec god, Quetzalcoatl, took the form of a huge feathered snake. In Christian art, the serpent lost its former beneficence, and became a symbol of Satan, evil, heresy, and sin. In classical ornament, the coiled serpent with tail in mouth was a usual form for a ring or bracelet: snakes adorned the rod of Aesculapius, *q.v.,* and the caduceus, *q.v.:* the complicated interlacing of ancient Scandinavian and Celtic ornament is a form of serpentine symbolism, also associated with dragon mythology, and later with the Christian cross (see *Runic knot*). Ecclesiastical sculpture, carving, and metalwork includes many representations of the snake: in heraldry it appears coiled, knotted, gliding, open-mouthed, fanged, and most often, twisted into a circle. See also *Asp, Dragon, Genius* and *Uraeus*.

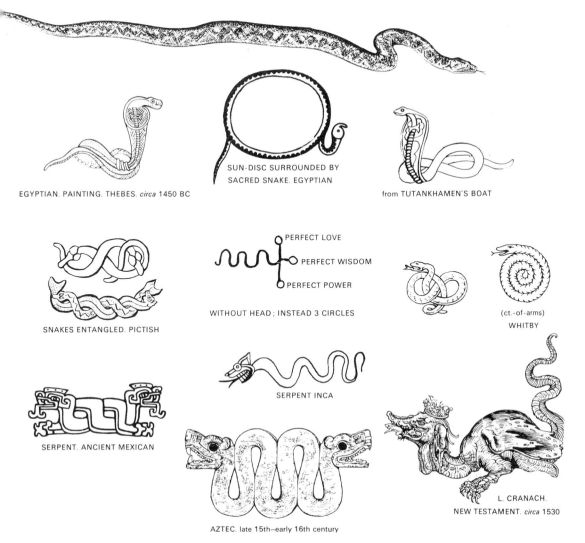

EGYPTIAN. PAINTING. THEBES. *circa* 1450 BC

SUN-DISC SURROUNDED BY
SACRED SNAKE. EGYPTIAN

from TUTANKHAMEN'S BOAT

SNAKES ENTANGLED. PICTISH

PERFECT LOVE
PERFECT WISDOM
PERFECT POWER

WITHOUT HEAD; INSTEAD 3 CIRCLES

(ct.-of-arms)
WHITBY

SERPENT. ANCIENT MEXICAN

SERPENT INCA

AZTEC. late 15th—early 16th century

L. CRANACH.
NEW TESTAMENT. *circa* 1530

195

DOUBLE-HEADED SERPENT

SERPENT NOWED.
HERALDIC

SERPENT AND CHILD.
DUKES OF MILAN.
HERALDIC

from BIBLE. WITTENBERG 1541

Shaft ring: see *Annulet.*

Shakefork: the heraldic term for a variation of the pall, *q.v.*, in which the limbs of the Y-shaped figure are pointed and end short of the edges of a shield.

Sharawadgi or sharawaggi: this word, first used in England by Sir William Temple in his *Essay on Gardening*, written about 1685, describes irregular or asymmetrical composition in decoration.

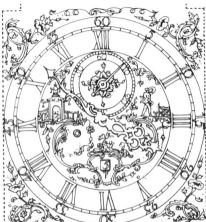

Shell: as a decorative motif, the escallop and nautilus (see these entries) have been used since Graeco-Roman times, and the shell ornament was characteristic of rococo, *q.v.* Among the Eight Buddhist Emblems of Happy Augury is a conch shell device, and the *buccinum* was the original inspiration for the trumpet known as a buccina, *q.v.* Different forms of shell motif were popular as carved decoration on furniture during the late 17th and throughout the 18th centuries. As a heraldic device, the escallop occurs most frequently, but whelk shells are also used. See also *Coquillage.*

SCALLOP SHELL. ROMAN MOSAIC. 2nd Cent. AD

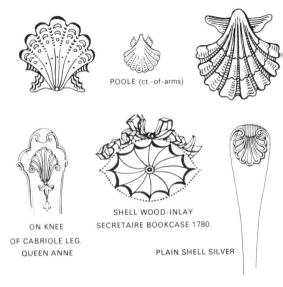

POOLE (ct.-of-arms)

ON KNEE
OF CABRIOLE LEG.
QUEEN ANNE

SHELL WOOD-INLAY
SECRETAIRE BOOKCASE 1780.

PLAIN SHELL SILVER

Shield: originally an essential part of defensive armour, the shield was used for displaying armorial bearings and personal devices to identify the bearer. It assumed and retained an important place in heraldry, and the shape has played a significant part in heraldic design. The heraldic shield is divided by lines, *q.v.*, into fields, upon which appear the charges that form a coat of arms: the dexter side covers the right side of the bearer, the sinister side covers his left side, and to a spectator these terms appear reversed. A shield with rounded base, indented to form a waist, and with a pointed top, is an important Buddhist symbol, often combined with the triratna, *q.v.*

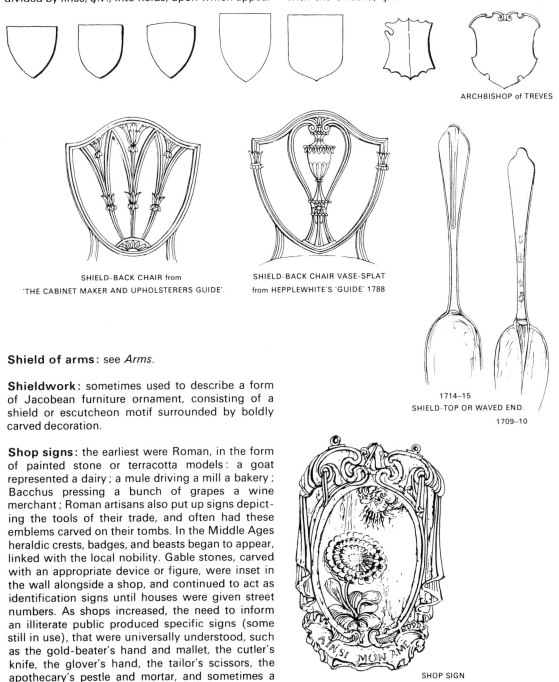

ARCHBISHOP of TREVES

SHIELD-BACK CHAIR from
'THE CABINET MAKER AND UPHOLSTERERS GUIDE'.

SHIELD-BACK CHAIR VASE-SPLAT
from HEPPLEWHITE'S 'GUIDE' 1788

1714–15
SHIELD-TOP OR WAVED END.
1709–10

Shield of arms: see *Arms*.

Shieldwork: sometimes used to describe a form of Jacobean furniture ornament, consisting of a shield or escutcheon motif surrounded by boldly carved decoration.

Shop signs: the earliest were Roman, in the form of painted stone or terracotta models: a goat represented a dairy; a mule driving a mill a bakery; Bacchus pressing a bunch of grapes a wine merchant; Roman artisans also put up signs depicting the tools of their trade, and often had these emblems carved on their tombs. In the Middle Ages heraldic crests, badges, and beasts began to appear, linked with the local nobility. Gable stones, carved with an appropriate device or figure, were inset in the wall alongside a shop, and continued to act as identification signs until houses were given street numbers. As shops increased, the need to inform an illiterate public produced specific signs (some still in use), that were universally understood, such as the gold-beater's hand and mallet, the cutler's knife, the glover's hand, the tailor's scissors, the apothecary's pestle and mortar, and sometimes a rebus. See also *Inn signs*.

SHOP SIGN
PLUS MARIGOLD

SHOP CARD

Siren: in Greek mythology, a sea nymph, half woman, half bird. The sirens were supposed to have lured sailors to destruction by their song, and when out-classed by the singing of Orpheus sailing with the Argonauts, they plunged into the sea and were turned to rocks.

TWIN-TAILED SIREN.
ROMAN PAINTING

GERMAN RENAISSANCE.
LUNEBERG MUSEUM

LOUVRE

Sixfoil: heraldic term for a six-petalled flower.

Skull: also called a death's head, emblematic of death and decay: usually appearing in conjunction with crossbones, *q.v.*, and sometimes with an hour glass and the figure of Time holding a scythe. Frequently used on 16th century tombstones in England, though not in the mid 17th, nor was it used again until the 18th century as a tomb and memorial ornament, and an undertaker's shop sign. In heraldry, a skull sometimes replaced the crest over the shield in a funeral escutcheon, to indicate that the dead person was the last of his line. The skull and crossbones on the flag of a vessel indicated a pirate (see *Pirate flag*), and the device has also been used on labels of containers of poisonous substances.

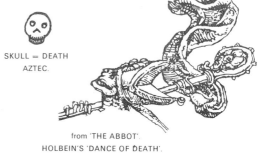

SKULL = DEATH
AZTEC.

from 'THE ABBOT'.
HOLBEIN'S 'DANCE OF DEATH'.

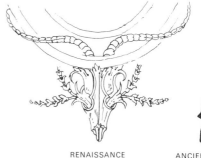

RENAISSANCE   ANCIENT MEXICAN

Snake: see *Serpent*.

Snarework: see *Guilloche*.

Solar symbols: see *Sun signs*.

Spades: the device used for one of the four suit signs on English playing cards: the French *piques* are identical: developed from the leaves (*blatt* or *grün*) and swords (*spadi* and *espados*) of the German, Italian and Spanish packs respectively. The sign has at various times represented knights and aristocrats, and symbolised justice and violence. See *Playing cards* and *Suit signs*.

Spandril: the triangular space enclosed by the curve of an arch, a horizontal line drawn through its apex and a vertical line from its springing.

Spandril-piece: the small cast-brass ornament used in the spandril of a clock face : in the triangular area delimited by the circle of the dial of the face and the right angle of the clock's casing.

BRACKET-CLOCK. KINGWOOD. *circa* 1670

THOMAS TOMPION. *circa* 1690

LONG-CASE CLOCK. *circa* 1700
FINIALS and QUARTER COLUMN at back.

Spectacle pattern: a device of considerable antiquity and uncertain meaning, found on Celtic crosses in Scotland : two circles, connected by an upper and lower curved line, the whole crossed by an oblique line, itself embellished.

from the ABERLEMNO CROSS

Sphinx: a fabulous monster, of Egyptian origin, later adopted with variations, by the Assyrians, Greeks and Romans. In ancient Egypt it was regarded as a sacred representation of the power and attributes of certain deities and Pharoahs, and was used always as a religious symbol and never ornamentally. The Egyptian sphinx was male, with the recumbent body of a lion, and usually with the bearded wigged head of a man (supposedly the reigning Pharoah), but also with the head of a ram, hawk or falcon (see *Andro-sphinx, Crio-sphinx, Hieraco-sphinx*), sometimes with hands instead of paws. The Assyrian version was originally a winged lion or bull, with the head of a luxuriantly bearded man; later Assyrian variations had a woman's head on the recumbent body of a winged lion. The Greek version, later adopted by the Romans, was also a winged recumbent lion with the head and bust of a woman. The religious significance of the Egyptian sphinx was forgotten, and it was used as an ornamental device by the Greeks and Romans; in French and Italian Renaissance decoration (though much distorted); in the late 18th and early 19th century revival of French interest in Egyptian antiquities (see *Empire style*); and in its pure classical form by such practitioners of the Neo-Classical style, *q.v.*, as Robert Adam (1728–92).

EGYPTIAN

GREEK

*WINGED AND SKIRTED. NIMRUD

FRENCH EMPIRE

WINGED SPHINX. IRAN. 2nd Cent. BC

from an ETRUSCAN TOMB

POMPEIAN

ROMAN

Spindle-and-baluster: an alternative term for baluster-and-spindle. See *Baluster*.

*from 'THE NEW BIBLE DICTIONARY' ed. J. D. DOUGLAS. Fig XXX, by kind permission of THE INTER-VARSITY PRESS. Also illustration to BULL= double capital; MENORAH=Roman and PAPYRUS=cyperus papyrus.

Spindle-and-bead: a term used by cabinet-makers and turners, for a moulding enrichment consisting of a series of alternate astragals or beads, and short rounded spindles.

Spiral: a continuous coiled line; a circular motif, used singly or in series, or combined with other curved flowing lines to form an intricate pattern. An ancient device closely linked with the primitive sun-snake, *q.v.*, it appears on Bronze Age weapons, armour, and utensils: used in Chinese decoration of the 13th to 10th centuries BC and known as thunder pattern. Characteristic of Celtic ornamentation when, starting from a fixed point, two or three spiral lines form an intricate design of coils within coils. (See *Trumpet pattern*). In classical decoration the spiral is the basis of the scroll and volute (see these entries): in Gothic ornament spiral foliage devices adorned crockets, capitals and spandrils.

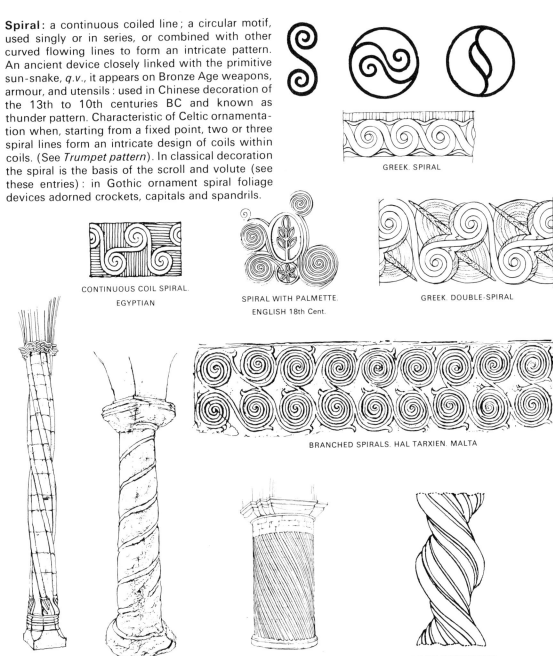

GREEK. SPIRAL

CONTINUOUS COIL SPIRAL.
EGYPTIAN

SPIRAL WITH PALMETTE.
ENGLISH 18th Cent.

GREEK. DOUBLE-SPIRAL

BRANCHED SPIRALS. HAL TARXIEN. MALTA

SPIRAL-COLUMN.
BRUNSWICK. 15th Cent.

SPIRAL-DECORATION.
NORMAN COLUMN. NORWICH

ITALIAN RENAISSANCE.
PALAZZO MUNICIPALE. PERUGIA

Spiral turning: a variation of barley sugar twist, *q.v.*, in which the decorative turning (see *Turned ornament*), took the form of a tighter spiral around the legs and stretchers of late 17th and early 18th century furniture: a closer and more delicate spiral twist appeared after the mid 18th century on bed-posts and the pillars of claw tables.

Split baluster: a baluster, *q.v.*, split vertically and applied as surface decoration: the split may be exactly central, or off centre, so that an exact half or more of a section may be employed. Used on furniture and chimney pieces during the late 16th and throughout the 17th centuries. See also *Split turning*.

SPIRAL from 4-POSTER BED.
ENGLISH. 1755

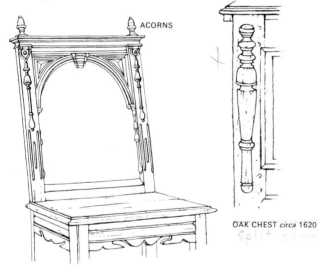

ACORNS

OAK CHEST *circa* 1620

ARCADED CHAIR: ENGLISH mid 17th Cent.

Split bobbin: a bobbin split centrally, and applied as surface decoration on mid and late 17th century furniture. See *Bobbin turning* and *Split turning*.

Split turning: turned units, split centrally, either in a half or larger section, and applied as surface ornament on late 16th and 17th century joined chests, cupboards and chair backs: the process was used by country makers until the mid 19th century. See *Turned ornament*.

Spotting: powdered, *q.v.*, decoration, forming equidistant, widely-spaced geometrical motifs.

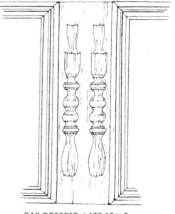

OAK DRESSER. LATE 17th Cent.

Spur: the basically triangular decoration from the circular base moulding on, and to the corners of, the plinth of a Gothic column.

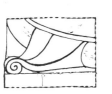
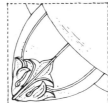
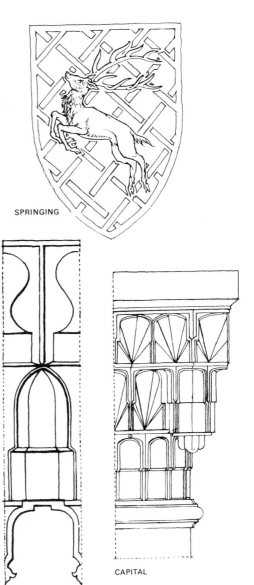

Stafford knot: see *Knot*. Well known as a pottery mark.

Square: a primal figure of four equal sides and four right angles. Apart from universal decorative application, is emblematic of the heavens, the elements, the four Evangelists, the Earth's four corners: the Inca Empire under Pachacutec was known as 'The Land of Four Corners'; and the four compass points. The innate stability and order of its form has given rise to such colloquial expressions as 'fair and square', 'all square'.

Stag: an important heraldic device: the stag, with a full head of antlers, is usually shown leaping.

SPRINGING

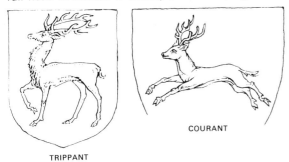

COURANT

TRIPPANT

Stalactite ornament: used in Saracenic architecture, where abrupt angles were concealed by stalactite-shaped vertical carved motifs, or brackets, and also in the Rococo style of the 18th century.

CAPITAL

203

Standard: this flag is named after the vertical pole from which it flew. The original heraldic standard, first used in the reign of Edward III, was long, narrow, tapering or double-tailed: it bore heraldic devices, badges, livery colours, mottoes, but not a coat of arms, though modern heraldic standards do display the coat of arms, badge and motto. Present day military standards are almost square, and the rectangular flag known as the Royal Standard is more truly a banner, *q.v.*

HENRY V

EGYPTIAN.

ASSYRIAN

ROMAN

Star: a geometrical motif, formed by joined points placed equidistantly within the circumference of a circle: usually possessing five, six, eight, or ten points. A primitive sun sign, *q.v.*: used in ancient Egypt to decorate the ceilings of tombs and temples, five-pointed and arranged in patterns of square or equilateral triangles. As a ceiling ornament, and a device used in powdered, *q.v.*, decoration, it has long been popular. The star has been employed as a Christian and Jewish symbol, and appears also in the symbolism of witchcraft and alchemy. In heraldry, it is called an astroid or estoile, and has six or more straight or wavy rays: the Scottish straight-rayed molet, *q.v.*, when unpierced, is known as a star, and as a molet when pierced. See also *David's shield* and *Pentacle*.

Star of David: see *David's shield*.

Step ornament: a pattern of rectangles, arranged diagonally or in squares, that formed a geometrical motif frequently used in Byzantine and Romanesque mosaic decoration.

Stepped fret: a decorative motif used by the Aztecs of Central America, *c*. AD 800.

DOUBLE-STAR. BABYLONIAN.
LOUVRE MUSEUM

SARACENIC MOSAIC. MONREALE

Stiff leaf: used in Early English Gothic decoration as a continuous band carved on foliated capitals: based on the trefoil, *q.v.*, the three-lobed leaves have a strong mid-rib, or a hollow in the central lobe: in more elaborate versions the tips of the lobes curl over towards each other.

Stopped channel fluting: flutes that are partially filled with a convex moulding or ornament. See *Fluting*.

Strap-and-jewel-work: modern term for the decorative use of turned ornament, such as balusters, lozenges, and other components of strapwork, *q.v.*, split and applied to a flat surface. Used on furniture during the 17th century. See *Split turning*.

Strapwork or strap ornament: intricate patterns of interlaced lines and scrolls, interspersed with geometrical figures, probably originated in Antwerp early in the 16th century. By the end of that century it had spread over Europe, with slight regional variations, and was popularised by Flemish and German copy books. Arabesques, grotesques, cartouches, shields, diamonds, lozenges, and oval forms were framed by strap-shaped members, often with scrolled ends or fitted into rings. Architectural motifs, classic columns, mouldings, ornaments and broken frets were later incorporated, and strapwork was illustrated in the works of Jan Vredeman de Vries (1527–c. 1604) of Antwerp, and Wendel Dietterlin (1550–99) of Strasbourg: the plates published by Dietterlin were complex, ornate and overpowering. Strapwork was widely used during the 16th and 17th centuries, on ceilings, pilasters, panels, plasterwork, furniture and chimney-pieces, and by enamellers and goldsmiths. A modern term, seldom used, is prismatic ornament.

FRENCH. CARVED PANEL

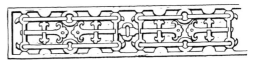

CARVED PANEL. LATE 16th Cent.

ELIZABETHAN. LATE 16th Cent. PLASTERWORK

16th Cent. PANEL
FRENCH.

ELIZABETHAN. LATE 16th Cent. PLASTERWORK

205

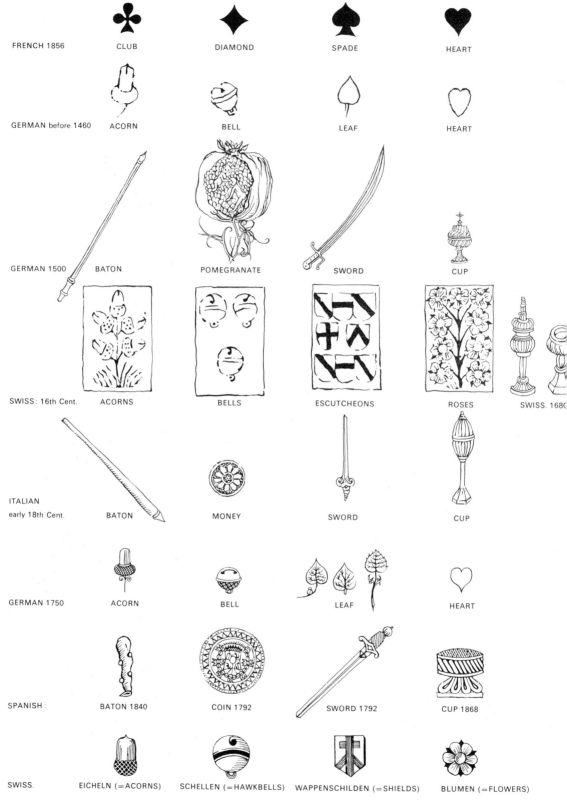

FRENCH 1856	CLUB	DIAMOND	SPADE	HEART
GERMAN before 1460	ACORN	BELL	LEAF	HEART
GERMAN 1500	BATON	POMEGRANATE	SWORD	CUP
SWISS: 16th Cent.	ACORNS	BELLS	ESCUTCHEONS	ROSES	SWISS. 168(
ITALIAN early 18th Cent.	BATON	MONEY	SWORD	CUP
GERMAN 1750	ACORN	BELL	LEAF	HEART
SPANISH:	BATON 1840	COIN 1792	SWORD 1792	CUP 1868
SWISS.	EICHELN (=ACORNS)	SCHELLEN (=HAWKBELLS)	WAPPENSCHILDEN (=SHIELDS)	BLUMEN (=FLOWERS)

Strawberry Hill Gothic: a modern term, applied to the light, gay, whimsical versions of Gothic that prevailed during the second half of the 18th century. Derived from the elegant experiments in the Gothic taste, made by Horace Walpole (1717–97) at his house, Strawberry Hill, Middlesex, in collaboration with Richard Bentley (1708–82) and John Chute (1701–76). See also *Gothic Revival*.

Striges: see *Fluting*.

String-course: a narrow continuous horizontal band or moulding on the face of a building. It may be decoratively carved and projecting; but when of brick and built-in is effected by a change of colour only.

Struck moulding: a moulding worked directly on a surface, as distinct from a planted moulding, *q.v.* See also *Stuck moulding*.

Strung coin: see *Money moulding*.

Stuck moulding: although a corruption of the term struck moulding, *q.v.*, it is occasionally used as an alternative term for planted moulding, *q.v.*

Subordinary: heraldic term for a variation of an ordinary, *q.v.*, to which it ranks as a device of secondary importance.

Suit signs: very early Chinese playing cards, *q.v.*, bore devices of coins, strings, myriads and tens of myriads, that imitated the value symbols on the paper currency then in use: these devices distinguished the four suits: as playing cards spread throughout the East and to Europe, the symbolism of the signs was lost, they acquired new meanings, and many variations in suit names and symbols appeared. The modern suit signs of spades, clubs, diamonds and hearts can be traced to the signs on 14th century Italian and 15th century Spanish cards, where they had become swords (spades), batons (clubs), coins or danari (diamonds) and cups or chalices (hearts). In 15th century France, the signs appeared as lance points (spades), clover leaves (clubs), arrowheads (diamonds) and hearts; German suit signs of the 16th century showed leaves (spades), acorns (clubs), hawks or bells (diamonds), and hearts. The joker plays no part in these ancient devices: of mid 19th century American origin, it first appeared on playing cards in 1887.

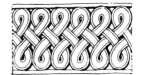

CARVED STRING. MUSEUM BRESCIA

Sun: a planetary symbol: also an heraldic device, sometimes given a human face, and surrounded by straight or wavy rays. It may be shown rising, setting, or shining from behind a cloud. The primitive religious symbols connected with the sun are dealt with under sun signs, *q.v.*

RISING SUN

DEMI-SUN IN HIS SPLENDOUR

SUN IN HIS SPLENDOUR

Sun god sign

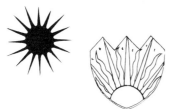

Sun god sign: a primitive sun sign, *q.v.*, consisting of an equilateral cross, sometimes with a central circle.

Sun signs: sun worship practised by primitive peoples continued in other forms and within many religions, and innumerable devices symbolising the sun and associated deities were devised. The origin of many present-day motifs may be found in sun signs of extreme antiquity, whose old meaning has long been forgotten: these symbolic representations, first used in primitive nature worship, survive as forms of geometrical decoration based on the circle, line, and S-curve. They include the star, sun god sign, sun-snake, swastika, triskele and wheel cross. See these entries.

SUN-GOD EMBLEM.
from CANAANITE HAZOR
14th—13th Cent. BC

SUN EMBLEMS. ANCIENT MEXICO

Sun-snake: one of the early sun signs, *q.v.*, in the form of an S, sometimes with a small circle in its centre. When additional S-shaped arms were added it became the double sun-snake or swastika, *q.v.*, and triskele, *q.v.*, and is the basis of spiral and scroll devices.

Sun wheel: see *Tchakra*.

Sunburst: American term for a lunette ornament with conventional sun rays: used on mid 18th century colonial furniture. In heraldry the term describes a device of the sun's rays appearing from behind a cloud, used as a badge by the English kings, Edward III and Richard II.

SUNBURST. BADGE of RICHARD II

SUNBURST

SUNBURST

Supporters: heraldic term for the ornamental accessories, in the form of human, animal or fabulous creatures, which appear in pairs, flanking a shield: very rarely a shield has a single supporter at the back. See *Heraldic ornament*.

Sunk moulding: a moulding that lies flush and covers a joint between two surfaces with different levels.

Surmount: a term used to describe cresting, *q.v.*, on a chair back.

ENGLISH OAK CHAIR. 1630

Swag: sometimes used as an alternative for festoon, *q.v.*, it specifically refers to a festoon composed of folds of draped cloth. Of classical origin, this motif was widely used from the late 16th to the late 18th centuries.

Swan: genus cygnus. Large web-footed water bird, with long, elegantly curved neck. and in most species snow-white plumage. Sacred to Apollo and Venus; symbol of excellence; in heraldry of gracefulness. Black, device of Josephine Bonaparte.

(HERALDIC) NAIANT

Swan-neck: in architecture, a term for ogee, *q.v.*, shapes, particularly applied to the curve in a staircase handrail where it joins a newel post. In cabinet-making, a broken pediment formed by two S-curves, facing inwards, is known as a swan-neck or scrolled pediment; in America as a goose-neck.

MIRROR. ENGLISH *circa* 1730

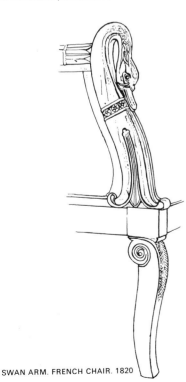

SWAN ARM. FRENCH CHAIR. 1820

SWAN-NECK or BROKEN PEDIMENT. BUREAU. mid 18th Cent.

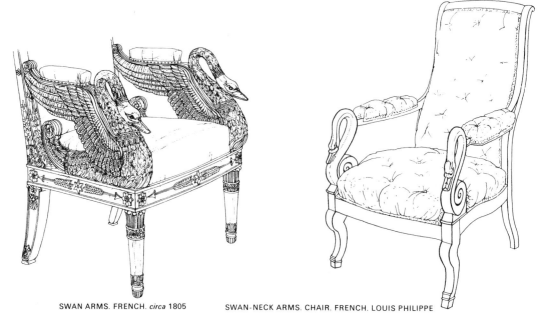

SWAN ARMS. FRENCH. *circa* 1805   SWAN-NECK ARMS. CHAIR. FRENCH. LOUIS PHILIPPE

Swash letters: typographical term for decorative italic letters with additional curls and flourishes, used in conjunction with ordinary italic letters: normally appearing at the beginning and end of a word, and chiefly used on title-pages.

ABFFGHKKLNOPYz   CASLON

ABCDFGHJMNPQ QRU&   GARAMOND

Swash turning: ornamental turning cut obliquely to the axis of a leg or stretcher. See *Turned ornament.*

Swastika: since prehistoric times this primitive sun sign, *q.v.*, has appeared with innumerable variations in pagan mythology and religious symbolism. In ancient nature worship the swastika was of great importance, representing the sun itself, planetary rotation, the regular procession of the seasons, the harmonious correlation of the forces of nature. Basically, it consists of two S-curves at right angles (sometimes called a tetraskele): the device called a double sun-snake is a multi-armed curved swastika: a Greek cross with the extremities bent backwards at right angles is the better known form, and the term 'gammadion' refers to this variation, which has the appearance of four Greek gammas joined at the bases. Many theories exist about its true meaning, but in general it has denoted good fortune, happiness and well-being, and remains a good luck emblem in the East. Used ornamentally, in the ancient and classical world, the device has adorned coins, pottery, mosaics, tombs, funerary monuments, and in association with the Christian cross, has been found in the catacombs and on Celtic gravestones. Alternative names include croix cramponée, croix gammée, the Anglo-Saxon fylfot (four-footed), and Thor's hammer.

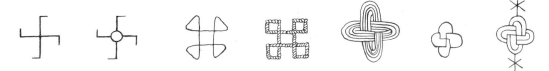

SWASTIKA IN CENTRE OF LABRYNTHINE DESIGNS KNOWN AS SOLOMON'S KNOT: i.e. WITHOUT BEGINNING OR END

Swelled rule: in typography, a decorative rule, *q.v.*, thick in the middle, tapering to a fine line at each end: the swollen central part may be engraved with ornament, or may have a central gap filled by small ornamental devices.

Sword: as an heraldic device, usually shown straight-bladed, cross-hilted, and unsheathed: an emblem of Christian saints and martyrs, including St Paul, St Alban, St Adrian, and the Archangel Michael. Crossed swords have been used as a pottery and ceramic mark in England and on the Continent.

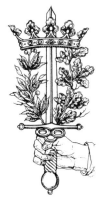

HERALDIC

DEVICE from TAROT CARD

Symbolic ornament: ornament that conveys an idea or association of ideas, by means of a sign, emblem, device or figure. The religious emblems of the ancient world and the Middle Ages were used, not as decoration, but to represent deities and their

211

attributes, natural forces, virtues, vices, and to reinforce faith and piety. Renaissance ornament was often symbolic, but was wholly decorative in character.

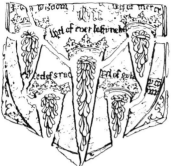

SACRED PASSION. STAINED GLASS

SACRED PASSION SYMBOLS. WOOD

SYMBOLS OF SUPREME POWER.
EGYPTIAN. SCEPTRE AND WHIP

MANDORLA
SYMBOL OF THE INTERSECTION OF THE
TWO SPHERES : HEAVEN and EARTH

SHRI- YANTRA MANDALA

CALENDAR STONE. AZTEC. 1481

MANDALA PATTERN=GROUND PLAN OF
THE BOROBUDUR TEMPLE

FRAMING OF A MANDALA

THUNDERBOLT FROM NIMRUD RELIEF

THUNDERBOLT. NABATEAN

Symmetrical fret: a simple fret with a pattern formed by a continuous series of equally spaced horizontal and vertical keys. See *Fret*.

T

Tablet: in architecture and cabinet-making, a flat surface, slab or panel with a decorative device or inscription carved on it : in medieval architecture the term denoted a band or label, *q.v.* : in the late 18th and early 19th centuries the name tablet-top was given to a chair with a shaped tablet forming the top rail of the back.

ARM CHAIR. REGENCY. WITH LATTICE BELOW TABLET

Tablet flower: sometimes used to describe a four-leaved flower, *q.v.* with four petals surrounding a raised or sunk centre, often employed as a moulding enrichment in Gothic architecture.

Tace: see *Tau cross*.

Tall cross: see *Tau cross*.

Talon-and-ball: see *Claw-and-ball*.

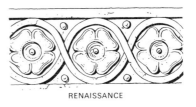

RENAISSANCE

Talon moulding: see *Ogee*.

Tarot: the collective name given to the pack of 108 cards that includes 22 so-called 'high' cards bearing allegorical pictures, as follows: the illusionist, the Popess, the Empress, the Emperor, the Pope, the lovers, the chariot, justice, the hermit, the wheel of fortune, force, the hanging man, death, temperance, the devil, the tower, the star, the moon, the sun, judgement, the world, the fool. The origin of the tarot pack is obscure : it has been suggested that the 22 pictorial devices formed part of ancient Egyptian hieroglyphic records, where they possessed important philosophical meanings ; or that the pack was a subsequent addition to the 52-card pack of playing cards, *q.v.*, brought from the Far East by travellers and gypsies, and was used for the Italian game of *tarrochi*, still played in southern and central Europe ; another theory is that they were a form of educational game for children in an illiterate world. The 22 pictorial cards became closely linked with fortune-telling, witchcraft, black magic and heresy and later, with mathematical science and theories : modern court cards have almost certainly developed from them. See *Playing cards, Sword*.

Tau cross: a T-shaped cross, the limbs often slightly splayed : when they are straight it is sometimes called a tall cross. Other names are gibbet cross, from its likeness to a form of primitive gibbet, St Anthony's cross, *q.v.*, and tace.

Tauro-centaur: see *Bucentaur*.

Taurus: the bull : the second sign of the Zodiac. See *Zodiacal devices*.

Tchakra: an ancient symbol connected with sun-worship, also called the sun wheel or wheel of fire : as the sacred wheel of Brahmanism, it is an emblem of Brahma and Vishnu. Alternative spelling Chakra : see *Wheel*.

Tears: in glassmaking, the air bubbles deliberately trapped in the stems, bases or finials of drinking vessels to provide decoration.

Telamones: see *Atlantes*.

Term, terminal figure or terminus: also called a herm or therm, this is a column or pedestal, round or rectangular, tapering towards the base, surmounted by a carved head or bust, of a man, woman, or pagan deity. Fireplace openings and chimney-pieces in the 16th and 17th centuries were often flanked by terms: also used on overmantels and bedheads, and in the 18th century, crowned by a capital, as stands for lamps or candelabra, or to support sculptured groups used in parks and gardens as ornamental boundary marks.

CHIPPENDALE'S DIRECTOR 3rd EDITION
TERM FOR BUSTOS

from ENGLISH early 17th Cent. CHIMNEY-PIECE   GARDEN EXAMPLE

Tetraskele or tetraskelion: a swastika, *q.v.*, with rounded ends to the four backward curving arms.

Therm: see *Term*.

Therm window: see *Diocletian window*.

Thor's hammer: see *Swastika*.

Thread-and-shell: an ornamental termination on spoons and skewers, used in the 17th and 18th centuries, consisting of a shell device enclosed between two narrow lines ending in spirals.

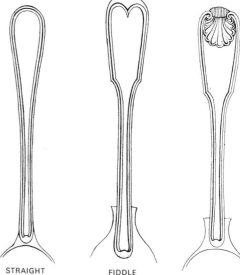

STRAIGHT
DOUBLE THREADED   FIDDLE
DOUBLE THREADED   SHELL and THREAD

Thread circuit: see *Trailed ornament.*

Three-legged cross: see *Triskele.*

Thunder pattern: see *Spiral.*

Thyrsus: a long light staff, entwined with leaves or ribbons: the ornamental head usually consisted of a pine cone, *q.v.*, but sometimes of ivy or vine leaves: originally a spear, the point concealed by the decorative head, this rod was carried during rites and festivals in honour of Dionysus or Bacchus.

from CAMEO. NAPLES MUSEUM

Tiger: in heraldry, when this animal appears in its natural form it is known as a Bengal tiger: the heraldic tiger or tyger, is more like a lion, with a downward tusk at the end of its nose.

HERALDIC TYGER

Toad back moulding: cabinet-maker's term for a moulding with two ogee, *q.v.* curves separated by a bead, which suggests the shape of a toad's back. Used on chair and table legs in the late 18th century. See *Moulding.*

Tondino: an archaic term for astragal, *q.v.*

Tooth moulding or tooth ornament: see *Dog tooth ornament.*

Torse: see *Crest-wreath.*

Torus: a large convex moulding, sometimes called a round, generally used in column bases. See *Moulding.*

Tracery: ornamental stonework formed in the upper part of a Gothic window, by the branching and interlacing of the mullions: also used to describe the surface decoration of vaulted ceilings, panelling, blind arches, canopies, and the glazing bars of bookcases and china cabinets. The word was first used in the 17th century.

Trademarks: in classical times, makers of pottery and building materials stamped their goods with a distinctive mark; later, artists and craftsmen marked their work with individual devices, that often took the form of a rebus, *q.v.* The modern trademark, that may be a rebus, or a design symbolic of the product, acts protectively against imitations, and confirms that the product is the work of a specific maker.

WILLIAM CAXTON'S. 1487–89

C: 1879–20th Cent.

BURLEIGH WARE EST. 1851 MADE IN ENGLAND

1930

Baguley Rockingham Works

1842–55

DENBY TRADE MARK CHEF WARE

1895–1910

BOVEY POTTERY ENGLAND

1949–56

BRITISH ANCHOR 1884–1913

B and Co: 1896–1900

POOLE ENGLAND

TRADE MARK EBD BURSLEM.

1875–92

by kind permission of
MARKS & SPENCER LTD:

Trade tokens

by kind permission of
CALLARD & BOWSER LTD

WARWICKSHIRE

CORNWALL

YORKSHIRE

Trade tokens: this form of local or regional currency, as opposed to the legal currency of the realm, was used intermittently in England from the reign of Edward I until 1821: in order to meet a shortage of low-value coinage, it was minted by employers and traders as small change, that was accepted regionally: the largest issues were in the mid 17th, end of the 18th, and beginning of the 19th centuries. Trade tokens bore a great variety of devices that form an historical and industrial record: they included representations of national and local figures, pictorial interpretations of political slogans, and scenes of agricultural and industrial life and activities.

DERBYSHIRE

PERTHSHIRE

STAFFORDSHIRE

by kind permission of B. A. SEABY LTD

WILTSHIRE

FLINTSHIRE

IRELAND

Trail: see *Vignette.*

Trailed ornament or trailing: in glassmaking, the ornamentation of a surface by a pattern of narrow looped threads of glass applied and melted in: known as thread circuit when they decorate the rim or neck of a vessel.

Treacle moulding: cabinet-maker's term for a moulding of quarter round (see *Boultin*) section, hollowed on the underside, and used on the lower edge of a hinged lid, that can then be gripped and raised. See *Moulding.*

Trecento: Italian art and ornament of the 14th century, that marked the transition from medieval to Renaissance forms. A combination of Byzantine, Saracenic, Gothic and classical architecture and decoration, the Trecento style is characterized by intricate tracery, formalised foliage, interlacing and rounded arches. See also *Cinquecento* and *Quattrocento.*

Tree of life: see *Sacred tree.*

Trefoil: an architectural and heraldic term for a figure of three equal arcs or lobes, separated by cusps, *q.v.* A motif in Gothic tracery, panelling and carved woodwork; sometimes called a cockshead. In Byzantine art it appeared as a variation of the nimbus, *q.v.*, a symbol of the Trinity, and was adopted as such by St Patrick. In heraldry, the three-lobed leaf is usually shown with a short stalk attached. See also *Foil* and *Trefoil foliage.*

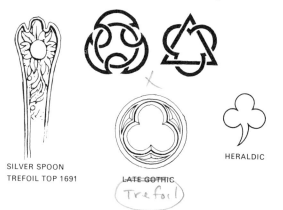

SILVER SPOON
TREFOIL TOP 1691

LATE GOTHIC
Trefoil

HERALDIC

Trefoil foliage: also called Early English leaf, a Gothic foliage motif of twining three-lobed leaves, frequently used to decorate capitals.

Trellis: a rectilinear arrangement of thin wooden or metal slats, intersecting each other at right angles or diagonally: a term often used as an alternative to lattice work, *q.v.* It has been suggested that the device originated with the pattern formed by the alternating strands of primitive weaving.

Tresse: a term sometimes used to describe interlaced bandelets, *q.v.*, that adorn mouldings.

Tressure: heraldic term for a narrow border, usually double, within the edges of a shield: it may incorporate fleur-de-lys motifs.

Triad: a decorative device composed of three comma-like shapes, possibly related to the triskele, *q.v.*: the Japanese 'mitsu tomoe'.

Triangle: a figure bounded by three straight lines: a basic decorative motif, used universally. Symbolically, represents to Christians the concept of The Trinity: to the Babylonians the Universe, Heaven and Earth. Symbol of the body, mind and spirit of the human family: the Egyptian hieroglyph for the Moon. Three triangles meeting at a central point was an ancient symbol for the Godhead.

Trident: a three-pronged spear, borne as a sceptre in representations of the Hindu god, Siva, the Greek Poseidon and Roman Neptune: used as an heraldic and decorative device symbolising dominion over the sea: as a ceramic mark it has appeared on Nantgarw and Swansea porcelain. Possibly originating as a primitive representation of lightning, the motif has a close affinity with the trisula and Buddhist triratna, *q.v.* The trident was used in the Roman Empire as a gladiator's weapon, a goad for horses and, in the form of a three-pronged fork, as a fish spear.

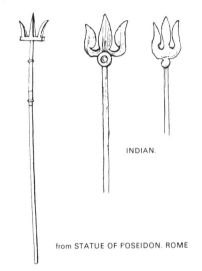

INDIAN.

from STATUE OF POSEIDON. ROME

Trifid: an ornamental device used during the 17th and 18th centuries on forks and spoons, in which the ends were divided into three sections by deep clefts or notches: sometimes called dog's nose pattern.

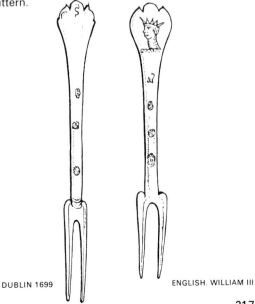

DUBLIN 1699   ENGLISH. WILLIAM III

Triga: a sculptured group consisting of a chariot drawn by three horses, and a charioteer.

Trigram: a device composed of three lines, or of three strokes, running parallel to each other: the word also means a three-letter inscription, and is a generic term for any figure composed of three strokes. An ancient Buddhist divinatory symbol known as the Eight Trigrams, contains the Yang and Yin, *q.v.*, device in the centre.

SKY

VAPOUR OR DAMPNESS

FIRE OR LIGHT

THUNDER

WIND

WATER

MOUNTAINS

EARTH

PA KUA or EIGHT TRIGRAMS

Triple guilloche: see *Guilloche*.

Triple open twist: see *Open twist*.

Triquetra: a three-pointed device of three equal arcs of circles interlaced to form a continuous figure. Of primitive origin, this motif was widely employed in Celtic art. Also symbolic of the Trinity. The word is sometimes used as an alternative for triskele, *q.v.*

Triquetrum: a primitive device in the form of three radiating axes, associated with the rotary movement of the sun, and having an affinity with the sacred wheel of Hinduism and Buddhism.

Triratna: this trident-shaped device, an important Buddhist symbol, appears over gateways and entrances in the East, often in combination with the Buddhist wheel and shield emblems, and sometimes with a human face. See also *Triskele*.

Triskele or triskelion: a three-armed figure that developed from a Y-shaped primitive sun sign, *q.v.*, symbolic of rotary motion: the arms may be angular, or end in curves or scrolls. Sometimes called a triquetra, this ubiquitous device, with many variations, was usually connected with the worship of pagan sun deities: it has been suggested that the arms were transformed, first into the legs of animals sacred to sun gods, and then into the three revolving human legs joined at the thighs (sometimes called the three-legged cross) that is a familiar version of the sign. Various theories exist to account for its adoption as the emblem of Sicily and the Isle of Man: the three-legged triskele was a coin and decorative device in Greece, *c.* 600 BC, and a little later in the Greek colony of Sicily: here (where it has been known as the sign of Trinacria, the ancient name of Sicily, literally land of three capes), the shape of the island may have influenced its adoption. It appears on 14th century monuments and regalia of the Isle of Man, and its migration there may be connected with Henry III of England's short reign as King of Sicily, and the annexation of the Isle of Man from Norway by Alexander III of Scotland in 1266. See also *Swastika*.

Trisula: an ancient Eastern symbol, of obscure meaning. In its simplest form it consists of a disc surmounted by a figure that resembles the shape of the Greek *omega*, but this basic shape is barely recognisable in the numerous and elaborate variations that have been discovered. It has appeared as a religious emblem of the Hindu god, Siva, and notably in Buddhism, where it is linked to the triratna, *q.v.*: throughout the Far and Middle East as an ornamental adornment of balustrades and porticoes, jewellery, and as a coin device: and in Greek mythological ornament: the trident, caduceus and winged globe (see these entries) are closely affiliated.

Triton: a merman: the upper part of the body that of a man, the lower of a fish: used as an heraldic device, and in maritime ornament. In Greek mythology, Triton was the son of Poseidon.

GREEK

from ETRUSCAN EMPHORA

GREEK

SION HOUSE

Trophy: a decorative group of weapons, armour, musical instruments, or floreated motifs, with ribbons and garlands, used as carved inlaid or painted ornamentation. The motif originated in the ancient Greek practice of hanging on trees the weapons abandoned by a defeated enemy. See also *Musical symbols*.

WAR TROPHY. VERSAILLES.
GIRARDON 1627–1715

True cross: an heraldic device, symbolic of the Crucifixion both through form and material representation.

Trumpet pattern: a spiral motif, typical of Celtic art, that occurs in illuminated MSS, stonework and metalwork, *c.* AD 300–1250. It consists of two or three C-shaped spiral lines starting from a fixed point, and terminating in the centres of each other's coils: the long curved spaces formed between the lines resembled the ancient Irish trumpet: the motif is sometimes called a divergent spiral.

IRISH.

Tudor flower or Tudor ornament: a motif that occurs in late English Gothic architecture. It consists of a formalised flower on an upright stalk, with square flat petals or foliage, the indentations of the leaves often marked by drilled holes. Used in series in brattishing, *q.v.*, borders, cresting and running decoration, and as a terminal ornament.

Tudor rose: the name usually given to the conventional heraldic rose, *q.v.* Widely used as a carved enrichment in Tudor architecture and woodwork.

Turned ornament: turnery, or turning, by means of a lathe on which cutting tools could be rotated, to produce ornamentally curved surfaces, was practised in Egypt as early as 1300 BC, and subsequently throughout the ancient world of the Middle East, Greece and Rome, and in medieval Europe: there, ball-and-ring turning was used on the arms, legs and stretchers of stools and chairs. As the technique improved in the 16th and 17th centuries, posts, spindles, legs and balusters on furniture were given elaborate curved forms that included a variety of spiral twists. See *Ball, Bobbin, Spiral* and *Swash turning,* also *Barley sugar twist, Baluster,* and *Open twist.*

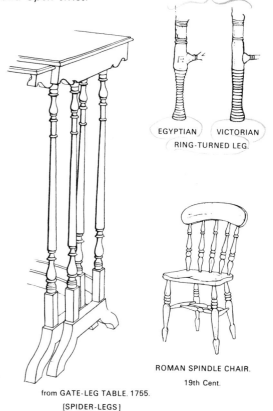

EGYPTIAN / VICTORIAN
RING-TURNED LEG.

ROMAN SPINDLE CHAIR.
19th Cent.

from GATE-LEG TABLE. 1755.
[SPIDER-LEGS]

Typographic ornament: the decoration of printed work by rules, printers' flowers and vignettes (see these entries), originated in the ornamental borders and initial letters of early illuminated MSS: for some time after the invention of printing, such ornaments were applied by hand by rubricators and illuminators.

U

Udjat, utchat or uẑat: an ancient Egyptian religious emblem representing the eye of Horus or Ra, the sun god, and symbolising his power: two eye emblems denoted the protection of both sun and moon. It has been suggested that the long-tailed R used in medical prescriptions is derived from this primitive sign.

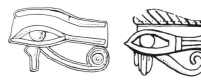

from LACHISH

Umbrella: an ancient Oriental symbol of royal dominion, dignity and power, and one of the Eight Buddhist Auspicious Signs. (See *Buddhist emblems*.) Umbrellas were also emblems of sovereignty and distinction in ancient Egypt, Assyria, and Greece.

Undulate band: a decorative band consisting of a continuous flower, fruit or foliage device, with the main stem of the plant running along the centre of the band in a gently curving wave-like form. See also *Vertebrate band*.

RENAISSANCE

INDIAN CORN. ITALIAN

Undy: see *Wavy*.

Unicorn: a fabulous white monster, bearded, with the head and body of a horse, cloven hoofs, tufted hocks, a lion's tail, and a long twisted horn projecting from the centre of the forehead: an heraldic device, notably as a supporter in the Royal Arms of England and formerly those of Scotland: one of the Queen's beasts, *q.v.* A primitive lunar symbol, and a medieval Christian symbol of chas-tity, associated with much myth and legend, its horn was alleged to be an antidote to any poison, and during the Middle Ages the animal was a favourite heraldic supporter in the arms of apothe-caries and, because of the supposed value of the horn, was also used as a trade sign by chemists and goldsmiths.

FRENCH. OAK CHIMNEY-PIECE early 16th century

Union Jack: see *Banner.*

Uraeus: a serpent motif of the ancient world, particularly associated with the Egyptian winged globe, *q.v.*, where two snakes encircled the central disc, coiling upwards on each side from the base, with heads raised, and sometimes crowned: also used on religious head-dresses, and above doorways and on tombs and mummy-cases: variations of the symbol appeared throughout Asia Minor, related to the winged globes of Assyria, Chaldea, and Phoenicia.

Urdy: heraldic term for an ornamental line like a row of pointed battlements. See *Line.*

Urella: see *Caulicoli.*

Urn: originating with the Graeco-Roman practice of cremation and of subsequently displaying the urn-shaped vessel containing the ashes in a house or on a monument; long used as a funerary ornament: some examples include flames issuing from the top, signifying eventual resurrection. During the 18th century knife-cases in the form of painted or inlaid urns were made, and the device was widely used in architecture and the decoration of furniture, notably as a terminal ornament on pedestals and finials.

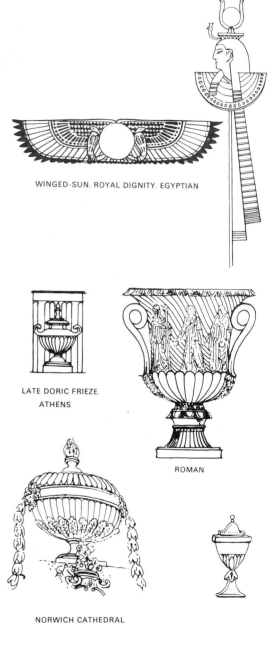

WINGED-SUN. ROYAL DIGNITY. EGYPTIAN

LATE DORIC FRIEZE. ATHENS

ROMAN

NORWICH CATHEDRAL

Utchat: see *Udjat.*

Użat: see *Udjat.*

TOMB OF PASHED.
RAMESSID PERIOD. XIX–XXth dynasties

Vane: see *Weather vane*.

Vase: a broad vase with a narrow neck—more like a squat bottle—was one of the Eight Buddhist Auspicious Signs. (See *Buddhist emblems*.) In classical times, a domestic utensil and associated with burial rites, it was often placed on a tomb as a container for provisions and offerings for the dead. As a decorative device, it became popular during the late 17th century, when it appeared in various forms: urn-shaped examples were used as terminal ornaments throughout the Georgian period.

ENGLISH LIBRARY-TABLE. DECORATIVE INLAY. *circa* 1770.

ADAMESQUE

Venetian window: also called a Palladian window, serliana, or serlian motif, it had three divisions, the central one arched and wider than the flat-headed ones on each side.

after C. CAMPBELL 18th Cent.

Vermiculation: an ornamental treatment of stone surfaces; an imitation of the irregular shallow channels and eaten appearance of worm-infested wood.

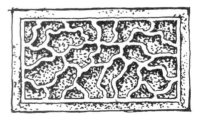

Vertebrate band: a decorative band, consisting of a continuous flower, fruit or foliage device, with the main stem running horizontally down the centre like a straight spine. See also *Undulate band*.

ITALIAN RENAISSANCE

Vesica piscis: a pointed oval form resembling a fish's bladder, sometimes called a mandorla, and frequently used as an aureole, *q.v.*, enclosing a representation of Christ, or the Virgin and Child. The close association of the fish, *q.v.*, with Christianity accounts for the long use of this device in religious symbolism: it appeared in the form of a panel in Gothic architecture, and on medieval ecclesiastical seals.

TYMPANUM VESICA PISCIS. LA CHARITÉ Sr. LOIRE

VESICA PATTERN. CORK (IRELAND) GLASS

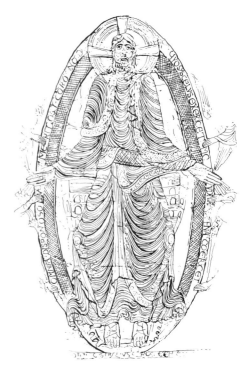

AUTUN CATHEDRAL. 12th Cent.

Vignette: an ornamental head- or tail-piece in a book, consisting of a small picture, scene, or trophy of weapons, foliage or musical instruments, without a border, and with the edges of the device shaded off: foliated ornaments on early illuminated MSS were called vignettes. Also used to describe a continuous Gothic moulding enrichment of vine leaves, grapes and tendrils, sometimes called a trail, and in Decorated architecture, a vine scroll. See also *Vine* and *Musical symbols*.

PRINTERS' VIGNETTES

THOMAS BEWICKE 1753–1828

from THE MONTE SANTO DI DIO. FLORENCE 1477

from TOMB OF NAKHT. THEBES. 1420–1411 BC

Vine: a decorative motif of great antiquity and universal use. In ancient China it took the form of a realistic trail of grapes, leaves and tendrils, and later a highly stylised type of scroll. In Egypt, it appeared in combination with the lotus, ivy and papyrus as an adornment to capitals, and a decoration on tomb ceilings: the Assyrian version was much more formal, revealing symmetrical arrangements of branches and square grapes. Originally sacred to Dionysus (Bacchus), the vine, with ivy, was the Roman sign for a tavern (see *Inn signs*). Formalised vine ornament was used throughout Graeco-Roman, Byzantine, Gothic and Renaissance decoration: the device was revived in the 18th and early 19th centuries. Combined with ears of wheat, it is a symbolic motif of the Eucharist. See also *Vignette* and *Wheat*.

MOORISH

BYZANTINE

POMPEIAN. SILVER INLAY ON BRONZE

OCCUPYING VESICA SHAPE

BYZANTINE. RAVENNA

BEDDINGTON

EARLY GOTHIC VINE-SCROLL

DEVON

CONGRESBURY

BOVEY-TRACEY

ARQUES. NORMANDY

ENGLISH. VINE WITH TENDRIL

VENICE

PERSIAN.

ITALIAN 1619

Vine scroll: see *Vignette*.

Virgo: the virgin : the sixth sign of the Zodiac : see
Zodiacal devices.

CHRISTCHURCH

Vitruvian scroll: a continuous series of undulating convoluted scrolls, having the appearance
of a regular line of curling waves: derived from the
Roman architect, Marcus Vitruvius Pollio: the motif
was revived in the 18th century. Also called running
dog, running scroll, and wave scroll. See *Knurl foot.*

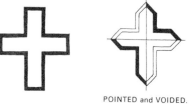

SILVER

Voided cross: a plain cross, *q.v.*, with an open
centre, giving the impression of one cross imposed
on another.

Voiders: see *Flaunches*.

POINTED and VOIDED.
DUKINFIELD (ct.-of-arms)

Volute: architectural term for the spiral scroll
ornaments flanking an Ionic capital. A smaller
version appears on Corinthian and Composite
capitals, and the device is also used to decorate
consoles and brackets. The form may be derived
from the outward curling sepals of the Egyptian
lotus, a shell, or an inward curving animal's horn.

IONIC

Vulture: a motif widely used in ancient Egypt,
shown with outstretched wings and grasping
sacred symbols in its claws: it appeared as ceiling
decoration in temples, and as an adornment for
breast ornaments of the dead.

EGYPTIAN. depicting VULTURE-GODDESS, GOLD CLOISONNÉ

of UPPER EGYPT. GOLD CLOISONNÉ

EGYPTIAN.

Waterleaf: a motif in the form of a broad flat leaf, used on late 12th century capitals, with a tapered lip curving to meet the abacus.

ENGLISH 12th Cent.

Waterleaf-and-tongue: a motif with a broad, flat formalised lotus or water lily leaf alternating with a dart-shaped tongue.

Watermark: an ornamental device, crest, or monogram, impressed into paper during manufacture as a maker's mark. Used by official organisations for whom large supplies of paper are regularly made.

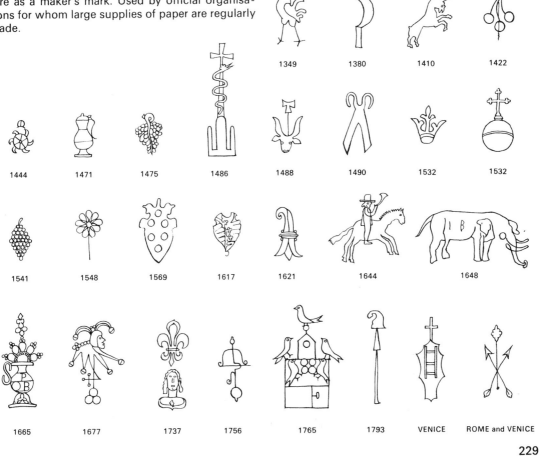

1349   1380   1410   1422

1444   1471   1475   1486   1488   1490   1532   1532

1541   1548   1569   1617   1621   1644   1648

1665   1677   1737   1756   1765   1793   VENICE   ROME and VENICE

229

SIENA   ROME and VENICE   VENICE

ITALIAN DAMASCENE WORK. 16th Cent. [Watered pattern]

Wave moulding: in architecture, a wave-like band of alternate slight convexities and concavities. In cabinet-making, an undulating band of some decorative wood, used as an applied moulding.

ENGLISH *circa* 1770

WAVE AND LOTUS. EARLY GREEK

OCCUPYING WAVED STALK SPACE

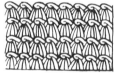

JAPANESE

Wave scroll: see *Vitruvian scroll*.

Waver dragon: see *Wyvern*.

Wavy: heraldic term for an ornamental undulating line; also called undy. See *Line*.

Weather moulding: see *Label*.

Weather vane: also called a fane or vane, and probably of Saxon origin. A metal plate or pointer, used on the top of a spire or the finial of a cupola, usually of wrought iron and generally incorporating crossed arms showing the four points of the compass, fixed to allow movement so it may turn to show the direction of the wind. The pointer is usually an ornamental motif, commonly an arrow or cock, but animals, fish, insects, human figures, inanimate objects, religious and heraldic devices are also used: the vertical post may be decorated with intricate scrolls, foliage and curlicues.

VIKING

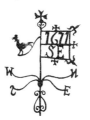

STRAP & BUCKLE BADGE

Weepers: small sculptured figures placed in niches in the sides of medieval and early 17th century tombs: they often represented the friends or children of the dead person; also called mourners.

Wheat: the wheatsheaf is a common heraldic device, known as a garb: ears of wheat, combined with the vine, form a symbolic motif of the Christian Eucharist: a mid 18th century chair with the back splat in the form of a conventionalised wheatsheaf, is known by the modern term of wheatsheaf back.

JOHN OF WHETHAMSTEDGE

HERALDIC

WHEATSHEAF SPLAT. ENGLISH

PLATE XVI.
CHIPPENDALE'S DIRECTOR. 3rd EDIT:

VERONA

ST MARIA DEI MIRACOLI.
VENICE

Wheel: one of the oldest symbols of the sun, the spokes representing rays, used thus in Buddhist, Hindu, Greek and Mithraic religious symbolism: the wheel appeared as an ornament on the capitals of Buddhist edict columns in India, *c.* 250 BC, and the device of a wheel surrounded by flames is one of the Eight Buddhist Auspicious Emblems. (See *Buddhist emblems.*) In heraldry, the usual form is a wagon wheel with decorative spokes. Wheels of Providence, intended to represent the vicissi-

tudes of human existence, were introduced as decorative motifs in sculpture, glass and painting, in medieval Christian churches: the circular wheel or rose window is filled with tracery, the slender stone members radiating outwards from the centre, like spokes. Wheels form the backs of some late 18th century chairs, and a type of Windsor chair has a wheel device pierced in the back splat: both types are known as wheel back chairs. See also *Catherine wheel, Tchakra,* and *Wheel cross.*

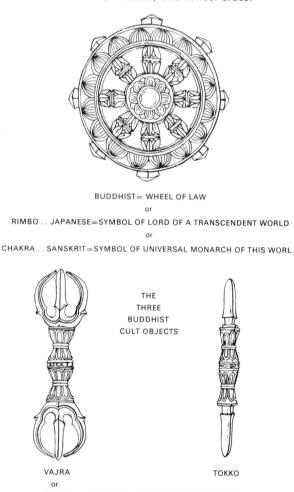

BUDDHIST= WHEEL OF LAW
or
RIMBO . . JAPANESE=SYMBOL OF LORD OF A TRANSCENDENT WORLD
or
CHAKRA . . SANSKRIT=SYMBOL OF UNIVERSAL MONARCH OF THIS WORLD

THE THREE BUDDHIST CULT OBJECTS

VAJRA
or
KONGO . . JAPANESE=ATTRIBUTE OF THE DIVINITIES
or   (sometimes with four or five points. illust: shows three)
VAJRA . . BUDDHIST=DIVINE WEAPON IN ANCIENT POETRY

TOKKO

CAPITAL. MUSEUM. SĀRNĀTH

SOLAR-WHEEL

SOLAR-WHEEL OF THE HORIZON COMBINED WITH A ROSE

ROUND WINDOW. NIKOLAI CHURCH. WISMAR

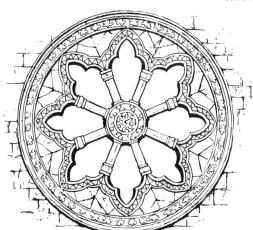

WHEEL-WINDOW

WHEEL OF LAW
(alternative name :—a DHARMACAKRA)
from SURYA DEUL TEMPLE. KONĀRAKA

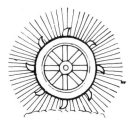

CATHERINE WHEEL RAYONNY
by kind permission of
SOUTH EASTERN ELECTRICITY BOARD

DEMI-WHEEL ON
CREST WREATH

COG WHEEL.
HERALDIC

HERALDIC

WHEEL-BACK CHAIR. ENGLISH. 1850 onwards

233

Wheel cross: a circle enclosing a cross: originally a primitive sun sign, *q.v.*, from which the rouelle, *q.v.*, and Christian wheel cross—a cross with slightly splayed limbs enclosed in a circle—evolved.

CELTIC. IRELAND

CROSS of the SCRIPTURES. 10th Cent. CLONMACNOISE

NORMAN

EARLY ENGLISH

DECORATED

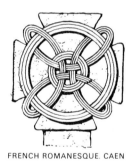

FRENCH ROMANESQUE. CAEN

Wheel of fire: see *Tchakra*.

Whorl foot: furniture-maker's term for a leg ending in an upturned scroll. See also *Knurl foot*.

ENGLISH. MAHOGANY. 1760 onwards

Willow pattern: an underglaze blue printed pattern used for the decoration of earthenware, occasionally gilt-edged. Probably the most famous of all such printed patterns; first used by the firm of Thomas Minton, who is accredited with the design, Stoke-on-Trent, England, between 1796–1806. This pattern's usage has been continuous, even to the present day; and is a true 'Chinoiserie', being without a Chinese prototype either in decoration or legend.

Winged globe: variations of this ancient Egyptian motif existed throughout the Middle and Far East, in Greece and Rome. The Egyptian prototype was of religious importance, symbolising protection in life and death, and eternal life, and used as an ornament above temple entrances, on cornices and pylons, and as a decorative device on tomb-ceilings, mummy-cases, and in ivory and bronze objects. Combining various forms associated by the ancient Egyptians with the sun—the disc, goat or ram, sparrowhawk, serpent—the device consisted of a central globe, around which twined two snakes (see *Uraeus*), surmounted by long curving animal horns, the whole resting on two wide outspread wings. The Assyrians, who used the motif as a religious and military emblem, added the winged and feathered figure of a god in the centre of the globe.

ASSYRIAN

GLOBE OF PERFECTION. PEKING

ASSYRIAN

Wivern: see *Wyvern*.

Wreath: in the ancient world, wreaths of foliage, flowers, or ribbons were worn as emblems of victory in war, success in the games, or to designate a sacrifice. In heraldry, the word means a circular garland of entwined leaves, flowers and sprays, worn on the head: also called a chaplet or garland. See also *Crest-wreath*.

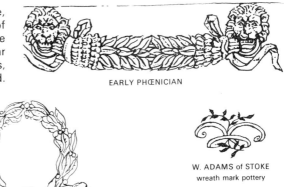

EARLY PHŒNICIAN

OF VICTORY. ALTAR PANEL. EAST FRANKISH 919 AD

W. ADAMS of STOKE wreath mark pottery

LOUIS XVI ORMOLU

ARA PACIS. ROME

WREATH MARKS. POTTERY

E. WOOD & SONS:
BURSLEM

HENSHALL & CO: BURSLEM

Wyvern, wivern, or waver dragon: a fabulous heraldic beast, a two-legged dragon, winged, the hind quarters serpentine and ending in a forked tail. As the emblem of the Kings of Wessex in Saxon England, the wyvern was the device borne on the English standard at the Battle of Hastings.

XY

Y-tracery: tracery with mullions branching at the top to form a Y. See also *Intersected tracery*.

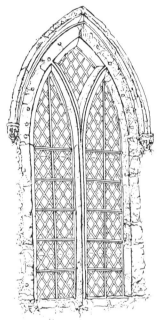

ALL SAINTS. MARKHAM CLINTON. NOTTS. 13th Cent.

Yachting style: a name given to Art Nouveau, *q.v.*, in 1896, by Edmond de Goncourt, in whose opinion the design of furniture in the style was based on ships' portholes.

Yakshi: an Indian nature spirit associated with fertility: this figure has been widely used as a motif in the decoration of the wall-railings which encompass a sacred Buddhist enclosure.

CHULAKOKA DEVATÀ DIVINITY. from BHĀRHUT

RAILING-PILLARS WITH YAKSHĪS from BHUTESAR

from JAISINGHPURA

Yale: a fabulous heraldic creature, of Roman origin : a large, goat-like animal, cloven-hooved, the tongue protruding, and with horns which could be moved back and forth at will. The Yale of Beaufort is one of the Queen's beasts, *q.v.*

Yang and Yin: an ancient Chinese symbol for the two cosmic souls representing Male and Female parts of the Universe. Universalism defines Yang as a universal, supreme *'shen'* or deity, Yin as a universal *'kwei'*; both self-dividing into an infinite number of *'shen'* and *'kwei'*; a particle of both when deposited in a human forms one of his two souls. All good proceeds from *'shen'* and all evil caused by *'kwei'*; both belong in the Order, as light and darkness, warmth and cold; as every year the vicissitudes of these souls cause the Seasons and related phenomena. Life thereby is a continuous creation and destruction, and a never ceasing re-absorption of these particles. Yang is elevated far beyond Yin, as far as Heaven is elevated beyond its counterpart Earth. All harm and all beneficence is with the authorization of the chief *'shen'* Heaven. The symbol appears in the centre of the Buddhist device known as the Eight Trigrams.

YANG-YIN SURROUNDED BY EIGHT TRIGRAMS

Z

Zigzag: a chevron, *q.v.*, motif, of great antiquity, used to represent water in ancient Egypt, and in early Scandinavian decoration to denote lightning: a characteristic Norman and medieval moulding enrichment. The term is often used to mean a chevron.

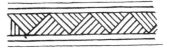

SAVAGE

FRENCH

PRINTER'S BORDER

Zigzag-and-ball: a Norman moulding ornament, consisting of a continuous chevron, enriched with a pattern of small circles, sometimes containing stars.

Zigzag band: a Chinese device, derived from the zigzag lozenge, *q.v.*, in which a continuous design is formed by such lozenges laid end to end; sometimes each contains a decorative leaf, animal or geometrical motif: the band may have originated from an arrangement of interlocking T-shapes that formed half lozenges.

HINDO

Zigzag lozenge: an early Chinese ornamental motif composed of three lozenge shapes linked or merged together. See also *Lozenge, Open zigzag lozenge,* and *Zigzag band.*

Zodiacal devices: the signs of the Zodiac are: 1 Aries, the ram; 2 Taurus, the bull; 3 Gemini, the twins; 4 Cancer, the crab; 5 Leo, the lion; 6 Virgo, the virgin; 7 Libra, the scales; 8 Scorpio, the scorpion; 9 Sagittarius, the archer; 10 Capricornus, the goat; 11 Aquarius, the water-carrier; 12 Pisces, the fishes. The Zodiac, or 'Path of the Creatures' was the old name for a celestial path divided into twelve sections, whose course lay through constellations bearing the names of living things, each traversed annually by the sun. In the ancient world

ARIES
21st MARCH–20th APRIL

239

the twelve signs were connected with the seasons, had mystical and astronomical associations, and each was believed to rule over one of the twelve months of the year. The signs appeared as mythological and symbolic devices in Graeco-Roman ornament; they have also been associated with the twelve tribes of Israel, and the twelve Apostles. In the modern world, apart from their astronomical significance, they denote horoscope readers, palmists and fortune tellers.

TAURUS
21st APRIL–20th MAY

GEMINI
21st MAY–21st JUNE

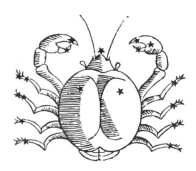

CANCER
22nd JUNE–23rd JULY

LEO
24th JULY–23rd AUG.

VIRGO
24th AUG.–23rd SEPT.

LIBRA
24th SEPT.–23rd OCT.

SCORPIO
24th OCT.–22nd NOV.

SAGITTARIUS
23rd NOV.–22nd DEC.

CAPRICORN
23rd DEC.–20th JAN.

SIGNS OF ZODIAC TAKEN FROM
'POETICON ASTRONOMICON' by
C. HYGINUS, VENICE 1485,
AND 'DE MAGNIS COPIUNCTIONIBUS' by
ALBUMASAR- AUGSBURG 1489

by courtesy of the
VICTORIA AND ALBERT MUSEUM

AQUARIUS
21st JAN.–19th FEB.

PISCES
20th FEB.–20th MARCH

Zoomorphic ornament: the use of animal forms, real or fabulous, to compose symbolic or decorative devices. In China, *c.* 1300–1000 BC, an important zoomorphic motif, widely used, showed two creatures facing each other in profile in such a way that the two heads formed one full face: this animal 'mask' was known as *t'ao-t'ieh*. Ancient Celtic and Scandinavian ornament contains interlaced zoomorphic ornament. See *Hom* and *Lion*.

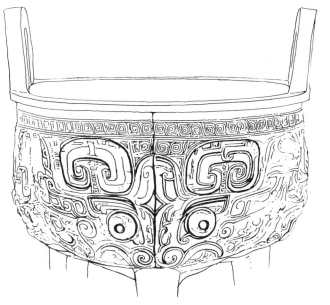

CHINESE *TING.* BRONZE late 2nd millennium BC.

PUEBLO

Zophorus or Zoophorus: a decorative frieze in which animal as well as human figures are shown. See *Scroll.*

241

A SELECT BIBLIOGRAPHY

Adeline's Art Dictionary (J. S. Virtue & Co. Ltd, 1891).

Analysis of Ornament by Ralph N. Wornum (Chapman & Hall, 1879).

Art Nouveau by Mario Amaya (Studio Vista Limited, 1966).

Art Nouveau by S. Tschudi Madsen (World University Library, 1967).

Boutell's Heraldry, revised by C. W. Scott-Giles and J. P. Brooke-Little (Frederick Warne & Co. Ltd, 1950).

British Pottery Marks by G. Woolliscroft Read (Scott, Greenwood & Son, 1910).

Chessmen by A. E. J. Mackett-Beeson (Weidenfeld & Nicolson, 1968).

Chess Sets by F. Lanier Graham (Studio Vista, 1968).

Chinese Art by William Willetts (Penguin Books Ltd, 1958).

Church Wood Carvings (*A West Country Study*) by J. C. D. Smith (David & Charles, 1969).

Concise Glossary of Terms used in Grecian, Roman, Italian and Gothic Architecture, A by J. H. Parker (James Parker & Co., 1879).

Decorative Heraldry by G. W. Eve (George Bell & Sons, 1897).

Design Motifs of Ancient Mexico by Jorge Enciso (Dover Publications Inc., New York, 1947).

Dictionary of Roman and Greek Antiquities, A by Anthony Rich (Longmans, Green & Co., 1873).

Dictionary of Terms in Art by F. W. Fairholt (Virtue, Hall & Virtue, 1854).

Dictionary of the Architecture and Archaeology of the Middle Ages, A by John Britton (Longman, Orme, Brown, Green, and Longmans, 1838).

Egyptian Decorative Art by W. M. Flinders Petrie (Methuen & Co., Ltd, 1895 ; 2nd edition 1920).

Encyclopaedia of Chinese Symbolism and Art Motives by C. A. S. Williams (The Julian Press Inc., New York, 1960).

Encyclopaedia of Cottage, Farm and Villa Architecture and Furniture, An by J. C. Loudon (Longman, Rees, Orme, Brown, Green and Longman, 1833).

Encyclopaedia of Ornament, The by Henry Shaw (William Pickering, 1842).

English Churchyard Memorials by Frederick Burgess (Lutterworth Press, 1963).

English Gothic Foliage Sculpture by Samuel Gardner (Cambridge University Press, 1927).

Englishman's Chair, The by John Gloag (George Allen & Unwin Ltd, 1964).

Evolution of Architectural Ornament, The by G. A. T. Middleton (Francis Griffiths, 1913).

Five Hundred Years of Printing by S. H. Steinberg (Penguin Books Ltd, 1955).

Flags of the World by H. Gresham Carr (Frederick Warne & Co. Ltd, 1961).

Grammar of Ornament, The by Owen Jones (Day & Son Ltd, 1856).

Handbook of Designs and Devices by Clarence P. Hornung (Dover Publications Inc., New York, 1946).

Handbook of Ornament, A by Franz Sales Meyer (Dover Publications Inc., New York, 1957).

Heraldry by J. S. Milburne (W. & G. Foyle Ltd, 1950).

Heraldry Simplified by W. A. Copinger (Manchester University Press, 1910).

High Victorian Design by Nikolaus Pevsner (Architectural Press, 1951).

Historic Ornament by James Ward (Chapman & Hall, 1897).

History of Architecture on the Comparative Method, A by Sir Banister Fletcher, revised by Professor R. A. Cordingley (Athlone Press, 1967).

History of Chess, A by H. J. R. Murray (At the Clarendon Press, Oxford. 1913, 1962).

History of Playing Cards, A by Catherine Percy Hargrave (Dover Publications Inc., New York, 1966).

History of Signboards, The by Jacob Larwood and John Camden Hotten (John Camden Hotten, 1867).

Illustrated Glossary of Architecture, 850–1830 by John Harris and Jill Lever (Faber & Faber, 1966).

Illustrations of Ancient Art by the Rev. Edward Trollope (George Bell, 1854).

Introduction to Typography by Oliver Simon (Faber & Faber, 1946).

Japanese Decorative Art by Martin Feddersen (Faber & Faber, 1962).

Leaves of Southwell, The by Nikolaus Pevsner (Penguin Books Ltd, 1945).

Manual of Heraldry, The edited by Francis J. Grant, W. S. (John Grant, Edinburgh, 1924).

Manual of Historic Ornament, A by Richard Glazier (B. T. Batsford Ltd, 1899).

Mediaeval Carvings in Exeter Cathedral by C. J. P. Cave (Penguin Books Ltd, 1953).

Migration of Symbols, The by the Count Goblet d'Alviella (University Books, New York, 1956. First published in Paris, 1892; English translation by Constable & Co., London, 1894).

Nature in Ornament by Lewis F. Day (B. T. Batsford, 1896).

Parthians and Sassanians by Roman Ghirshman, edited by André Malraux (Thames & Hudson, 1962).

Pattern, A Study of Ornament in Western Europe from 1180 to 1900 by Joan Evans (Clarendon Press, 1931).

Picts, The by Isabel Henderson (Thames & Hudson, 1967).

Pioneers of Modern Design by Nikolaus Pevsner (Penguin Books Ltd, 1960).

Playing Cards by Roger Tilley (Weidenfeld & Nicolson, 1967).

Primitive Art by Leonhard Adam (Cassell & Co., 1963).

Principles of Ornament, The by James Ward (Chapman & Hall, 1899).

Printed Book, The by Harry G. Aldis (Cambridge University Press, 1947).

'Printers' Flowers and Arabesques' by Francis Meynell and Stanley Morison (*The Fleuron*, No. 1, 1923).

Pocket Book of Collectors' Terms by Michael Goodwin (Country Life Ltd, 1967).

Short Dictionary of Furniture, A by John Gloag (George Allen & Unwin Ltd; revised enlarged edition, 1969).

Social History of Furniture Design, A by John Gloag (Cassell & Co., 1966).

Stones of Venice, The by John Ruskin.

Style in Ornament by Joan Evans (Oxford University Press, 1950).

Styles of Ornament, The by Alexander Speltz (Dover Publications Inc., New York, 1959).

'Symbols and Emblems in our Churches', a paper given on behalf of the Preston Church of England Society, by T. Harrison Myres, FRIBA, on 24 February 1890.

Symbols for Designers by Arnold Whittick (Crosby Lockwood & Son Ltd, 1935).

Symbols, Signs and their meaning by Arnold Whittick (Leonard Hill (Books) Limited, 1960).

Weather Vanes of Norwich and Norfolk, The by Claude J. W. Messent (Fletcher & Son Ltd, Norwich, 1937).

INDEX OF PERSONS AND PLACES